Chinese Investment in Africa

China leads the world when it comes to investment and influence on the African continent. The extent of Chinese investment in Africa is well known and much has been written about China's foray into Africa. However, most of the available material has approached this issue by looking at China as the 'new colonialist' – more interested in Africa's vast natural resources than working in partnership for sustained development. Whilst China's interest in Africa's resources is evident, it is just half of the story.

China's foray into Africa goes beyond its appetite for natural resources and into the realm of geopolitics and international political economics. For example, China is all too aware of how it can cultivate Africa's support on global issues at the United Nations and at other international fora. Breaking free from the binary arguments and analysis that characterize this topic, Professor Abdulai presents a refreshing perspective, arguing that China's foray into Africa can produce win–win outcomes for China and Africa – if Africans really know what they want from China.

Hitherto, each African country has tended to engage China with an individual wish list, acting in isolation and not as part of a wider continent (indeed, Africa and the African Union do not yet have a coordinated policy towards China). For Africa to be able to do that, it needs to know where China is coming from, the factors that contributed to its awakening and success, and the benefits and possible pitfalls of this foray, in order to better position itself for a win–win engagement with China.

This book will be a valuable read for policy makers, think-tanks and students of Africa–China studies programmes alike.

David N. Abdulai is an internationally renowned academic and the author of numerous books. He is president and CEO of the African Graduate School of Management and Leadership in Ghana. His most recent book is titled *African-Centred Management Education: A New Paradigm for an Emerging Continent*.

Chinese Investment in Africa

How African Countries Can Position
Themselves to Benefit from China's
Foray into Africa

David N. Abdulai

Routledge
Taylor & Francis Group

LONDON AND NEW YORK

First published 2017
by Routledge

2 Park Square, Milton Park, Abingdon, Oxfordshire OX14 4RN
52 Vanderbilt Avenue, New York, NY 10017

Routledge is an imprint of the Taylor & Francis Group, an informa business

First issued in paperback 2020

British Library Cataloguing in Publication Data
A catalogue record for this book is available from the British Library

Library of Congress Cataloging in Publication Data
A catalog record for this book has been requested

ISBN: 978-1-4724-8021-7 (hbk)
ISBN: 978-0-367-59575-3 (pbk)

Typeset in Bembo
by Deanta Global Publishing Services, Chennai, India

For My Father
"It is a terrible thing to see and have no vision"
—Helen Keller

Contents

Figures

Tables

Preface

It is unimaginable that just a little over 30 years ago, during the era of China's "Great Leap Forward," experiment under Mao Tse Tung, about 20 million Chinese died of starvation (Xun, 2012; Dikötter, 2010). Fast forward to 2015–2016 at the time of writing, when an emerging China is an economic and military power to reckon with in global economic and political affairs. China is the second largest economy in the world after the US, with a US$10.35 trillion economy. In terms of Africa, it is now its largest trading partner, with total trade between the two exceeding US$10 billion in 2000.

China's emergence and its impact on global economic and world affairs can be regarded as one of the most important phenomena of the twenty-first century, if one takes into consideration the kind of sorry state the country was in during the era of Mao Tse Tung. Its foray into Africa,[1] one of the richest continents in terms of natural resources but the poorest in terms of development, adds an interesting dimension to the narrative as it pertains to China's emergence. This foray into Africa has not gone down well with many of Africa's former colonial masters as well as the US and other important players in the global economy who are also interested in Africa's rich natural resources. But these players also see their influence in the region been challenged by an emerging China's current engagement with Africa. These dynamics, in my view, make this topic interesting but also important in global geopolitics and economic relations.

Africa's experience with previous forays into the continent during the colonial and post-colonial periods, and specifically during the era of the Cold War, has left a bitter taste in its mouth, so to speak. During the colonial era, African countries watched helplessly as they were exploited by their colonial masters with minimal or no development. The Cold War era also saw African countries being used as pawns between the East and the West, former Cold War combatants in their strategic and geopolitical interests. At the end of the Cold War, Africa was left with nothing. Angola, for example, was completely ruined because of a prolonged war linked to the Cold War. Commenting on colonialists and colonialism, the late Patrice Lumumba, the first democratically elected leader of the Democratic Republic of the Congo (DRC) (whose death has been allegedly attributed to Belgium and the Central Intelligence Agency (CIA))

(De Witte, 2003; Devlin, 2008; Gerard and Kuklick, 2015) said, "the colonialists care nothing for Africa for her sake. They are attracted by African riches and their actions are guided by the desire to preserve their interests in Africa against the wishes of the African people. For the colonialist all means are good if they help them to possess these riches," (Lumumba, 1961). It is thus imperative that Africa looks at China's current engagement with the continent critically. Could the foray being made by an emerging China into the continent produce the same results as before, or would this time be different? How are African countries going to make sure that China's engagement with the continent does not produce the same results as before? How are they going to position themselves adequately to benefit from China's current engagement with the continent?

In order for African countries not to repeat the mistakes of the past as it pertains to previous forays of foreign countries into the continent, they need to plan, prepare and position themselves well to benefit this time around with China's foray into the region. This book is thus written to offer some guidance to African leaders and policy makers on how they can achieve such a goal. It offers an entirely different approach on how this can be achieved. It suggests that the first place to start in this positioning for African countries is to know where China came from, that is, its history and politics – specifically, the factors that contributed to its emergence as an economic and political power. The book further suggests that African leaders and policy makers ask themselves the probing question of why China is interested in Africa. A thorough and critical analysis of such a question on their part should help African countries develop strategies that will help them position themselves adequately to benefit from China's foray into the region; specifically, to leverage on these investments to contribute to Africa's growth and development efforts. Is this possible? Can Africa and indeed the African Union (A.U.) and regional economic communities (RECs) on the continent be able to come together to develop a common strategy or a unified policy towards China? Some people may have their doubts. However, in this book, some suggestions are offered as to how African countries could do that. Furthermore, the book offer suggestions to African countries on how to develop a forward-looking vision, working with the Chinese to enhance their relations moving forward to ensure a win–win outcome in this engagement.

The genesis of this book can be traced back to the time I was living and working in Asia; specifically, when I was the dean of the faculty of Business and Law at Multimedia University in Kula Lumpur, Malaysia. It was at this time that China was just emerging as an economic and political power to be reckoned with. This emergence attracted my interest and, with subsequent research, led to the publication of my first book on China titled *An Emerging China and its Impact on ASEAN*. When I moved to South Africa to become the CEO and executive director of the University of South Africa's Graduate School of Business Leadership, I continued my research on China but now with a focus on China–Africa relations. While in South Africa, I was fortunate enough to be invited to give talks on "An emerging China and its impact on Africa" and "Doing business with the Chinese" at numerous fora in southern Africa. I eventually gave my inaugural lecture to become a full professor at the Graduate School of Business Leadership, at the University of South Africa on China and Africa. This cumulative research work on China and countries of the Association of South East Asian Nations (ASEAN), and on China and Africa from my days in Asia to date and the experience gained on the topic have resulted in the writing of this book. The journey has been long; I have learnt so much in the process, and there is still so much more to learn about China's engagement with Africa. There is also so much written about China and so many books that speak to the importance of an emerging China in our world today. Even though this is supposed to make any researcher's work easy, it actually complicates it, in my opinion. At the end of it all, it is a joy to be able to add another book to this long list of books on China, which I think is one of the important phenomena of our time. This is also an effort to share this information with the reading public.

I could not have been able to accumulate so much of this information and these ideas and views about China without the help and support of so many people in diverse ways. Indeed, there are so many to mention in this brief preface. However, some of these people need special mention here, for without their vision, effort and support this book would never have been possible or even conceived. For their help, I am most grateful. They include Dato Ng Tieh Chuan, who was instrumental in getting MPH Publishing in Malaysia to publish my first book on China. The publication of my first book on China served as an impetus to continue with my research on the emergence of China, even when I moved from Malaysia to South Africa. The numerous organisations and individuals in southern Africa who invited me to talk on China and Africa, and the authorities at the University of South Africa who accepted my topic on China and Africa for my inaugural lecture, also deserve recognition here. Even though I am not a China–Africa scholar, the encouragement in these diverse ways increased my interest in pursuing research in this area, resulting in this book.

However, this book would have not seen the light of day in its current form if the commissioning editor and the editorial board of Ashgate and Gower Publishing had not shown interest in the book. My Ph.D. dissertation chair, Professor Joe Szyliowicz of the Josef Korbel Graduate School of International Studies at the University of Denver, has played an important role in the writing of this book. At a lunch meeting during one of my annual visits to Denver, Colorado, many years ago, Professor Szyliowicz offered a preliminary critique of and pointers for the initial draft of this book. He has also offered his much-cherished critique of the most recent draft of the manuscript as well as pointing to some publications to read that enhanced the book. I will forever be grateful to him for his continued guidance and support of my work since I left graduate school almost two decades ago. Another graduate school professor of mine when I was a Master's student at the School of International

Service at American University in Washington, D.C., Professor Fantu Cheru, also took time out of his busy schedule to comment on the draft manuscript. Dr. Yaw Ansu, a renowned economist, formerly with the World Bank and now the chief economist at the African Center for Economic Transformation (ACET) also took the time to comment on the initial draft of the manuscript. His unique observations and suggestions from a policy perspective have contributed a lot in giving balance to this book, otherwise written from a general reader's perspective. My good friend Bunmi Makinwa, former director of the United Nations Population Fund (UNFPA) Africa Region, also offered his much-appreciated insights into the initial draft of the manuscript while on assignment in Ethiopia. Bunmi's unique observations and critique prompted me to address in the book some of the neglected issues concerning China's investment in Africa.

To all these mentors and professors of mine, I am truly grateful, and I feel really fortunate to have benefited from their insights and contributions, which have gone a long way to make this book what it is today. As we say in Ghana, *Me da mu asi* – thank you; according to an old African saying, "by standing on your shoulders, I am able to see over the marketplace." I will also like to thank the staff of the African Graduate School of Management and Leadership for their secretarial work on the manuscript. My final thanks go to my family, who, during the December 2015 holidays, gave me the space and support to edit and re-write numerous sections of this book because of the constantly changing events in the global economy and that of China as well. Despite the acknowledgement of the contributions made by all those mentioned and not mentioned in the writing of this book, they are in no way responsible for any errors, omissions or faults in it. A book like this will definitely have some errors, as well as omissions or parts that some people will not agree with. All such errors, omissions and faults remain mine. The current Chinese engagement and investment in Africa is a fascinating and timely topic. I hope this book will encourage others to research other dimensions of the topic.

David N. Abdulai
Accra, Ghana
February 2016

Note

1 Africa as used throughout this book refers to Sub Saharan Africa, unless otherwise noted.

Acronyms and Abbreviations

AFRICOM	US–Africa Command
ACET	African Center for Economic Transformation
AGOA	Africa Growth and Opportunity Act
ASEAN	Association of South East Asian Nations
A.U.	African Union
BOT	Build Operate Transfer
CCP	Chinese Communist Party
CCPIT	China Council for the Promotion of International Trade
CIA	Central Intelligence Agency
CIC	China Investment Corporation
CLM	China Luanshya Mine
CNMC	China Non-Ferrous Metal Mining Company
CNOOC	China National Offshore Oil Corporation
CNPC	China National Petroleum Corporation
COMNC	China Oil Multinational Corporation
CSFAC	China's State Forum Agribusiness Corporation
CSTP	Cultural, Scientific and Technology Protocol
DRC	Democratic Republic of Congo
EACTI	United States–East Africa Counter-Terrorism Initiative
ECOWAS	Economic Community of West African States
EPA	economic partnership agreements
ETC	Economic and Technical Corporation
FDI	foreign direct investment
FOCAC	Forum on China–Africa Cooperation
GATT	General Agreement on Trade and Tariffs
GDP	gross domestic product
GLF	Great Leap Forward
GNPOC	Great Nile Petroleum Operating Company
HIPC	heavily indebted poor countries
ICB	Industrial and Commercial Bank of China
IDA	International Development Association
IMF	International Monetary Fund
IPR	intellectual property rights

JETRO	Japanese External Trade Organisation
JV	joint venture
KCM	Konkola Copper Mines
LCM	Lwanshya Copper Mine
LDC	less developed countries
MDGs	Millennium Development Goals
MFN	most favoured nation
MNC	multinational corporation
MPLA	Popular Movement for the Liberation of Angola
NFCA	Non-Ferrous Africa Mining Corporation
NAFTA	North American Free Trade Area
NATO	North Atlantic Treaty Organisation
NICs	newly industrialised countries
NPC	National People's Congress
OAU	Organisation of African Unity
OECD	Organisation for Economic Corporation and Development
OMNC	oil multinational corporations
OPEC	Organisation for Petroleum Exporting Countries
PEPFAR	President's Emergency Plan for Aids Relief
PRC	People's Republic of China
RECs	regional economic communities
RMB	Rimimbi
ROC	Republic of China
SADC	Southern Africa Development Community
SANANGOL	The National Fuels Society of Angola
SEZ	Special Economic Zone
SINOPEC	China Petroleum and Chemical Corporation
SMEs	small and medium-sized enterprises
SOE	state-owned enterprise
TA	technical assistance
TICAD	Tokyo International Conference on African Development
TRIPS	Trade Related Aspects of Intellectual Property Rights
TSCTI	Trans-Sahara Counter-Terrorism Initiative
UDI	Unilateral Declaration of Independence
UNCTAD	United Nations Conference on Trade and Development
UNFPA	United Nations Population Fund
UNITA	National Union for the Total Independence of Angola
WIPO	World Intellectual Property Organisation
WTO	World Trade Organization

Introduction

Introduction

China's emergence as an economic and political force was envisioned long ago by one of the great leaders of France—Napoleon Bonaparte. In 1803, he observed that China was like a sleeping giant and that when she awakens, she will astonish the world. His exact words were, "there lies a sleeping giant. Let her sleep, for when she wakes she will shake the world" (Bertrant, 1916). Napoleon's vision and prophecy has come true, and China, the sleeping giant, has awoken and is shaking the world, so to speak, in numerous ways: politically, economically, socially and technologically. This is making the traditional global powers uncomfortable, and they have every reason to be. Amongst many of the discomforts that China's emergence has created in politics, trade, economics and technology is its having to face allegations that it manipulates its currency, it does not compete fairly, and it does not respect the human rights of its citizens, to mention just a few. Some of these allegations can be observed as having some merit, and others do not. A rather important discomfort that China has created is its current increased engagement with Africa, a region long regarded by Africa's traditional allies as "*la chasse gardée*" literally translated as "their hunting grounds" or their "spheres of influence"; hence, nobody should tamper with "their Africa."

The view of this book is that China's current increasing engagement with Africa has its advantages and disadvantages as well as critiques. But before this can be thoroughly ascertained, an in-depth understanding of where China came from and how that has driven and is driving its developmental trajectory even today and the way China sees itself amongst the league of nations is of immense importance. Justice will not be done to the reasons behind China's current engagement and investment in Africa if the aforementioned issue is not dealt with. Some have questioned why so much history and background on where China came from is given in the early chapters of this book. Others have also observed that the author should have gone straight to the issues surrounding the China–Africa engagement. Such observations are right, but this author believes that the past informs the future. According to Theodore Roosevelt, the twenty-sixth president of the US, "the more you know about the past, the better prepared you are for the future" (Wills, 1937). The more Africans know about China's past and their own past, the more they will be able to prepare for their future and their engagement with China in its current entry into Africa. They are therefore more likely not to repeat the mistakes of the past.

But history is very important as a teacher for any person or country that wants to develop. History presents those living in the present with the opportunity to analyse past events and see where others went wrong or where they were right, or why decisions were taken at a certain time. This allows those living in the present to make informed decisions to guide their growth and development into the future. History, for Africans, can be likened to the anthills of the Savannah. According to the late Chinua Achebe, a renowned African writer, "the anthills of the Savannah survive the bushfires of the Savannah to be able to tell the new grass what transpired last year" (Achebe, 1987). Revisiting China's history as it pertains to its emergence in this book is a step in this direction.

From research, looking at where China came from, its impoverish background and the factors that have driven and are driving its development, this author believes that so far the benefits from China's investments and current engagement with Africa outweigh the costs as it pertains to Africa's development trajectory vis-à-vis how the continent has been treated by its formal colonial masters and the West in general. These observations are detailed in the book. The aim of this book, therefore, is to look at Chinese investment in Africa, the importance of such investment and how African countries can position themselves to benefit from China's current foray into Africa. The initial chapters of the book therefore look at Sino-African relations from a historical perspective to situate correctly this narrative of Chinese investment in Africa.

China–Africa relations date back to between 202 B.C. and A.D. 220 and were mainly confined to trade relations. But the well documented contacts between China and Africa were the voyages made by the Chinese admiral Zheng He in October 1415, during the era of the Ming dynasty. He led his fleet of ships four times to the east coast of Africa, with stops in Somalia and Kenya (Snow, 1988). To further prove that China–Africa relations took place way beyond the time the first "White man" set foot on African soil, the *Da Ming Hun Yi Tu*, a Chinese map that confirms the contact between Chinese and Africans pre-dating the European "discovery" of Africa, was shown to the South African Parliament by the Chinese ambassador to South Africa in 2002 (Guijin, 2004). The history of Sino–China relations, post Zheng He, dates back to 1960, when Premier Zhou Enlai made his ten-nation tour of Africa in December 1963 and January 1964. Zhou visited Egypt, Algeria, Morrocco, Tunisia, Ghana, Mali, Guinea, Sudan, Ethopia and Somalia. On this tour, he espoused China's "Five Principles of Peaceful Coexistence":

1   Mutual respect for each other's territorial integrity and sovereignty
2   Mutual non-aggression

3   Mutual non-interference in each other's internal affairs
4   Equality and cooperation for mutual benefit
5   Peaceful co-existence.

These five principles have since formed the basis of China's foreign policy decisions. China's non-interference in Africa's internal affairs in its investment and aid decisions are a case in point. Zhou's visit was followed at a high level by the visit of former Chinese president Jiang Zemin to Africa in the year 1996. Jiang visited Kenya, Egypt, Ethiopia, Mali, Namibia and Zimbabwe. The visit was aimed at strengthening the solidarity and cooperation between China and African countries. China's forays into and contact with Africa thus date back to 202 B.C. and A.D. 220, but the most notable are the voyages made by Zheng He in 1415.

So why is the current foray of China into Africa such a big deal? Why is it that China's current engagement with Africa is regarded as a "new colonialism"?

Is it because of the fact that the China of today is an emerging power on the global scene with the requisite resources to flex its muscle? Is it also because China's current foray into Africa has introduced an element of competition between it and Africa's traditional allies, who regard this new competition as "a new Scramble for Africa," referring to China's foray into Africa and the quest for the latter's resources. Competition is good, and if this competition between China and Africa's previous traditional allies leads to increased demand for Africa's natural resources and an increase in aid and investment, Africa stands to gain. From this author's perspective, this increased competition could be one of the major reasons for such a reaction. But beyond that, what is also new is that China's approach in its dealings with Africa in its current engagement with the continent is different and unique. Africans see the Chinese treating them as equals, devoid of the "lecturing" they receive from the West, which they regard as condescending and patronising. China's non-interference policy in Africa's politics or the internal affairs of African countries irks the West. The West's engagement with Africa from the observation of most African leaders has mostly been in its incessant interference in Africa's internal affairs. Furthermore, its aid to Africa often comes with conditionalities, and African leaders feel that all they get from the West is "too much talk" on human rights and the rule of law, while the practical needs of their people, like investments in infrastructure and industries, are neglected. Whiles others might disagree with this view, the facts on the ground as it pertains to China's current investment in Africa proves it – they are preferred as partners to their development than the West.

Also, while the global financial crisis engulfed and seriously impacted the economies of Western countries, China's economy chugged along through the crisis, albeit not as fast as in its early stage of growth. This thus gave African countries the perception that China must be doing something right. They thus welcome its current engagement with Africa. There is an African proverb that goes, "not even frowning frogs can stop the cows from drinking from the pond. Despite the "frowns" and unhappiness of Western countries that the Chinese are in Africa, their previous *"chasse gardée"*, there is nothing they can do to stop them. But this book is not about the rivalry between China and the West over Africa. This book is written for Africa, its people, leaders and policy makers on how they should effectively handle China's current investment in Africa in order to be able to benefit from it by learning from their past engagement with the West. It is more about how African countries can benefit from China's financial and technological investments in Africa by positioning themselves well and effectively to leverage on these investments for their sustainable growth and development. Very little has been written on this issue as it pertains to the current Chinese engagement with Africa.

Chapter 1 of this book will start by looking at the awakening of China, the sleeping giant, specifically looking at China from the era of Mao Tse Tung and his Great Leap Forward policy as well as his introduction of the Cultural Revolution and the disastrous consequences that such policies had on China. Chapter 2 will then look at the era of Deng Xiaoping and his "Opening-Up" policy as well as the factors that contributed to China's awakening. One of the most important factors that also contributed to China's awakening is its entry into the World Trade Organisation (WTO). China's current status as an important global economy would not have been the case if it had not joined the WTO. This will be looked at in Chapter 3 of this book. It must be mentioned here that Chapters 1–3 of this book have benefitted a lot from my previous work and book, *China's New Great Leap Forward: An Emerging China and its Impact on ASEAN*. Chapter 4 will explore the specific reasons why China is interested in Africa. It will look at specific reasons why China is investing in Africa, in what sectors and the resources involved. Furthermore, Chapter 5 will explore the benefits that will accrue to Africa with China's current engagement with the region, especially Chinese investment in Africa. The criticism of this foray will be examined critically in Chapter 6. The effort here is to strike a balance between those who see China's current engagement with Africa as beneficial and those who don't, and the attendant reasons.

In Chapter 7, we will explore the issue of Chinese migration to Africa as a result of Chinese investment in Africa and the impact of such migration on China–Africa relations. This issue is an entirely new development that has not been anticipated by either side. This issue is one of the silent challenges of this engagement but both sides have ignored it or have decided to sweep it under the carpet. Its potential impact on China–Africa relations cannot be emphasised enough. Chapter 8 will look at how African countries can position themselves to benefit from China's foray into Africa. This chapter is more about some suggestions and observations from the author on how this can be achieved. Very little has been written on this issue. For this to happen, Africa needs a strategy to engage China. Does it have one? Can it have one because of the divergent interest amongst African countries? Chapter 9 will look at China's current engagement with Africa and the impact that it has on external players like Europe, Asia, America, Japan and multilateral institutions who also have interests in Africa. Chapter 10 will look at the way forward for Africa and China by exploring the prospects for their engagement into the future. This chapter is more concerned with what China and Africa can do to enhance this relationship to ensure its sustainability and produce win–win outcomes for both parties. The final chapter of this book concludes by pulling all the chapters in the book together.

1 The Sleeping Giant has Awoken
China's New Great Leap Forward

1.1 Introduction

Any effort at understanding China's current engagement with Africa, and indeed its current foray into and investment in Africa, require delving deep into its background and the history of where China came from to where it currently is today. For African countries, the benefit of understanding this history will help them position themselves well in their current engagement with China. In this book, this history will start with the era of Mao Tse-Tung (also known as Mao Zedong). This is because it is when modern political and economic relations between China and Africa began.

This relationship started in 1950, when China signed official bilateral trade agreements with Algeria, Egypt, Guinea, Somalia, Morocco and Sudan. To strengthen these relations, Mao sent Zhou Enlai on a ten-country tour of Africa between December 1963 and January 1964. Hence, any talk about current Chinese investment or engagement with Africa will not be complete without mentioning the effort of Mao Tse-Tung in this respect. When it comes to China, it can be argued that the awakening of China and its growth to its current state can be attributed partly to Mao. His failed policies, which resulted in the death of over 20 million Chinese due to starvation during the "Great Leap Forward" era, made China opt for a better economic system, market socialism, in the 1970s, under the leadership of Deng Xiaoping. This section of the book will therefore look at who Mao Tse-Tung is, how he ascended to power, his failed policies, and their impact on the rise of today's China, linking that to its current engagement with Africa. The section will also look at the rise of Deng Xiaoping and how his prudent policies set the foundation for the growth of modern-day China (Dillion, 2015).

One of Mao's famous quotes in his *Little Red Book* reads, "It is well known that when you do anything, unless you understand its actual circumstances, its nature and its relations to other things, you will not know the laws governing it, or know how to do it or be able to do it well" (Mao, 1936). The irony of this statement is that China's Great Leap Forward effort under Mao did not follow the leader's own wisdom. The consequences were obvious – millions of Chinese peasants died of starvation, and the effort was a total failure. In this book, this event, China's Great Leap Forward, sets the stage for us to be able to look back at the China of yesterday to see the sorry state that it was in – a far cry from what it is today – and how that informs China's rise. Fast forward to another era and a quote by another Chinese leader, Deng Xiaoping, from his pragmatic speech delivered at the Third Plenum of the 11th Central Committee of the CCP held in December 1978: "It doesn't matter if it is a black cat or a white cat, as long as it can catch mice it's a good cat" (Xiaoping, 1962). This observation by Deng captures his pragmatic approach to the development of China, devoid of dogma and ideology, which has helped to usher the country from the sad chapter of Mao's era to its current trajectory of prosperity and growth. This latter chapter in China's developmental trajectory is regarded by this author as China's "new" Great Leap Forward. It is a contrast with the Great Leap Forward era under Mao, where his failed economic policies resulted in the death from hunger of over 20 million Chinese (Xun, 2012). The contrast can also be seen with China's current prosperity, which has made it one of the top economies in the world and a country to be reckoned with in global affairs.

This prosperity has seen China develop with an average growth rate of about 10 percent for the last 20 years and of late a growth rate around 9.7 percent. However, recent Chinese growth rates have not been impressive (see Figure 1.1). But the previous impressive growth rate has enabled the country to move over 300 million people, a significant majority of its population, out of poverty in a rather short time. Although the country still faces the challenge of a good majority of its population still living in poverty, particularly in its hinterlands; this is a far cry from the millions who died of starvation during the period of the Great Leap Forward under Mao Tse-Tung. Even though much still needs to be done, the achievements of China so far in this arena cannot be ignored.

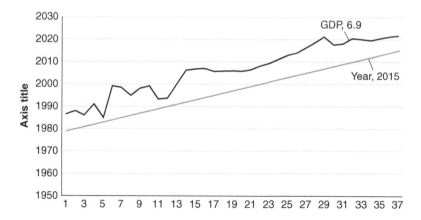

Figure 1.1 Chinese Real GDP Growth, 1979–2015 (percent).

Source: Based on Chinese GDP data Compiled by Author.

This chapter will start by looking at two significant incidents during the era of Mao Tse-Tung specifically during the time of his Great Leap Forward initiative and also Mao's Cultural Revolution and its contribution to China's underdevelopment and ironically, its development as well.

The chapter will continue by looking at Deng Xiaoping's era and how it was a remarkable change from Mao's. It will also examine Deng's opening-up policy and will link that to the ushering in of what I think is China's "new" Great Leap Forward era, an era characterised by the opening up of China, the liberalisation of its economy, the forging of diplomatic relations with other countries, its joining of the World Trade Organization (WTO), and the reform of the country's institutions as well as the witnessing of a period of rapid growth and development, amongst other things. It is also this growth of China that has contributed to its companies venturing abroad. The venturing of Chinese companies abroad sets the stage for us to look at China's current foray into Africa in the subsequent chapters of this book. This background, it is hoped, will help African policy makers and leaders to some understand China and how to deal with the Chinese as they currently invest in Africa.

1.2 Mao Tse-Tung and China's Great Leap Forward

Any attempt to write about the socio-political and economic development of modern-day China will be incomplete without referring to Mao Tse-Tung (Mao Zedong). This book is no exception. Mao is regarded as the principal founder of the People's Republic of China (PRC), and his name is synonymous with Maoism, his political philosophy, which is more of an ideology based on Mao Zedong's thought. Its focus was on China's peasantry as a revolutionary force. Mao believed that if the peasantry were well mobilised, they could become a positive force for change and could undertake a "people's war." It was also under Mao's rule that two significant events in the history of China took place, the Great Leap Forward concept and the Cultural Revolution (Kissinger, 1979 [2011]). The impact of each of these events on the socio-economic and political history of China and the Chinese psyche could go on in perpetuity because of the indelible and devastative impact they had on the Chinese people. But this could also be looked at from the viewpoint that the negative impact of these policies made the Chinese people look for alternative options that they felt were better than Mao's; that would lead to their socio-economic development.

Mao was born into a peasant family on December 26, 1893, in a village called Shaoshan in Hunan Province. In 1819 he graduated from Changsa teacher training college and, after a brief stint in the national army, he went to work at Beijing University as a library assistant. It was while working at Beijing University that Mao was reported to have been converted to Marxism by Li Ta-chao, the head of the library; and Chen Tu-shui, a professor of literature at the same university. In 1921, Mao found the Chinese Communist Party (CCP) in Shanghai, which allied in 1923 with *Koumintang*, (the Nationalist Party) to fight against feuding local warlords. In 1925, Mao concentrated all his efforts on rural China in organising the peasantry, a move that eventually made him break away from the mainstream Communist party after *Koumintang* forces put down a peasant uprising known as the "Autumn Harvest." The organisation of the peasants was to eventually sow the seeds of his rise to power in the 1930s and 1940s. Fast forward to 1949 when Peking (Beijing) fell to Mao and Chiang Kai-Shek was forced to withdraw to Formosa (Taiwan). This allowed Mao to declare the establishment of the People's Republic of China on October 1, 1949.

At the age of 56, Mao became chairman of the CCP with Chou-En-Lai, Lin Piao and Liu Shao-chi helping him to carry out his ideological work. In the early years when Mao was at the helm of the CCP, dissenters were executed or sent to prison or for re-education (brainwashing). At first, Mao modelled his socialist society on that of the former Soviet Union. He later developed a Chinese alternative to that of the Soviets, which reflected the diverse Chinese populations, his experience with peasants and socialist society, and his disdain for bureaucracy. Mao's alternative model tried to integrate intellectuals with peasant guerrilla leaders as an economic and social strategy.

This concept was referred to by Mao as "mass-line" leadership. Stalin, the Soviet leader at that time, condemned Mao for this alternative model, and by 1956, Mao reacted and made public his policies. One of these was his "let a hundred flowers bloom" proclamation. His intent here was to encourage criticism of the bureaucracy by intellectuals. He miscalculated, thinking these criticisms would be minor. When they were not, he launched an "antirightist" campaign and crushed this group. He labelled those intellectuals who disagreed with him and spoke up as "rightist" and jailed, killed or exiled most of them. Those that remained were forced to align with his thinking or had to go underground. But one of the policies that Mao will be most remembered for is the Great Leap Forward (GLF) initiative (Abdulai, 2007).

The GLF initiative was rolled out in 1957 and it was an attempt by Mao to substitute a bureaucratic system for a cellular one. It was his effort to rapidly transform China from an agrarian economy into a rapid and industrialised and collectivised communist economy. The GLF initiative was a system modelled on that of the Paris Commune of 1871, a system of local communes that were autonomous. It was thus Mao's aim with this initiative to make Chinese communes autonomous in their development and enable them to work on projects with a common ideology as the unifying force. Others regarded the GLF initiative as Mao's deliberate attempt to break away from the Soviet model of socialism by developing a Chinese version that he had thought about during his years in Shaanxi. But also it emanated from the bad blood that had evolved between Mao and the Soviet leadership. This strengthened his resolve to see through this vision. The kind of Chinese socialism that Mao was advocating was one that placed importance on moral and material incentives. Thus, it encouraged the people to leap into the lower stage of communism. This leap, it was hoped, would help

China overtake the West in industrial and agricultural development within a few years.

Under this initiative, rural communes were to practice self-reliance as the fundamental principle. The family played a limited role, and collective farms were merged into larger units. Since all Chinese were to engage zealously in physical labour to transform their country, Communist Party cadres were no exception to this rule. Backyard furnaces were developed and metal pans and pots as well as other utensils were collected to make steel to develop tools. Communes were to grow their own food. Even though such initiatives could be regarded as a great idea, they flopped, with serious consequences. For example, as it pertains to agriculture, chaos ensued, and this was heightened by poor weather and a poor harvest, with most of the communal leaders, who were afraid to disappoint Mao, falsifying the amount of grain produced. Thus, the great downfall of the initiative was due to lies. Community leaders lied about an abundant harvest, which was not the case.

Furthermore, Mao, who was rather stubborn and arrogant, refused to see or hear talk from anyone about the failure of his initiatives. Hence, nobody dared to give him any such news. The consequence was one of the greatest famines in history. It led to the death of about 14–20 million Chinese between 1960 and 1962 (Xun, 2012; Dikötter, 2010). This failure was a blow to the CCP and led to the forced retirement of Mao; he was subsequently relegated to the "second line" in the decision-making hierarchy in the CCP, with Liu-Shaoqi and Deng Xiaoping taking charge. But Lui and Deng's leadership did not last long, as we will find out later (Abdulai, 2007).

1.3 Mao Tse Tung and the Cultural Revolution

Those who counted Mao out when he was forced to retire were mistaken. He found a way to come out of "retirement" to launch the Great Proletarian Cultural Revolution (1966–69). The Cultural Revolution was Mao's attempt to give Chinese youth a taste of revolutionary struggle, for he felt that the old Communist Party members were corrupted and infected with Soviet-style revisionism, a style he tried to break away from much earlier when he fell out with the Soviet Union. Some saw the Cultural Revolution as a shrewd way devised by Mao to claw his way back to power, restore his name and seek revenge on his enemies for his humiliation. Jiang Qing, Mao's wife, was known to have relentlessly egged her husband on to reclaim power using the Cultural Revolution as the tool. The target of the Cultural Revolution was the "Four Olds." These were *old customs*, *old habits*, *old culture* and *old ways of thinking*. Some believed that the idea of the "Four Olds" was a clever way for Mao to get rid of his enemies but disguised them in a brilliant ideological way as an effort to remove "bourgeois" and "intellectual" influences and the exploiting class whom he felt were a threat to the Chinese revolution. Mao, who was a consummate strategist, knew that by labelling his enemies as "bourgeois" or as "enemies" of the revolution, it was easy to eliminate them. It is akin to the proverbial "giving a dog a bad name to hang it."

The movement spread to Beijing from Shanghai and in the process consumed some of the top cadres of the CCP, such as Luo Ruiqing, and also saw the purging of Deng Xiaoping. The youth who were now mobilised by Mao into the Red Guards attacked and almost destroyed the party establishment. Mao then brilliantly executed his strategy by stepping in to stop the chaos created by the Red Guards, using the army to restore order and to consolidate his power. During this era of the Cultural Revolution, the Red Guards also attacked authority figures, and sometimes humiliated even their parents and others in public. Chinese intellectuals during this time were put to work in rural areas, toiling away at demeaning jobs that required physical labour. Former mayors and provincial officials were reported to have been put to shame, forced to wear dunce caps and their faces smeared with ink. Landowners had their hair cropped and were forced to bow before crowds. Families were broken and fathers were exiled to work in rural areas with hard labour for dubious denunciations. Sometimes, some of these families were turned in by students who were against their parents for not supporting the Cultural Revolution (Piore, 2003).

An excellent lecture by Li Zhensheng, *Red-Color News Soldier*, offers a pictorial glimpse into Mao's Cultural Revolution. One of the reasons why Li's lecture is important as a glimpse into this era is that he was one of the young photographers that covered Mao's Cultural Revolution for a Communist newspaper in Heilongjian province. Most people during this period committed suicide and those who could flee did. The Cultural Revolution later fell into chaos and plodded along until 1968 when Mao got disenchanted with the chaos and began to impose order using the army. Mao ordered millions of the Red Guards to be resettled in far-off inhospitable parts of China. Thus, the fire of the Cultural Revolution went out in 1969, but aspects of it lingered on until the death of Mao on September 9, 1976. Today, Mao's Cultural Revolution is often referred to as the "Ten Years of Upheaval" or *dong-luan* in Chinese because of the suffering, divisiveness and bitterness it caused. The death of Mao ended the *dong-luan* and introduced a new era of "opening-up" led by Deng Xiaoping.

1.4 Era of Deng Xiaoping

Deng Xiaoping (Teng Hsiao-p'ing) was born in Jiading in the Sichuan province of China. He studied in France and Moscow and served the CCP in various capacities until he succeeded Mao after his death in 1976. Deng had worked with Mao, joining him in the 1930s and participating in the Long March in 1934–35. He was elevated to the CCP's Central Committee in 1945 after serving in several positions in the CCP under Mao. When the National Government collapsed in 1949, Mao set up a Communist government in its place. It was in this government that Deng had the opportunity to rapidly move up the ranks under Mao's patronage. Thus, by 1952, he had risen to the position of vice premier. Between 1956 and 1966, he served as General Secretary of the CCP. When Mao went into forced retirement after the disastrous failure of the GLF experiment, Deng exhibited his pragmatism in his opposition to Mao as part of the radical attacks he made against Mao during this time. In hindsight, these attacks were a miscalculation on the part of Deng. When Mao re-emerged during the era of the Cultural Revolution, Deng was purged. It was only after Mao's death that Hua Guofeng reinstated him in 1977. Deng later forced Hua out of office in 1980 and became the leader of China.

It was Deng who set the People's Republic of China on the path of reform and liberalisation and opened it up to the outside world. His "Open Up" policy, *Kaifang*, is credited with China's rise. This, to many, has changed China into what it is today. Deng started in 1978 to stabilise and strengthen China and its economy. He called for "Four Modernisations" – agriculture, industry, the military, and science and technology. In agriculture, peasants were allowed for the first time to lease land and could sell their harvest at markets. Thus, the agricultural communes, established by Mao, were discontinued. As part of Deng's industrialisation efforts, he established Special Economic Zones (SEZs), where foreign investments were encouraged and foreigners were allowed to establish factories. This was a huge departure from the Great Leap Forward initiative of Mao.

He also modernised the military by improving their weapon systems and technology. The modernisation of the Chinese army is being continued by subsequent Chinese leadership and has attracted concern from the US and other Western countries (see Cheung, 2014). According to the Federation of American Scientists, China is estimated to have an arsenal of about 180 active nuclear warheads and a total of 240 warheads as of 2009. In terms of warheads, China is ranked third in megatonnage and it could double the number of warheads on missiles that could threaten the US by the mid-2020s (Kristensen et al., 2011).

China is also reported to have a huge cache of small arms and weapons, too numerous to name here. The country also has other military weapons that are of deep concern to the US Pentagon. According to a 2014 report released by the Pentagon to US Congress on the advancement in Chinese military weaponry, these weaponry include China's first modern aircraft carrier called *Liaoning*, stealth fighters, jet fighters, huge plane carriers, nuclear submarines, missiles, guided missile destroyers, and intermediate range ballistic missiles (LaGrone and Majumdar, 2014). Roger Cliff (2015) gives a detailed assessment of China's military capabilities in his book *China's Military Power: Assessing Current and Future Capabilities*.

Segal and Yang (1996), in their edited lecture *Chinese Economic Reform: The Impact on Security*, view China's increased economic power translated into an unqualified increase in its military power, and the attendant fear of such an authoritarian, military behemoth. In an effort to enhance its science and technology capacity, thousands of Chinese students were sent abroad by Deng to study science and technology to return and improve on China's science and technology efforts. China is reaping some of these benefits today as many of those sent to study science and technology abroad are back home, contributing to the growth and development efforts of the country.

Deng also engaged in political and economic diplomacy to break China's decades of isolation. For example, in 1978, he visited Japan despite the long-standing frosty relationship between the two countries, and in 1979 he visited the US. He negotiated the return to Chinese sovereignty of Hong Kong from Britain in 1997 and Macau from Portugal in 1999, all in a strategic effort to build China's economic and political might. The brilliant policies pursued by Deng contributed to the rise of today's China.

But there are some who are of the view that Deng was not the principal architect of these sweeping reforms and changes that led to the rise of China. David Shambaugh (1984), a professor at George Washington University in Washington, D.C. in the US and a biographer of Zhao Ziyang, the late former general secretary of the CCP, holds the view that Zhao was the principal architect of the sweeping changes that began in China in the 1980s under Deng. It is reported that Zhao was the one who pushed for the development of coastal provinces into Special Economic Zones. He was also the one that advocated agricultural reforms, price reforms, and industrial reforms. According to Shambaugh, all these ideas were Zhao's, but it was Deng that got the credit (Yardley, 2005).

Even if it was so, one cannot lose sight of the fact that it was Deng that brought Zhao to Beijing in 1980 and made him deputy prime minister. He was later elevated to the position of prime minister and later made the general secretary of the CCP, and he was regarded in many circles as Deng's heir apparent. He fell out of favour with Deng after the Tiananmen Square incident, when he was stripped of his power for his support of the students during the 1989 pro-democracy demonstration and pushed into obscurity. He was put under house arrest for 15 years, and he died in Beijing in 2005. In his book *Prisoner of the State*, Zhao detailed how he agreed that the CCP should look for ways to ease tension with the student protestors at Tiananmen Square. He wrote that by standing up against the conservative elements of the government, he knew that he had sealed his fate (Zhao, 2009).

But the truth is that Zhao had miscalculated and hedged his bets in favour of the students, thinking that they could topple the CCP. Someone like Zhao, who was part of the inner circle of the CCP, should have known that the CCP does not tolerate dissent and thus will do everything in its power to crush any such dissent. The brutal crushing of the Tiananmen Square student demonstrations is a testimony to this fact.

Thus, any time the story of China's rise is told, Deng's Opening Up strategy and his liberalisation policies will be remembered (Dillion, 2015). But Deng will also be remembered for the Tiananmen Square massacre. Ironically, it was Deng's economic and social reform policies that are regarded as having unleashed the political and social aspirations of the people, particularly the young generation of Chinese. The socio-political aspirations of the young generation, and the unwillingness of the CCP to compromise, led to the massacre. When Deng came under intense criticism from the US over the Tiananmen massacre, he spoke out vociferously against the US, saying, "the United States has blamed us for suppressing the students. But didn't the US itself call out police and troops to deal with student strikes and disturbances, and didn't that lead to arrests and bloodshed? It suppressed the students and the people, while we put down a counter-revolutionary rebellion. What right has it to criticize us" (Xiaoping, 1989).

Apparently, Deng was referring to the putting down of student protest in the US during the Civil Rights and Vietnam War eras as cases in point. He was referring to anti-Vietnam protests at Kent State University in Ohio on May 4, 1970, where the US National Guards shot and killed four young students. The shooting resulted in four million students going on strike in 450 universities and colleges in the US Deng was also referring to the violent quelling with water hoses, dogs, and police batons of civil rights demonstrations in the US in the 1960s, when African-Americans protested against racial segregation and discrimination. These included nonviolent and civil disobedience protests, such as the Montgomery bus boycott, the Selma to Montgomery marches, and the Greensboro sit-ins, to mention just a few.

After the Tiananmen incident, Deng resigned from his official posts but wielded authority behind the scenes to enable him continue with the promotion and implementation of his economic reform policies. His health took a turn for the worse in the 1990s and, with the fear of a power struggle ensuing on his death, Deng installed Jiang Zemin as his handpicked heir. He died on February 19, 1997, from his prolonged illness. Some Asian leaders like Lee Kuan Yew, the late first prime minister of Singapore, looked back at the Tiananmen Square incident with the view that China would have been worse off today if the protesters had succeeded in toppling the Communist authorities. According to Lee, Deng's action to crush the protest was to save China; he argues that democracy is not a necessary precondition for economic progress and may in some instances even retard the creation of wealth. He added, "I do not believe that if you are a libertarian, full of diverse opinions, full of competing ideas in the market place. Full of sound and fury, therefore you will succeed" (*New Straits Times*, 2004d, p. 21).

Of course, there are those who will disagree with Lee's views on this issue and indeed he is entitled to his view. From the time he ruled Singapore until his retirement as prime minister and also until his death, Lee Kuan Yew was an autocrat and did not whole-heartedly believe in some of the tenets of Western democracy. For example, he did not believe, as is the case in Western democracies, that the media is the "Fourth Estate." He did clamp down hard on dissent and on political opponents as prime minister. I think no one can tell if China would be worse or better off today if the protesters of Tiananmen Square had succeeded. Yet, all will agree that the Tiananmen Square incident will form an important part of the modern history of China, no matter which side of the fence you are on as it pertains to Lee Kuan Yew's views (Abdulai, 2007).

Jiang Zemin, who took over from Deng, was born on August 17, 1926, in Yangzhou city in China. He studied electrical engineering at Jiatong University in 1947. He joined the CCP in 1946 and held many high-level positions, including the post of minister of electronics and industry from 1983 to 1985 and Mayor of Shanghai from 1985 to 1989. He became general secretary of the Communist Party in 1989 and president of China in 1993. Jiang continued the policies of Deng such as the liberalisation of the economy, and he initiated as well as engineered China's entry into the WTO with his premier Zhu Rongji. Zhu Rongji was the brains behind the implementation and shepherding in of the reforms during their era. Zhu's book *Zhu Rongji on the Record: The Road to Reform (1991–1997)* gives details of how these reforms were undertaken.

Jiang did all this, yet maintained a strong grip on political power. He also made efforts to create a name for himself and to even influence the CCP by developing a new ideology for the party. He came up with concepts like "Spiritual Civilisation," and by this his intention was that the Chinese people should be able to find a balance between spiritualism and the materialist civilisation they were now confronted with. He also came up with the "Three Representation" concept. By this concept, Jiang Zemin was calling on his party to represent the "interest of the masses" (it was more of a representation of Mao's order), the "interests of productive forces" (a concept that identifies more with Deng's era) and the "interests of the new advanced culture" (a view from his period and beyond and where China needs to go).

When Jiang was first appointed as the successor of Deng, many were those who internally and externally wrote him off as awkward and unimpressive. Some even regarded him as bland and felt that he was a convenient tool of the CCP to be effective, and thus would have to depend on Deng, who handpicked him, in order to survive. Those who were quick to write off Jiang were mistaken. In fact, his unimpressive and sometimes even aloof persona was his strength and masked a skilful politician who was able to rise through the byzantine web of the Chinese political structure and system. He held on to power until 2001, when he decided to step down and chose Hu Jintao to be his successor. Even with Hu as the president, Jiang still held on to the position of chairman of the State Military Commission, undoubtedly a powerful position that enabled him to control China's army.

The view held by some was that it was a shrewd way for Jiang to wield power behind the scenes. Jiang finally stepped down from his position as head of the armed forces in September 2004. It was reported that behind the scenes, pressure was put on him by the Central Committee members to retire, following the footsteps of the late Deng Xiaoping (*New Straits Times*, 2004a, p.28). In March of 2005, China's parliament voted overwhelmingly to accept the resignation of Jiang from the position he had held for 15 years.

1.5 Deng and the "Opening-Up" Policy

China's incredible growth today would not have been possible if the economy had not been opened up and reforms were not begun by Deng Xiaoping. Deng's "opening-up" and reform policies can be credited for the economic gains China is enjoying today (Kissinger, 1979 [2011]; Dillion, 2015). It all started when he took over power in 1976. His first bold economic reform that points to such an opening up was to put into place the Household Responsibility System that made rural farmers responsible for their plots of land. For the first time in history, these farmers were allowed under this system to sell their produce on the open market after meeting a state quota obligation. This new radical policy by Deng unleashed a productivity surge that provided a bumper harvest. It also sparked the individual initiative in rural farmers, and, for the first time, most of these people could participate in the market in a small way.

As part of the opening-up policy, Deng introduced the "Four Modernisations." These modernisations were to begin to develop those aspects of the Chinese economy that would lead the country on the road to economic development. These were agriculture, industry, the military, and science and technology. In agriculture, he dismantled the old communes, and peasants were free to sell their harvest in markets. The setting-up of Special Economic Zones (SEZs) was a way to modernise Chinese industry. In these SEZs, foreign direct investment (FDI) was encouraged through tax incentives, and foreigners were allowed to establish industries in these zones. To invigorate these SEZs, Deng undertook his now famous "Southern Inspection" trip in 1992. This trip was in the tradition of some of China's great emperors like Kang Xi and Quan Long, which were usually undertaken to see how successful their policies were.

Deng wanted to see whether the SEZ model he introduced could be adopted around China. In his modernisation of the military, Deng made sure that they were provided with new weapons and up-to-date training under this policy. To modernise China's science and technology capabilities, Deng sent many Chinese students abroad to study and acquire skills in this rather important area. These students were then to return and help in its development efforts. Deng's investments are paying off, as most of these students are returning and are contributing to the vibrant Chinese economy we are seeing today (*The Star*, 2003, p. 34).

But Deng's opening-up policy was not only confined to the aforementioned four areas. He also gradually started to open up China diplomatically. For example, in 1978, Deng toured Southeast Asia and Japan. In 1979, he visited the US. In 1980, he negotiated the return to Chinese sovereignty of Hong Kong from Britain, which became a reality in 1997; and Macau from Portugal, which happened in 1999. All these were important events that in a way have contributed and set China on the way to its current economic achievements. For example, starting in 1992, the fruits of Deng's opening-up policies were seen in the expansion of the economy to 14.2 percent. It grew to 13.5 percent in 1993 and 12.7 percent in 1994, and the growth dropped to 10.5 percent in 1995 (Panitchpakdi and Clifford, 2002).

Between 1978 and 2000, the average economic growth of the Chinese economy was 9 percent annually. By the time Deng died in 1997, the reform process he put in place to move the country along had taken root, and his hand-picked successor, Jian Zemin, was sure to keep on with the reforms; he did so until he also handed over power to Hu Jintao in 2000. Hu Jintao led China from 2000 to 2012. He was born on December 21, 1942, in Taizhou, Jiangsu province. He graduated from Tsinhua University as an engineer. As president of China, he presided over a decade of consistent economic growth and development in the country. During his tenure, he introduced the Scientific Development Concept. The aim of such a concept was to build China into a harmonious socialist society, prosperous and free of conflict. In his foreign policy, he continued to advocate China's peaceful development policy, and during his tenure, China's influence in Africa increased tremendously. Since then, Hu Jintao has handed power to another generation of leadership led by Xi Jinpin.

1.6 China's New Great Leap Forward

China's first GLF (1958–60) was in another time in the past. It was a time when China wanted to develop but failed miserably with severe consequences, resulting in the loss of millions of lives due to famine (Kissinger, 1979 [2011]). Today, China is witnessing a different GLF. This particular new GLF is seeing China attain the goals it once could only have dreamed of in the era of the first GLF under Mao. This comprises impressive economic growth rates, one of the fastest growing economies in the world and an impressive creation of wealth in the history of China. China's new GLF can be likened to a giant awoken from its long slumber as earlier predicted by Napoleon, and both developed and developing economies are paying attention.

Today's China is a far cry from the days of Mao and his GLF. China's new GLF has seen a true economic emergence of the country and has instilled pride and confidence in its people. Here are a few economic details that testify to such a fact. China's economy grew at an average of 9.1 percent annually between 1980 and 2000. Even during the Asian financial crisis, when most of the economies in Southeast Asia were witnessing negative growth, the economy of China continued to grow. In 2001, China's economy grew to 7.3 percent and to 8 percent in 2002. China's growth rates are expected to be sustained at an annual rate of 6–7 percent or more over the next 10 years. So far, China's economy has been growing at an average of 9 percent since 2003. Figure 1.1 shows China's growth since 1979. However, at the time of this writing, the Chinese economy is facing a slowdown in its growth. Its stock market recently (2016) was in turmoil and its currency was sharply depreciated, with the currency falling 1.3 percent to the US dollar (Wheatley, 2016;

Norbrook, 2015). This recent turmoil in the Chinese stock market and the recent slowdown in its economy does not mean that China's economic prowess has diminished. It is still the second largest economy in the world.

Exports in the country grew from US$10 billion in 1978 to US$278 billion in 2002, making China the sixth largest trading nation in the world at that time (Adhikari and Yang, 2002). Its share of global exports has tripled, and its share of world imports doubled from 1990 to 2002. For example, in 2001, China's exports rose by 23 percent to US$266 billion and accounted for 4.4 percent of all world exports. Its trade surplus in 2001 increased to over US$30 billion (*Economist*, 2003). China is the largest recipient of FDI in both regional and developing world terms. For the first time in 2002, FDI in China rose by 13 percent to US$52.7 billion, surpassing the US as the top FDI recipient according to UNCTAD (*New Straits Times*, 2003, p. B16). Furthermore, A. T. Kearney's FDI Confidence Index Survey of 2002 has China as the most attractive investment destination in the world, surpassing the US for the first time. China's foreign trade and foreign reserves have jumped from US$147.3 billion, US$20.6 billion and US$167 million to over US$1.4 trillion, US$851.2 billion and US$403.3 billion respectively (*China Daily*, 2004, p. 7).

Figure 1.1 shows the growth of the Chinese economy from 1979, when it was at 7.6 percent, to 2013, when it was at 7.3 percent. Except for the years 1981, when growth was 5.3 percent; and 1989 and 1991, when growth was 4.1 and 3.8 percent respectively, China's growth has averaged about 7 percent annually for the last three decades.

In addition, China's ascension to the WTO is another important event that contributed to its current economic growth. Even though China will be forced by the some of the WTO rules to open up its economy, the benefits of joining the WTO outweigh the costs. China will no longer have to go before the US Congress to get its most favoured nation (MFN) status renewed. It will have access to many markets around the world and, most important of all, it will attract more FDI into its economy. The issue of China's entry into the WTO is dealt with at length in Chapter 3 of this book. Thus far, this chapter has shown where modern-day China came from and how some of the events of the different eras have played a role in its economic emergence. African leaders and policy makers will do well to learn from China's growth experience and trajectory. Knowledge of this background will help them in their dealings with China.

The next chapter will look at some specific factors and issues that have contributed to China's economic emergence. The rationale for this chapter is to enable African policy makers in their dealings with China to appreciate the challenges China had to go through to attain its current economic might. As African countries and their leadership continue to look at China's mode of development and aspects they hope to emulate, this history and background of China's emergence could influence how they deal with China. It could also lead to their ability to learn from China's experience.

1.7 Conclusion

The most talked-about country in boardrooms around the world, in factories, in the strategy sessions of corporations, and amongst politicians and policy makers in both developed and developing countries is China. It is all about an emerging China and how it is going to affect their bottom line and their economies either positively or negatively. But that was not the case long ago. Until the end of the Cold War, China was synonymous with inferior goods, a poor struggling country, communism, and human rights abuses, to mention just a few. It was the same China that, under Mao Tse Tung, attempted to in his words to "surpass the West" in what he dubbed a Great Leap Forward. This effort failed miserably, leading to the starvation of millions of Chinese. Mao's Cultural Revolution was equally disastrous for China.

It was after Mao's death that Deng Xiaoping decided to change course and opened up the economy and the country to the outside world. His famous saying, "It doesn't matter if it is a black cat or a white cat, as long as it can catch mice it's a good cat" (Xiaoping, 1962) summarised his philosophy and pragmatism, which were the guiding force for the gradual modernisation of China and a move toward a market economy. His policies of the opening up of China and the subsequent restoration of diplomatic relations with most of the countries in the world saw prosperity come to China for the first tie. This has led to what this author terms in this book as "China's new Great Leap Forward."

After the Tiananmen Square incident, Deng took a back seat but handpicked Jiang Zemin to replace him and urged him to continue with the reforms. This Jiang did until the death of Deng in 1997. Jiang continued with the reforms until he also stepped down and chose Hu Jintao to replace him. Hu has also since step down, and Xi Jinping has been chosen to replace him. It is this continuation of the reform process and the opening-up policies started by Deng that is seeing China undertaking its new Great Leap Forward and becoming a global economic and military force to be reckoned with.

2 Some of the Factors that Contributed to China's Awakening

2.1 Introduction

The ancient Chinese philosopher Lao Tsu (570–490 B.C.) once said that "the journey of a thousand miles begins with a step." Similarly, the journey that saw China's emergence via reforms and the opening up of its economy began with one step. It started when Deng Xiaoping allowed peasants to lease land and sell their harvest in markets without any fear of reprisals from the central government or the Chinese Communist Party (CCP). Since taking those wobbly steps, the country has not looked back. The reforms and opening up have been gradual and at China's pace, but they have had a profound impact on the Chinese people and the world. As Deng Xiaoping once remarked, *Mozhe shitouguo he*, "we must cross the river by stepping on the stones" (Xiaoping, 1984). Deng's view was that China cannot afford not to open up but it must not rush the opening-up process for fear of unforeseen circumstances. Today, China has emerged as an economic as well as a political powerhouse on the global stage.

What are some of the factors and issues of both domestically and internationally that contributed to this emergence?

This chapter is going to look at some of these factors, which range from the desire on the part of China to reclaim its past pre-eminence, the failure of Mao's policies, and the collapse of the former Soviet Union to Deng's visionary and pragmatic leadership.

2.2 China's Desire to Reclaim its Past Pre-Eminence

The China of yesterday was a glorious one with a long history of impressive achievements and innovations. For example, gunpowder, paper, printing and the compass were invented in China. Ancient China also produced philosophers like Lao Zi, Sun Zi, Mencius and Confucius. It also boasts a long history of dynasties starting from the Xia dynasty in 2070 B.C. to the fall of the Qing dynasty in 1911. The Xia dynasty was overthrown by the Shang dynasty (1600–1046 B.C.). The Shang dynasty was followed by the Zhou dynasty (1046–221 B.C.). The Zhou dynasty was followed by the Qin dynasty

(259–210 B.C.). It was during the period of the Qin dynasty, under the rule of Emperor Qin Shi Huang, that the first centralised and unified feudal state in Chinese history was established. It is also important to note that it was under the rule of Emperor Qin that the first standardised written scripts, weights, measures and currencies were established. He also established the system of prefectures and counties. But the most outstanding development under Emperor Qin's rule was the building of the Great Wall of China, which stretches for about 5000 kilometres in the northern part of China and took a labour force of 300,000 12 years to build.

But everything has an end. The Qin dynasty ended when it was defeated by the Han dynasty (206 B.C.–A.D. 220). It was under this dynasty that handicrafts, agriculture and commerce flourished. The famous "Silk Road" had its beginnings during this dynastic period when Emperor Wudi expanded the territory of the empire from present day Xinjiang in the Central Plains to Central Asia and the east coast of the Mediterranean sea. It was also during this time that Buddhism spread to China and the paper-making technique was invented. Next came the period of the Three Kingdoms, which comprised the Jin dynasty (265–420), the Southern and Northern dynasties (420–589) and the Sui dynasty (581–618).

The Tang dynasty (618–907) followed the Sui dynasty. Under this dynastic period, technologies were enhanced for textile manufacturing and the production of pottery and porcelain as well as ship-building and smelting. During this time, China's influences reached far as cultural and trade relations were established with many countries, including Japan, Korea, India, Persia, and Arabia. The period following the fall of the Tang dynasty was one of wars. When it precipitated, the Song dynasty emerged (960–1279). During this dynastic period, China was the leader of the world in astronomy and in science and technology. It was during this period that movable type was first made from clay. This invention contributed to the increase in the number of lectures published during that time.

The Yuan dynasty (1271–1368) was established when the grandson of Genghis Khan, Kublai Khan, conquered the Central Plains, making Dadu, today's Beijing, his capital. Beijing, formerly known as Peking, is still the capital of China today. The Song and Yuan dynastic periods were also the time when four great inventions in the history of mankind emerged. These were papermaking, printing and the invention of the compass and gunpowder. After the Yuan dynasty, the Ming dynasty (1368–1644) emerged. It is reported that in this dynastic period, the largest-scale and the longest voyages before the time of Christopher Columbus were made. Table 2.1 shows a list of China's dynasties from Xia to Qing.

Reports have it that Zhu Di (1360–1424), the son of Zhu Yuanzhang, the founder of the Ming dynasty, sent a eunuch called Zheng He on these voyages. Zheng passed through South East Asia, the Indian Ocean, the Persian Gulf and the Maldives, reaching faraway places like Somalia, Kenya, and parts of the east coast of Africa (The story of the voyages of Zheng He has been made into a National Geographic T.V. documentary).

Table 2.1 China's Dynasties

Dynasty	Date
Xia	2070–1600 B.C.
Shang	1600–1046 B.C.
Western Zhou	1046–771 B.C.
Eastern Zhou Spring and Autumn period	770–476 B.C.
Warring States period	475–221 B.C.
Qin	221–207 B.C.
Western Han	206 B.C.–A.D. 24
Eastern Han	A.D. 25–220
Three Kingdoms	A.D. 220–265
Western Jin	A.D. 265–316
Eastern Jin	A.D. 317–420
Southern and Northern dynasties	A.D. 420–589
Sui	A.D. 581–618
Tang	A.D. 618–907
Five dynasties	A.D. 907–960
Northern Song	A.D. 960–1127
Southern Song	A.D. 1127–1279
Yuan	A.D. 1271–1368
Ming	A.D. 1368–1644
Qing	A.D. 1644–1911

Source: China 2003, 1st Edition, New Star Publications, Beijing, China.

Then, in 1644, the Manchus of northeast China established the Qing dynasty (1644–1911). By the early nineteenth century, the decline of the Qing dynasty set in. The dynasty's rulers fought with the British in 1840 as the latter wanted to protect its opium trade. In 1911, the Qing dynasty fell to Sun Yat-sen's 1911 revolution. This revolution was also to signal the end of over 2000 years of feudal rule in China, paving the way for the establishment of the Republic of China (1912–1949). This brief synopsis hopes to encapsulate some aspects of China's glorious past. It is also important to mention in passing that pre-Communist China also had a significant industrial development history (Chang, 2010).

The psychological significance of China's past pre-eminence in the world and the history and prestige of this past pre-eminence as detailed in this section, as well as all the numerous inventions that it presents, viewed cumulatively, is, in the opinion of this author, one of the driving forces behind the desire of modern Chinese leadership to see the China of today recapture such past pre-eminence. In a way, it thus contributes to a better understanding of some of the actions and thinking behind some of the decisions that have been undertaken by recent Chinese leadership. Some of these actions may seem bizarre to the outside world, but China's history has contributed to the emergence of the country as it is today and will continue to guide its leaders' decisions as it pertains to the future of China. As we are adequately advised by Niccolo Machiavelli in his book *The Prince*, "those who want to advance into the future must learn from the past" (Machiavelli, 1515 [2007]). The Chinese have taken this adage to heart. African leaders and policy makers can learn from this history. It will help them understand the psychology of Chinese leaders and the actions and thinking behind some of their policies and decisions concerning Africa, as well as their actions on the global stage. This could help African leaders and policy makers immensely in their negotiations and dealings with China.

2.3 The Failure of Mao's Policies

One of the factors that has contributed to the emergence of China today as an economic and political power are the lessons learnt from some of the failed policies of Mao. For any nation to progress, grow and develop, it must be willing to learn from the mistakes of the past. It must not dwell on the past, but the past must be the best guide for its future actions, making sure that it does not repeat mistakes. Mao's failed economic policies, from collective agriculture to his Great Leap Forward and Cultural Revolution policies, have contributed to famine and tyrannical rule and resulted in the ultimate retrogression of China during his era. It also brought about the closing of the Chinese society to the outside world. Speaking to some members of the Chinese Liberation Army in March 1981, Deng Xiaoping said,

> When the Great Leap Forward started, was there anyone who opposed it? But later some comrades including Mao Zedong himself found that there was something wrong with it. The two meetings comrade Mao convened in Zhengzhou were precisely for the purpose of rectifying the 'Left' errors in the Great Leap Forward. During the 17 years preceding the Cultural Revolution our work, in the main, proceeded along a correct path, though there were twists and turns and mistakes.
>
> (Xiaoping, 1981)

It can be deduced from this carefully worded speech by Deng that subsequent Chinese leadership after Mao did recognise that there were problems with some of his policies and ideologies. It was the harsh experiences under the Mao era that in a way hardened the resolve of most Chinese and their leadership not to repeat them again.

Mao's policies included the launching of mass campaigns, which he said would root out traitors, counterrevolutionaries and corruption; he introduced the "Three-Anti" as well as the "Five-Anti," campaigns that involved intense investigations into the private lives of Chinese citizens. In another campaign, "Let a Hundred Flowers Bloom, Let all the Schools of Thought Contend," he intended to encourage freedom of speech and establish a way for Chinese intellectuals to criticise the CCP. Mao thought such criticisms would be minimal. He was mistaken. The torrent of criticisms forced him to clamp down hard on these intellectuals who dared to criticise the CCP. He labelled them "rightist" and imprisoned and exiled most of them. This was the beginning of some of his failed policies. What subsequent Chinese leadership has learned from these failed policies and the willingness to change has also contributed to the emergence of China today.

It is no secret that for any nation to grow, it needs its intelligentsia, or what are referred to today as "knowledge workers." China's persecution of its "knowledge workers" during Mao's era was a grave error and had a severe impact on its growth and development for a very long time. In later years, when Deng took the helm of power, he spoke out against such repressions and tried to rectify them. In a speech in 1978, Deng said,

> We must firmly put a stop to bad practices such as attacking and trying to silence people who make critical comments, especially sharp ones, by ferreting out their political backgrounds, tracing political rumours to them and opening "special case" files on them…but of course we must not let down our guard against the handful of counterrevolutionaries who still exist in the country.
>
> (Xiaoping, 1978)

Also in 1958, Mao's policies saw the introduction of the Great Leap Forward (GLF) initiative. He wanted to overtake the West in industrial and agricultural production in a few years. He wanted to achieve in minimal time a feat that had taken the West many years to accomplish. The results were disastrous, yet Mao was stubborn and refused to hear about any failures. Hence, peasants falsified grain production numbers because they were afraid to report any bad news to the leaders. The result was a catastrophe of enormous proportions, leading to the death of millions of Chinese. Because of this failed policy, Mao was forced to retire, but not for long. He fought his way back by mobilising the youth into what was called the Red Guards, and they attacked and destroyed the CCP establishment. He accused the Communist Party cadres of not living up to the ideas of Communism and reverting to Soviet-style revisionism. But Mao's main aim was to restore his name after his humiliation due to the failure of his GLF policy. It was also a way to seek revenge against his enemies. This led to chaos, death and destruction. Even Mao became disenchanted with the trajectory of the Cultural Revolution, but it was too late and it had gone too far.

The fire of the Cultural Revolution finally went out with the death of Mao in 1976. When Deng ascended the throne, he put the final nails in the coffin of the Cultural Revolution by crushing the "Gang of Four"—Jiang Qing, Zhang Chunqiao, Yao Wenyuan and Wang Hongwen. Party cadres and leaders who survived persecution under the Cultural Revolution vowed that they would never allow anything like that to happen again. Towards the last days of his life, even Mao accepted the fact that the Cultural Revolution was a failure. He said that "the Cultural Revolution has been a failure on two counts: One was 'overthrowing all' and the other was waging a 'full-scale civil war'" (Xiaoping, 1980).

All these failed policies of Mao have, in a way, contributed to the impetus of subsequent Chinese leaders, especially Deng Xiaoping, to look for the workable policies that have resulted in the emergence of China today. Even though Mao is still respected as the founder of the People's Republic of China and its socialist political ideology, his policies during his rule had a devastating impact on China's development. Deng Xiaoping hinted at this in the Third Plenary Session of the Eleventh Party Congress of the Chinese Communist Party in Beijing in December 1978, when he said "We must seek truth from facts" (Xiaoping, 1978). Euphemistically, Deng was quoting Mao, urging party members to realise the truth: that even though Mao was a great leader, the fact is that some of his policies were a disaster and had immense consequences for the Chinese people. It was thus Deng's way of urging them to embrace the opening-up policies he had introduced.

2.4 The Collapse of the former Soviet Union

The collapse of the former Soviet Union contributed, in a curious way, to the emergence of today's China. Both China and the former Soviet Union were Communist countries and the largest in the Communist world during the era of the Cold War. The collapse of the former Soviet Union brought about the end of the Cold War. It can be said that the collapse of the former Soviet Union represented somewhat of a learning curve for the Chinese in the opening-up process of their economy. Historically, China and the former Soviet Union had always had good relations during the era of Mao and Joseph Stalin. These relations ultimately went sour after the death of Stalin. When Mikhail Gorbachev took over power in the former Soviet Union in 1985, he endeavoured to restore the broken relations between China and the former Soviet Union that went back as far as the 1930s. The beginning of the troubled relations between the two countries was over ideological differences in their various versions of Communism as well as over the personal idiosyncrasies of Mao and Kruschev in the leadership of the Communist world.

When Stalin died in 1953, Mao felt it was now his turn to become the leader of the Communist world. Mao grew resentful of the new Soviet leadership under Kruschev, who did not regard him as such and refused to accord him the status he believed he deserved. In addition, Mao believed that the Soviet leadership at that time strayed away from the true Marxist–Leninist ideals of the struggle for the world triumph of Communism. This led to a split between China and the Soviet Union in 1960, a confrontation and subsequently a conflict. Border tensions even arose in 1969, leading to armed clashes between the two Communist countries along the banks of the Ussuri River on Damansky Island. Gorbachev's visit to China in 1989, therefore, was a way to find a lasting solution to this conflict between the two Communist countries and neighbours. It was during the meeting of Gorbachev and Deng that relations between China and the then Soviet Union were formally normalised.

When Gorbachev introduced his *Perostroika* – the reforming or restructuring of the Soviet system, politically, economically and socially (Gorbachev, 1988), he without caution undertook extensive reforms in quite a short space of time. The Chinese watched in horror as the Soviet Union collapsed in the wake of Gorbachev's hasty implementation of reforms and the opening up of its economy without the adequate checks and balances. Behind closed doors, most of the Chinese leadership, especially Deng, thought Gorbachev was foolish to embark on the political reform of the former Soviet Union without first undertaking economic reforms. To the Chinese leadership at that time, it was like putting the cart before the horse, so to speak. This, they saw, was going to be a recipe for disaster and would weaken Gorbachev's rule, and so it did. It also led to political unrest. States broke away and chaos broke out, and Gorbachev was eventually kicked out of power by the late Boris Yeltsin. But even after Yeltsin took over, there was still a certain amount of chaos in the country.

It was exactly this kind of chaos and political unrest that the CCP wanted to avoid. They understood in no uncertain terms that change was inevitable but that in any system of change, those who have benefited from the old regime will not be willing to let go without a fight. This observation was aptly captured by Machiavelli in *The Prince*, when he said that "it must be considered that there is nothing more difficult to carry out, nor more doubtful of success, nor more dangerous to handle, than to initiate a new order of things. For the reformer has enemies in all those who profit by the older, and only lukewarm defenders in those who would profit by the new order" (Machiavelli, 1515 [2007]). On the other hand, those that had not benefited from the old order wanted drastic change. These forces of push and pull, if not handled well, could result in chaos, and that is exactly what had happened to the former Soviet Union.

Consequently, when Deng undertook the opening up of China, the lessons of the collapse of the former Soviet Union were fresh in his mind. He made sure the power of the CCP was strong, and it is still so today. A testimony to this way of thinking was the clamping down hard on student protesters in Tiananmen Square and the purging of the Communist Party of leaders like Zhao Ziyang who were sympathetic to the students. It could be that this crackdown was due to Deng's fear that if he was lenient China might end up with a similar fate as the former Soviet Union. This author is sure that there are many views on the way the Tiananmen Square incident should have been handled. Such a debate is not the preoccupation of this book. What is clear is that Deng's opening-up process was gradual and that the fate of the former Soviet Union, the rapid opening up of its system, and its subsequent quick demise were fresh in the minds of the Chinese leadership at that time. In a strange way, the gradual opening up, in which it was ensured that economic reforms were afoot before China's attempt to open up politically, is partly due to the lesson they learned from the collapse of the former Soviet Union in their reform and opening-up process. It is also due to the fact that the CCP did not wish to lose control of the country and its grip on political power. This, in the view of this author, has contributed to the emergence of a strong and prosperous China, which is stable with a strong leadership.

2.5 Deng Xiaoping's Visionary and Pragmatic Leadership

Before a meeting of cadres of the Central Committee of the CCP in 1980, Deng said,

> Modernization is at the core of all these three major tasks, because it is the essential condition for solving both our domestic and our external problems. Everything depends on our doing the work in our own country well. The role we play in international affairs is determined by the extent of our economic growth. If our country becomes more developed and prosperous, we will be in a position to play a greater role in international affairs.
>
> (Xiaoping, 1980)

Such a poignant observation by Deng points to the vision and ideas that have guided his thinking. This pragmatic vision is what has contributed to the emergence of China today. Commenting on this new emergence of China because of Deng, the late Lee Kuan Yew, the first Prime Minister of Singapore said, "if I compare the China of today with the China I saw in the last days of the Mao era in 1976–79, it's so vastly different it's unimaginable" (Chang, 2001). Deng realised from the outset that without the opening up of the Chinese economy, the development of science and technology and the allowing of some freedoms under the Chinese Communist model, the country will never develop. He introduced the concept of the "four modernisations" in an effort to step up economic construction. According to Deng, economic construction is all about stepping up the drive of China's "four modernisations." This will enable China to build a strong economic foundation to help it modernise its national defence and science and technology.

In August 1980, Deng was asked by the late Italian journalist Oriana Fallaci whether his "four modernisations" policy, which was to bring foreign capital into China, would inevitably give rise to private investment and subsequently a miniaturised version of capitalism. He responded that no matter how much China opens up to the outside world and admits foreign capital, its relative magnitude will be small and would not affect China's socialist system of public ownership of the means of production. His answer to Fallaci was a take from his speech at the Twelfth National Congress, when he said,

> We will unswervingly follow a policy of opening to the outside world and actively increase exchanges with foreign countries on the basis of equality and mutual benefit. At the same time, we will keep clear heads,

firmly resist corrosion by decadent ideas from abroad and never permit the bourgeois way of life to spread to our country."

(Xiaoping, 1982)

However, he admitted to Fallaci that such a move might bring some decadent capitalist influences into China. "We are aware of this possibility; it's nothing to be afraid of" (Xiaoping, 1980). Deng was right. He would be turning in his grave today if he saw the amount of decadent capitalism that has invaded his country. Decadent capitalist influences and heightened corruption are some of the ills the CCP is fighting today as a result of its opening-up policies.

Indeed, the opening up of the economy has introduced corruption and a lot of economic crimes; this is still an issue and is one of the challenges facing China today. Before his death, Deng saw the increase in such economic crimes and sought to curb them. At a speech before the political bureau of the Central Committee in April 1982, Deng lashed out at the rise in economic crimes and argued for culprits to be dealt with mercilessly. He said,

A number of cadres have been corrupted in the brief year or two since we adopted the policy of opening up to the outside world and stimulating our economy. Quite a few are involved in economic crimes. These misdeeds are more serious than the crimes exposed in the days of the movements against the "three evils."

(Xiaoping, 1982)

He called for those involved in economic crimes to be expelled from the party, from the army and from public employment. He added,

The struggle against economic crime is one of the ways of ensuring that we keep to the socialist road and realise the 'four modernizations'. It is an ongoing struggle, a regular item of work. If we don't make it so, how can we talk about keeping to the socialist road? Without this struggle, the 'four modernizations' and the policy of opening to the outside world and stimulating the economy will end in failure.

(Xiaoping, 1982)

It seems that Deng is reaching out from his grave to fight "Decadent Capitalism" – or corruption – through the fifth generation of Chinese leaders in the persons of Xi Jinping and Li Keqiang. In the short time since they assumed power, they have jailed many senior party officials for corruption.

For example, Gu Janshan, a former senior military officer, was sentenced to death with a two-year reprieve for corruption. Ex-security chief Zhou Yongkang was jailed for life for bribery, abuse of power and disclosure of national secrets. In his speech as head of state, Xi said "we must resolutely reject formalism, bureaucratism, hedonism and extravagance and resolutely fight against corruption and other misconduct" (*Business Day*, 18 March 2013, p. 6).

Deng spent the rest of his life deepening the reforms that he set in motion and was succeeded by his handpicked loyalist Jiang Zemin. He died in 1997. Today, Deng would be greatly disappointed if he was to hear of the magnitude of corruption in China since the opening-up process. This corruption is hindering the reforms he put into place and has had the impact he predicted before his death. Nevertheless, Deng's policies and their impact on China and the contribution he made to its current growth and development trajectory will never be forgotten by the Chinese people. For example, during the recent celebration of the 100th anniversary of Deng's birth, Hu Jintao, the former president of China, praised Deng by saying, "the creative ideas of late leader Deng Xiaoping and the policies he put forward have provided a strong theoretical guidance to the continuous development of the cause of the Party and people" (*New Straits Times*, 2004c, p. 20).

On the same day, the *People's Daily*, one of the newspapers of the CCP, said it best in an editorial: "The most important historical contribution by comrade Deng Xiaoping is his great decision for reform and opening up and his creation of a road to socialist modernization" (*New Straits Times*, 2004c, p. 20). Deng's visionary and pragmatic leadership in steering his country on the road to modernisation by opening up to the outside world will remain one of the most important pieces in the modern-day history of China.

2.6 Deepening of Reforms and Modernisation Process by Subsequent Chinese Leadership

The role played by the continuity of the reform and modernisation policies instituted by Deng in the emergence of China cannot be overemphasised. These reform programmes have been built on and deepened by Jiang and the role played by subsequent generations of Chinese leaders (the third generation) in the emergence of China. Without this continuity, there would have been a danger of relapse of the fragile reform process after the death of Deng. This is because there were and still are internal interests who are against such reforms and will look for the least chance to destroy them. Jiang Zemin and his successor, Hu Jintao, continued with the reforms and also sought out ways to deepen them. As well as ushering China into the World Trade Organization (WTO), they also put into place the requisite laws that would contribute to a versatile business environment in China. Much has been done in this respect since China's opening up, but much still needs to be done. Jiang once observed that

A very important reason for China's backwardness after the 15th Century was that China's feudal rulers closed the door to international intercourse, indulged in parochial arrogance and could not stand the development of world science and technology. As a result, the Chinese nation sadly missed its historic opportunity.

(Liu, 2001)

During Jiang's tenure in power, he sought to change that, hoping that this time around, the Chinese nation would not miss this opportunity. With Zhu Rongji, they further opened up the Chinese economy and put into place some of the necessary laws to help the country grow. Zhu enacted tough macroeconomic measures to set the Chinese economy on a sustainable path of growth. He expunged low-tech projects and supported projects in transportation, energy and agriculture to encourage growth. He averted market fluctuations and focused on the strengthening of industry and agriculture during his time as premier. He was also credited with the large privatization program in China, which saw China's private sector grow massively. Zhu and Jiang started the process of punishing those government officials who were corrupt (Rongji, 2013).

Hu Jintao, who replaced Jiang, was elected president of the People's Republic of China on March 15, 2003. He was born in December 1942 at Jixi in Anhui Province. He graduated from Tsinghua University, majoring in the study of hydropower stations. Hu joined the CCP in 1964 and held several positions until he became vice president in March 1998 and vice chairman of the Central Military Commission in September 1999. Hu has already launched a proposal to develop the interior parts of China as a way of bringing about balanced development between the coastal and interior parts of the country, and efforts are being put in place to lift millions of rural poor out of poverty.

Under Hu's rule, China's parliament for the first time amended the constitution to protect private property that has been acquired legally. In a way, Hu can be said to be continuing with the "Three Represents" theory of Jiang Zemin, which stands for advanced productive forces, culture and all that is in the interest of the Chinese people (*New Straits Times*, 2004, p. B22). A speech given by Wen Jiabao, former China's premier in Hu's government at the 2004 legislative session in Beijing, captures the direction of Hu's government: "we must take more direct and effective policies…to strengthen, support and protect agriculture and increase rural incomes in line with the needs to balance urban and rural development" (*New Straits Times*, 2004e, p. B20). Going forward, the challenge that Hu's government faced was how to continue to deepen the reform process and harness the economy without widening the current yawning gap between rich and poor (Brown, 2012). Hu Jintao and Wen Jiabao were succeeded by Xi Jinping and Li Keqiang as president and premier of China, respectively.

Xi Jinping assumed office on 15 June 1953. He studied chemical engineering at Tsinghua University. He also studied Marxist philosophy and ideology education at postgraduate level at the same university, as well as a doctor of law (LLD) degree from Tsinghua. Xi was the Governor of Fujian province between 1999 and 2002. He was also governor of Zhejiang as well as CPP Secretary in the same province from 2002 to 2007. He became CPP Secretary in Shanghai in 2007. He served as vice president between 2008 and 2013. Xi was groomed to take over from Hu Jintao as the fifth generation leadership of China. Since Xi took over from Hu, he has initiated a serious and determined fight against corruption in China. Corruption has become endemic in China, such that over 20,000 individuals are convicted of corruption related crimes each year. Also, hundreds of Chinese officials have either been executed or sent to prison for life after being convicted of corruption (Wedeman, 2012; Jinping, 2014).

A few months into Xi's term, he outlined an "Eight Point Guide" to fight corruption. His "Eight Point Guide" listed rules aimed at introducing strict discipline to guide the conduct of party officials. His pronouncement and vow that he was going to root out "tigers and flies" is believed by many to mean high-ranking party officials as well as ordinary ones. It is reported that in just a couple of years into his term, he has brought cases against former Central Military Commission vice chairman, Xu Caihou; security chief Zhou Yongkang, who has since received a life sentence for bribery and abuse of power; and former senior military officer Gu Junshan, who was sentenced to death with a two-year reprieve for corruption (Jinping, 2014). At this writing, Guo Guang Chang, one of China's tycoons, often referred to as the "Chinese Warren Buffet," has been caught up in Xi's anticorruption drive. He has been detained by Chinese authorities to assist in certain investigations (*Financial Times*, 2015, p. 1). Xi also announced numerous legal reforms in 2014. His aim is to reform the legal system, which he believes is affected by corruption, thus making it ineffective. He has also initiated a more nationalistic as well as an assertive foreign policy aimed at projecting China onto the global stage, and he has also coined a phase, "the Chinese Dream," just like his predecessors. He sees his role as the leader of China as being to spearhead China's great revival (Hsiung, 2015). Xi's continuation of China's engagement with Africa, initiated by his predecessors, is laudable. In a 2015 meeting of the Forum on China–Africa Cooperation (FOCAC) in Johannesburg, South Africa, he announced a US$60 billion investment package for Africa.

2.7 Positive Response from the West and the Rest of the World

Even though much credit needs to be given to China, its leaders and its people for bringing about its current emergence, it is equally important to give credit to the West and the rest of the world for their positive response to efforts towards change in China. This has in many ways contributed to the growth of the Chinese economy, contributing to its emergence. The Chinese leadership had long realised that no country can be an island. That is why, during the opening-up phase of China to the world, Deng visited as many countries as he could and established diplomatic relations with many countries. Since this move, subsequent Chinese leadership have cultivated friendship with the West and other developing countries. This has, in turn, garnered a positive response from the West, particularly the US, and has made it possible for China to join the WTO, thus making it possible for China to open its markets to the rest of the world and vice versa.

The yearly MFN renewal process that gave China a headache in the US Congress is a case in point. If the West and other countries had not made it possible for China to join the WTO, it would still have had to go before the US Congress every year to renew its MFN status. If that had been the case, it would be highly doubtful that China could have achieved its current growth rates and hence its current emergence. Without China's membership of the WTO, it would also have been doubtful whether its markets would have been opened for other countries to take advantage of or that China would have had access to world markets, as is currently the case.

Similarly, a positive response from countries like Canada contributed to China's emergence. Canada supported China's accession to the WTO and never had an MFN debate in its parliament to determine annual renewals of trade with China. Indeed, Canada always had a long-standing history of constructive engagement with China. And this has also been the case in the European Union, which also played a positive role in China's emergence. It has been one of the largest donors of aid to China during its struggling years and even though it has from time to time spoken up about China's human rights record, it never stood in China's way in its efforts to develop. Thus the European Union's positive response towards China has, in numerous ways, contributed to its emergence. Countries in Africa and Latin America also played a positive role in China's emergence. The relationship between China and most of the countries in Africa and Latin America goes way back to the era of the Cold War. China has always supported liberation movements and socialist governments in these regions. In return, they have supported China, which, during the Cold War, had few allies and was rather ignored at many international fora.

Most of the countries that empathised with China were those in Africa, Latin America and the Caribbean. Countries in Asia also generally supported China in its emergence. Despite the difficult relations between China and some countries in the Asia region, they did not stand in the way of its emergence. The importance of this is that, if China had faced hostility from the West and most of the countries in the world, it would have been impossible for it to emerge today as an economic and political power. This is because it did not have the requisite technology or resources as well as fiscal and trained human capital to undertake its development. Thus a positive response from the West and the rest of the world and their contribution to China's emergence, directly or indirectly, cannot be emphasised enough. But one must add that all such responses were not for altruistic reasons. Indeed, each country might have looked at the situation from the perspective of the impact on their interests and economies.

2.8 Conclusion

Some of the factors that contributed to China's emergence as an economic and political power on the global stage can be attributed to its desire to reclaim its past pre-eminence as a great nation. In a way, Mao's failed policies have also contributed to the emergence of China today. The bitter experiences of Mao's GLF policy and the Cultural Revolution made the new leadership after Mao look for better alternatives. It took the visionary leadership of Deng, who opened up China and set it on the current path of growth, to achieve the economic emergence of China. Subsequent leadership, such as Jiang Zemin, Zhu Rongji, Hu Jintao and Wen Jiabao, must deepen and continue with the reforms. Certainly, the gradual opening up of the country by Deng, an approach maintained by the current leadership, was because of the experience from the collapse of the former Soviet Union, a Communist state, where the leadership lost control of the country as it rapidly opened up, leading to chaos and the breaking up of the different states. Finally, the receptiveness of the West and the rest of the world to China's opening up and their acceptance of China into the community of nations have also contributed to this emergence.

3 China's Entry into the World Trade Organisation (WTO)

3.1 Introduction

Another important contributor to China's current emergence, as a significant contributor to its current position as a global economic and political force, is its entrance into the World Trade Organization (WTO). China's efforts to transform its economy from a socialist to a free-market one have seen the lifting of the majority of its people out of poverty in quite a short space of time. The continuation of such reforms, according to the Asian Development Bank, has contributed to China's rapid economic expansion, resulting in the near elimination of extreme poverty in the country. This would contribute to about 78 percent of people in the country living on less than US$1 a day (*New Straits Times*, 2004b, p. B9). According to the *Economist* (2013), China has pulled about 680 million people out of misery from 1981 to 2010 and reduced has reduced its rate of extreme poverty from 84 percent in 1980 to 10 percent in 2013. Furthermore, its efforts at being accepted in the global family of nations (WTO) and becoming a part of the global economy of nations has contributed to its ability to attract foreign direct investment (FDI) to fuel the country's growth. Thus, if China's economy is to continue to grow, it needs to have access to markets and natural resources. One way China's leadership knew they could do that was to join the WTO. Joining the WTO was therefore one of the last hurdles that China had to clear to realise this goal. But membership of the WTO goes beyond just access to markets and resources for China; psychologically, it has also meant that the country has arrived on the world economic stage as a "player," so to speak.

Furthermore, it was an opportunity for China to shed its pariah status and the image of its distant past in the West as "Communist and dictatorial." In the context of Asian culture, joining the WTO was regarded as an opportunity for China to save face, (*mian-zi*) a very important issue for the country. After all, it belonged to all other international organisations but the WTO at that time. The concept of *mian-zi*, "face," is quite an important dynamic of the Chinese culture and indeed of most Asian cultures. Thus an elaboration of it is appropriate and will be addressed in Section 3.3.

This chapter will start out by looking at the importance of the WTO to world trade in this era of globalisation amid the cacophony of noise from pro- and anti-globalisation advocates. It will continue by exploring the reasons why China wanted to join the WTO, followed by a discussion of China's WTO membership accession process. The chapter will look at the implications for China and the rest of the world, particularly Asia, now that it has joined the WTO. These implications will entail benefits as well as costs. The chapter will conclude after the analysis of these important issues.

3.2 WTO and Global Trade

The importance of trade in today's global economy cannot be emphasised enough. Trade between nations not only fosters bilateral relations; it is also a source of income for most countries to grow their economies. The WTO was formed to further such global free trade. It was established in January 1995 as a replacement for the General Agreement on Tariffs and Trade (GATT). The WTO has at its heart about 28 agreements that serve as the legal ground rules for world trade. These agreements have as their objectives

- To help trade flow as freely as possible
- To achieve further liberalisation gradually through negotiations
- To set up an impartial means of settling disputes

These core agreements of the WTO are contained in the final act of the Uruguay Round of trade negotiations. Non-discrimination ("most-favoured nation" clause), freer trade, the encouragement of competition and the reduction of protectionism are some of the fundamental principles on which the WTO agreements are based. Because trade plays an important role in the development of nations, the WTO plays an important role in fostering free trade amongst nations. For the WTO to be able to undertake this role effectively, it has to walk a fine balance or it risks becoming a target of both developing and developed countries alike, which can accuse it of partiality. If that was to happen, the organisation would lose its credibility and effectiveness and the global trading system could collapse. For example, there are some in the developing world who see the WTO as nothing more than a powerful cabal that serves as a front for rich nations and large corporations. Others see it as an enforcer of a certain cruel "New World Order" (Panitchpakdi and Clifford, 2002). The November 1999 demonstrations in Seattle, Washington, which disrupted the WTO meeting held there; and the recent 2003 failed WTO talks held in Cancun, Mexico, and in Hong Kong in 2005 are held up by some to support the aforementioned views.

Developed countries and most of their citizens see it differently. They complain that free trade under the auspices of the WTO is seeing their jobs migrate to lower wage havens. India and China are some of the countries that have come under attack lately on this issue (*Business Week*, 2003; *Economist*, 2004, p. 3). In fact, it became one of the defining arguments in the 2004 US presidential elections between George W. Bush and John Kerry. Equally, it became part of the presidential election debate between Barack Obama and Mitt Romney in the 2012 US presidential campaign, and I am sure we have not heard the last word on this issue yet.

Other areas in which the WTO has come under severe criticism, particularly from developing countries, is the Trade-Related Aspects of Intellectual Property Rights Agreement (TRIPs). Under this agreement, substantive minimum standards and protections are accorded to virtually all areas of intellectual property rights (IPRs). Some of these include patent eligibility, requirements for the protection of plant varieties, copyrights for computer software and electronic transmissions, protection for well-known trademarks and effective measures to guard confidential information (Maskus, 2000). Under the agreement, adequate enforcement and administration as well as the incorporation of IPRs into the WTO's dispute resolution mechanisms are addressed. Most developing countries criticise the TRIPs agreement because they see prices of pharmaceutical products skyrocket as the developed countries exploit new seed varieties and genetic resources without adequate compensation. They also see these developed countries patent life forms, which they claim is a deliberate effort to limit their access to these resources and knowledge. Furthermore, they argue that most of these TRIPs agreements were reached without due consideration as to how developing countries can participate in them (Maskus, 2000; Correa, 2000).

All of the above discontents about free trade on the part of both developed and developing countries point to the importance of and need for an organisation like the WTO. The role of the WTO therefore can be likened to that of a football referee, making sure that all the players in the game abide by the same rules. Without the WTO, countries would undertake unilateral retaliatory measures that could have devastating impacts on global trade and the global economy, as evidenced by the depression of 1930.

That depression had an international dimension that this book is concerned with. The US maintained a regime of high tariffs on goods coming into the country, yet, at the same time, it made loans to foreign countries and tried to export its products. Other countries therefore could not sell their goods in the US market; consequently, they could not make money to buy American products or repay the loans they took from America. Other countries also copied the US and undertook unilateral measures and policies to advance their interests with little regard for the international trading system and the attendant economic consequences. Furthermore, as the domestic economies of various nations faced stiff competition from other nations, the pressure from the affected domestic constituencies in the country on the government of the day may have forced it to undertake protectionist measures in response to the pressure.

One of the important roles of the WTO is to help prevent countries undertaking such protectionist measures. Despite all its shortcomings, the role of the WTO in fostering free trade amongst countries cannot be emphasised enough. The opening up of free trade has afforded most countries in the developing world, for example in South East Asia (newly industrialized countries or

NICs), the opportunity to move the majority of their people out of poverty. Similarly, it has helped developed nations to create jobs at home and to maintain their high standards of living. It also serves as an honest broker and helps to mediate in trade disputes. It is for these reasons that the WTO should not be allowed to be captured by any single country or group of countries or ideological groups to further their interests and agendas. Rather, both developed and developing countries must make sure the WTO works for the benefit of all its members, rich or poor, small or big, influential or not. They must make sure that the organisation stands for free and fair trade unequivocally, today, tomorrow and into the distant future.

3.3 Why China Wanted to Join the WTO

The reform process put in place by the late Deng Xiaoping made China realise the true benefits of a market economy. And it also realised that, if the country is to truly benefit from the global economy, that it must be integrated into the world economy. One way of doing so was to join the WTO. But joining the WTO also meant that China, which had been closed to the outside world since 1949, would now be truly opened. Indeed, it would be one of the best ways for Chinese leadership to show to the world that the opening up of their country was a continuous process and thus would be a powerful symbolic political statement. But also, reformists within the country wanted very much for China to join the WTO because, as a rule-based organisation, it would help open some of the doors and minds of non-reformists who were against the reform efforts, thereby giving the country the impetus to continue with its reforms. Joining the WTO would also force the domestic opponents of change to find lesser reasons to fight change. This is because it would be much harder for them to fight the WTO compliance regulations. Reformers thus saw the entry of China into the WTO as contributing to the enhancement of the rule of law, transparency and accountability, as well as representing the potential to draw more FDI into the country.

Another reason why China wanted to join the WTO (the "economic United Nations [UN]") was because it was the only significant international organisation that it was not a member of. As international trade began to play an important role in globalisation and as China's own international trade began to increase, it was important for China to become a member of the WTO. Also, as previously mentioned, becoming a member of the WTO would help China save "face" (*mian-zi*). The concept of saving face in Asian societies, which is hierarchical, is a big thing. In Asian societies, people will go to great lengths to gain and preserve "face." Asians are rather jealous of their social reputation and will go to lengths to attain, maintain and guard against its loss. For example, it is common in Asia to see the wealthy or the pseudo-wealthy splurge on luxury cars and designer products to show to their relatives and their community that they have "arrived." A Westerner may ask why would Asians go through all this trouble to save "face"? This is because other people in their society have a strong tendency to use such semblance of success in their evaluative judgements of their status and hierarchy. In a nutshell, it is all about the social position they occupy in the social hierarchy (Ng, 2001). China's wanting to join the WTO was thus about its social hierarchy amongst the community of nations and the prestige that came with it.

Most foreign businessmen in China, particularly those from the West, fail to understand this issue and are thus baffled by it. They ascribe it to attitude, showmanship and scoring points on the part of their Chinese counterparts (*Economist*, 2004, p. 12). Such erroneous observations miss the point. One can therefore see China's accession to the WTO in this light amongst other analyses. Furthermore, the WTO accession will entail some diplomatic benefits for China. It would solve once and for all China's long-standing trade problems with the US. This is because previously every year, trade between China and the US was voted on in Congress. It was the US Congress that had to decide whether or not to renew or China's most favoured nation (MFN) status and what strings to attach to it. This did not augur well for China's growth and development efforts. China knew that if it joined the WTO, the long-standing trade problem it faced with the US would be normalised.

Economically, the benefit to China for joining the WTO is the market access opportunities it offers the country as well as the world at large. Before China joined the WTO, the World Bank observed that, by the year 2020, China's share of world trade could rise to about 10 percent, which will be next only to the US with 12 percent (World Bank, 1997). This could create another engine of demand for the world economy. China's huge population of 1.3 billion is a huge potential market for the world and a source of competitive labour. China also sees joining the WTO as a means of attracting investment for its development efforts and thus sees the rest of the world as a market for its exports and the provision of jobs for its citizenry.

3.4 China's WTO Membership Process

Having realised the enormous benefits for the country if it was to join the WTO, China's efforts to do so were relentless. The following is a brief narration of China's route to the WTO. The effort started in 1986 when China applied to join the General Agreement on Tariffs and Trade (GATT) talks, which started in 1987 as part of China's opening-up policy. Unfortunately, such talks came to a halt when, in 1989, China cracked down on the pro-democracy movement in Tiananmen Square. The talks continued seven months later, but by then, the bar of entry had been raised, resulting in the talks collapsing again in 1994. This resulted in China losing the opportunity to become a founding member of the WTO. In 1995, talks began again, and China was granted an observer status but not membership. Then, the 1997 Asian financial crisis slowed down the talks, which had been progressing rather well. After the dust of the Asian financial crisis settled, the negotiations continued and came to a halt again because of the bombing of the Chinese Embassy in Yugoslavia by the North Atlantic Treaty Organisation (NATO) in May of 1999. In July of the same year, the terms of entry were agreed upon between China and Japan, and, in November of the same year, between China and the US. The next agreement to facilitate China's entry into the WTO was between it and the European Union (EU), which was achieved in 2000. The final set of bilateral agreements that China signed before being accepted in the WTO was between it and Mexico and other major trading partners in September of 2001. By November of the same year, China was officially accepted as a member of the WTO. It formerly joined the organisation in December 2001. Table 3.1 offers a summary of China's route to the WTO from 1986 to 2001, when it was officially accepted as a member.

The road to Geneva for China was littered with a lot of obstacles, so to speak, as the summary in Table 3.1 shows. Most of these obstacles were political and economic ones. One of the big obstacles that stood in the way of China's membership of the WTO was the US. There was fear within the American political establishment about a massive loss of jobs in the textile and manufacturing sectors, and the attendant backlash from trade and labour unions that could result was something the government could not afford. Hence the Clinton administration at that time sought more provisions in its agreements with China to protect the aforementioned local constituencies in the US, a key democratic voting bloc. Then, on May 7th, 1999, another obstacle cropped up that impeded China's entry into the WTO. A NATO plane piloted by an American bombed the Chinese embassy in Belgrade. In this unfortunate incident, three Chinese in the embassy were killed. Although the US attributed this to an accident due to the usage of old maps, the Chinese government refused to accept the incident as an accident. The reaction from the Chinese public against the US was fierce. Demonstrations took place and tough words

Table 3.1 China's Long March to WTO Membership

Year	Progress/Status of Talks
1986	China applies to join GATT talks
1989	Talks suspended due to Tiananmen Square crackdown
1989	Talks resume seven months later
1994	Talks collapse again
1995	China granted observer status
1997	Talks slow down because of Asian financial crisis
1999 (May)	China halts talks because of the bombing of its embassy in Yugoslavia
1999 (July)	Entry terms agreed on between China and Japan
1999 (November)	Entry terms agreed on between China and the US
2000	Entry terms agreed on between China and the EU
2001 (September)	Entry terms agreed on between China and Mexico and other major trading partners
2001 (November)	China officially accepted by WTO as a member
2001 (December)	China formally joins the WTO as a member

Source: Compiled by author.

were uttered by angry Chinese towards the US. Even Hu Jintao, the former president of the People's Republic of China (PRC) and deputy president at the time of the bombing, had tough words for America. On state television, he referred to the attack as a "criminal act" on the part of the US. The soured relations between China and the US because of this incident were seen by some as jeopardising China's prospects for joining the WTO. The WTO talks, which were suspended for a while because of this incident, later saw China and the US sitting down to put to rest this regrettable incident. The clearing of this hurdle was the last one for China, opening the way for it to join the WTO. It was officially accepted as a member in November 2001.

3.5 China Joins the WTO: What were the Implications?

China's entry into the WTO had many benefits, which have already been delineated in Section 3.3. But the implications go beyond that. By joining the WTO, China agreed to abide by international norms and regulations concerning market access, removal of tariffs, non-tariff barriers and subsidies. Thus, morally, China has to comply with these international norms; if it fails to follow them, it will lose its international credibility or could face retaliatory measures from other members, and this could affect its growth and development efforts. It could also equally put its economy and reform process in jeopardy by discouraging the flow of FDI into the country, thereby affecting its growth process.

Furthermore, China's WTO ascension helped the country break local as well as departmental monopolies, which had proven rather difficult to break by reformers in the country. This is because the WTO rules require transparency in government contract processes, a just treatment of foreign businesses and compliance with international norms. It was the view of China watchers that reformers who were faced with tough opposition from within the country usually pointed to WTO rules and requirements as a justification for the requisite reforms they are undertaking (Furst, 2001). The country will continue to face such challenges concerning transparency, fair treatment of foreign businesses and compliance with international norms.

It should also be mentioned that China's entry into the WTO had a tremendous impact on its banks and financial institutions, which long enjoyed a monopoly of the Chinese market until its WTO entry. These banks and financial institutions, which have been shielded by the government, now have to face competition from foreign competitors for a share of the domestic Chinese market. Most of these Chinese banks and financial institutions were also saddled with non-performing loans. These competitive challenges have forced some of these banks to go out of business. But in the long run, they have also forced those that survive to become efficient.

The numerous non-performing loans of Chinese banks were due to monies lent to state owned enterprises (SOEs), most of whom are inefficient, bloated and bureaucratic. With China's entry into the WTO, doors opened and foreign competitors muzzled their way into China to compete with these SOEs.

This competition led to some dislocations for some of these inefficient SOEs, some of which had to disintegrate, resulting in many of their employees been laid off; this led to some social upheavals with attendant challenges for the CCP. Another important implication for China in joining the WTO was the fear by most Chinese at that time of "Westernisation" or Western influences, which they believed could cause the death of Chinese values and their replacement by Western materialistic values and decadence. Yes, China has in some ways seen the creeping in of Western values, especially amongst the youth and *nouveau riche*. But overall, it has not resulted in any serious dislocation in Chinese values.

Some of these concerns have occurred since China joined the WTO. Others see China's joining of the WTO as the end of the Communist Party because they saw it as giving up control over the economy as it "kow-tows" to WTO rules, and through the privatisation of SOEs. In fact, because of this view, most anti-reformists in China thus referred to the leadership of the country at that time as weak or traitors. They held the view that the Communist Party had sold out its soul to the West. Such fears can be appreciated for some in any nation going through a period of serious change after decades of knowing only one system – Communism. But equally afraid were the bureaucrats and those in the top cadres of the Communist system, who stood to lose their jobs and privileges and thus resisted any move to change. Fourteen years after China joined the WTO, however, the CCP has not lost its grip on the economy and political power in the country. It is still as powerful as ever.

China's entry into the WTO was observed to have short-term social consequences. There was the likelihood that it would put competitive pressures on the agricultural sector as well as the telecommunications and automobile industries. The fear was that its WTO obligations could cause farm incomes to fall and income disparities would result between rural agricultural and urban areas; the majority of China's population lives in rural areas, particularly in the central and western parts of the country. Furthermore, because most of these people are poor, China needed to act fast to avoid a social crisis. It would need to mobilise massive resources to help develop these areas in an effort to arrest poverty[1].

Sadly, as mentioned elsewhere in this book, even though China has significantly reduced extreme poverty in the country, a huge income disparity is growing amongst its people. As it pertains to the telecommunications sector, China would have not opened it to foreign competition without the pressure it faced from its WTO accession (Mueller and Lovelock, 2004). The sector has been forced to be competitive and efficient because of these foreign competitors. It was also forced to satisfy its customers as it continues to also restructure (Pangestu and Mrongowius, 2004). As it pertains to the automobile industry in China, WTO membership brought about reasonable lower prices and steeper foreign competition in the sector as many competitors entered the market (Francois and Spinanger, 2004).

Thus in hindsight, looking at China's growth trajectory as well as the current economic might of China in the global economy, one can say without any doubt that China's WTO entry has been worth it.

3.6 Conclusion

When Jiang Zemin and Zhu Rongji took over the stewardship of China, joining the WTO was one of the items at the top of their agenda (Rongji, 2013). They realised that if they were to be able to continue with the reforms and if the Chinese economy was to grow, they had no choice but to join the WTO. The membership of the WTO, which is often regarded as the economic UN, comes with numerous benefits as well as costs. WTO membership, they knew, would help spur their country's economic growth. It was also going to solve China's yearly MFN renewal process by the US Congress. These leaders also believed that joining the WTO would help China's reform process tremendously. Because the WTO is a rules-based system, reformers in China thus pointed to these rules to push through the requisite reforms. Thus, WTO ascension was seen as a weapon against the anti-reformers. It also enabled China to have access to other markets and resources from around the world. Above all, it helped China save "face" amongst its contemporaries in Asia and around the world.

But joining the WTO also had some consequences for China. It forced China to open its market to other countries, which resulted in many losing their jobs because of the non-competitiveness of most of its SOEs. Yet, if the costs and benefits of China's entry into the WTO are weighed, it is safe to say that the benefits to China outweigh the costs. It has led to the expansion of production, the growth and development of the country and the movement of most of its populace out of poverty. In the words of one of its celebrated leaders, "we can only improve our standard of living gradually, on the basis of expanded production. It is wrong to expand production without raising the people's standard of living; but it is likewise wrong – in fact impossible – to raise the people's standard of living without expanding production" (Xiaoping, 1980). For China, joining the WTO helped the country achieve this goal, but it also contributed to China's current emergence as an economic and political power.

Note

1 "Social Costs for China's Entry into the WTO," http://www.asiafeatures.com/business/0111,2915,02.html).

4 Why is China Interested in Africa?

4.1 Introduction

China's foray into Africa is a topic of much discussion at international fora and strategy sessions and meetings in Western capitals as well as in discussions in African capitals and in the classrooms of academic institutions around the world. Much has also been written about this topic in books, academic journals and magazines. This will continue to be so for some time; even as of the time of writing, discussions are still ongoing among numerous policy makers and China–Africa specialists and observers about China's current engagement and investment in Africa. Some see this current engagement negatively, others positively. Most of the discussions and observations pertaining to China's interest in Africa have to do with its quest for the continent's natural resources to fuel its booming economy. The observations of those who view China's interest in Africa negatively centre on the assertion by some that China is the "new coloniser" or "colonialist" and it is China's turn to "pillage" Africa – euphemistically put by some of these observers as "the Second Scramble for Africa." This is drawing an allegory of China emulating Europe's initial foray into Africa. Specifically, it is looking at China and comparing its current foray into Africa to what happened at the Berlin Conference of 1884–1885, which led to the "Scramble for Africa" and its resources by European countries. The difference here is that one country is involved as opposed to numerous countries.

Yes, it is partly true that China's current foray into Africa has to do with its interest in Africa's natural resources. But is China's interest in Africa based only on its demand for these resources? The answer is no. If the quest for natural resources was the only reason why China was interested in Africa, then Western countries would equally be guilty as it pertains to their interest in Africa. Western powers' interests in Africa, as well as those of China, go beyond natural resources. It also has to do with influence and dominance. African leaders and policy makers are not oblivious to such a fact. The same can be said of some emerging powers like India, whose voracious appetite for resources to fuel its growth and influence is seeing its increase engagement with Africa. China is therefore not any different to other countries in this regard. If China is only in Africa for its natural resources, why is it invested in non-resource-rich African countries such as Rwanda, Ethiopia and Eritrea? It's about influence and markets for its products. The aim of this chapter is to offer more insight into why China is interested in Africa and consequently its foray into the region. It is argued that China's interest in Africa goes beyond the search for natural resources. This interest was clearly delineated when former President Hu Jintao of China spoke before the Nigerian National Assembly in Abuja in 2006. According to Hu, China's partnership with Africa involves areas ranging from politics, economics and science and technology to culture, education and health, and he contended that China was ready to deepen Sino-African relations in these areas. Subsequent visits and utterances by Chinese leaders to Africa after Hu have all made it clear that their foray into Africa and their relations with African countries go beyond their quest for the continent's natural resources.

With these observations as the base, this chapter will look at some of these issues in detail. It will also look critically at the numerous reasons why China is interested in engaging Africa aside from its quest for Africa's natural resources. For African countries to be able to benefit from China's investment in Africa, it is important for their leaders and policy makers to really understand why China is interested in Africa. The Chinese just did not get up one day and decide that they want to invest in Africa. There must be a reason why a lot of thought went into the decision to invest in Africa. Through an understanding of this, it is hoped that African leaders and policy makers will be able respond adequately and position themselves in such a way that their respective countries can benefit from China's foray into the continent. So what are some of the reasons why China is interested in Africa? Sections 4.2–4.7 of this chapter offer some of these reasons.

4.2 Rekindling and Enhancement of Old Ties

China's current interest in and foray into Africa cannot be viewed in isolation from China's relations and links with Africa, which date back centuries. Official Chinese reports trace the links between China and Africa as far back as the Han dynasty (206 B.C. to A.D. 220). But it was during the Tang dynasty (A.D. 618–901) that the trade between China and Africa grew (Yuan, 2007). It is reported that around the eleventh or twelfth centuries, the people of Pate and Kilwa, who lived along the coast of East Africa, were shipping elephant tusks, rhinoceros horns, tortoise shell, aromatic woods, incense and myrrh to Southern China. Trade between China and Africa was further enhanced during the era of the Sung dynasty (A.D. 1127–1279). Evidence of objects of the era that were discovered around Somalia all the way down to Mozambique confirms the increasing trade between China and these countries along the Indian Ocean going way back. Furthermore, it was also during this period of the Sung dynasty that references to black people as *K'un lun* – "black as ink" – was common (Rotberg, 2008). China's earlier foray into Africa also dates back to the era of the well-documented voyages of Zheng He, who, during the Ming Dynasty, led his fleet of ships four times to the east coast of Africa (Snow, 1988).

In recent times, especially during the 1960s and 1970s, when many African countries were seeking to attain their independence from colonial rule, China offered significant financial, military and economic support to these countries. This, according to the Chinese was in solidarity with their "African brothers" fighting imperialist and colonial rule. Also in the 1960s and 1970s, China was viewed by most African countries as a champion of an alternative mode of development as viewed through the lens of a socialist ideology. Many were the African countries who found this ideology appealing and therefore subscribed to it in an attempt to distance themselves from their former colonial masters (Doriye, 2010).

Tanzania and Zambia are examples of the African countries that benefited from this early relationship with China in the 1970s. The Tanzania–Zambia railway was built by China during that time at a cost of US$412 million (Moritz, 1982). This railway (the Tazara railway), also known as the "Great Uhuru Railway," is still regarded as China's huge infrastructure project in Africa. The idea of the railroad is attributed to Cecil Rhodes's vision of a railroad linking British colonies from "Cape to Cairo." In the 1960s, Kenneth Kaunda, who was the independence-era president of Zambia, wanted to liberate his land-locked country from its dependence on the transport routes through the late Ian Smith's White-ruled Rhodesia (Zimbabwe) and apartheid-era South Africa. The idea to build the Tazara railway became more urgent when Smith, the then prime minister of Rhodesia (Zimbabwe), declared a Unilateral Declaration of Independence (UDI) from Britain on November 11, 1965, and threatened to cut Zambia's trade routes to the sea. This was because Kaunda and Nyerere supported black liberation movements in the region. The UDI was a unilateral breakaway from Britain, of which Rhodesia was a former colony.

The presidents of the newly independent Zambia and Tanzania, Kenneth Kaunda and the late Julius Nyerere, respectively, contacted the World Bank for funding for the railway but were refused, and their subsequent lobbying of Western countries for funding was unsuccessful. These two independence-era African leaders contacted Britain, West Germany, Japan, the US and the USSR, but all declined to fund the project. They then reluctantly turned to China, under Mao, as a last resort, and Mao agreed to fund and construct the railway line. In agreeing to fund and build the railway, Mao said to Nyerere, "You have difficulties as we do, but our difficulties are different. To help you build the railway, we are willing to forsake building railways for ourselves.[1]" Work began in 1970, with over 20,000 Chinese labourers employed to build what was Africa's longest railway, covering 1860 kilometres of track and serviced by 147 railway stations. The project was completed in 1975, about two years ahead of schedule, with China providing the initial rolling stock of 85 locomotives, 2100 freight wagons and 100 passenger coaches for use on the line (Raine, 2009).

The scale and the cost of the project and the commitment shown by the Chinese in delivering it on time in the face of the refusal of the funding of the project by Western countries and the World Bank is often pointed to by the Chinese as a symbol of their friendship with and commitment to Africa. It should be noted in passing that this was the period of the Cold War, and that perhaps the Western unwillingness to fund the project could be because they viewed the project through a Cold War lens. To build the Tazara railroad, the Chinese needed to bore ten kilometres of tunnels and construct 300 bridges, which needed shiploads of materials and equipment. It also involved dozens of Chinese ministries, which did put enormous pressure on Chinese aid (Brautigam, 2009). Five years after the railway was launched, it fell into disrepair due to a lack of maintenance as well as lack of technology transfers and capacity building on the part of the Chinese.

This is an important sustainability issue that African policy makers and leaders should seriously consider when it comes to such huge undertakings in Africa in the future, not only in partnership with the Chinese but also with other foreign governments and companies. This issue of sustainability is dealt with at length in the latter part of the book. Discussions are now ongoing to have a Chinese firm overhaul the railway. The Chinese Civil Engineering Construction Corporation, an SOE, has offered to refurbish the railway line and bring it up to date to contribute to the growth and development of Africa's Eastern Corridor. The Tazara railway will be refurbished in phases, starting with the line from Dar-es-Salaam to Morogoro, followed by the line from Morogoro to Dodoma. The Chinese believe that it will contribute to enhancing the old ties between China and Africa.

Thus according to the Chinese, a prosperous and developing China today wants to enhance and rekindle these old ties between it and African countries as they were in the 1960s and 1970s. Obviously, this is not for altruistic reasons but involves a clear understanding of the mutual benefits that will accrue for both China and Africa due to the rekindling of these old ties. African leaders and policy makers would also do well to recognise this fact to help them in effectively harnessing Chinese investments and its foray into the continent.

4.3 Africa's Abundant Mineral Resources

Africa is rich in mineral resources such as bauxite, cobalt, copper, diamonds, gold, phosphates, platinum and manganese, to mention but a few. The continent also has abundant oil deposits, particularly in Nigeria, Angola, Sudan, Guinea, Congo and Chad. It also has abundant fertile lands and a youthful population. Therefore, one of the important reasons for China's interest in Africa is undoubtedly its rich natural resources. China currently receives about a third of its oil imports from Angola, Sudan, Equatorial Guinea and the Republic of Congo. It is also looking to receive more supplies from Chad, Nigeria, Algeria and Gabon. For example, in 2006, the China National Offshore Oil Corporation (CNOOC) completed a deal with Nigeria whereby it acquired a 45 percent stake in an oil block at a cost of over US$2 billion. The oil field was scheduled to pump 225,000 barrels of oil a day in 2008. To offer an insight into

China's interest in Africa's natural resources, three countries randomly picked by this author – Angola, Zambia and Sudan – will be discussed as examples.

This first country is Angola. In 2005, China's Eximbank extended a $1 billion oil-backed loan to Angola. It was later increased to US$3 billion in 2006 for the rebuilding and upgrading of Angola's infrastructure, which had been destroyed during that country's civil war. But one cannot talk about China–Angola relations without mentioning the difficulty Angola faced in its efforts to raise funds for development after the country's civil war (1975–2002). The country approached international finance institutions (IFIs) for funding but was turned down due to poor standards of governance and transparency. Angola approached China as an alternative source to the IFIs for funds to rebuild their war-torn economy. China agreed to help Angola. For China, cultivating a relationship with Angola, the second largest African oil producer after Nigeria, was rather important in terms of potential oil exploration contracts to ensure its energy security (Corkin, 2008). Thus, in 2004, the Chinese Exim bank extended an oil-backed line of credit to the amount of US$2 billion to Angola. The loan was doubled to US$4 billion in 2006, which made China the biggest player in Angola's post-war construction effort. An additional US$500 million was negotiated and added to the amount to help integrate the infrastructural developments into the national economy.

Angola's relations with China go way back to when China used to support the Popular Movement for the Liberation of Angola (MPLA) in the 1960s and 1970s. China switched its support from the MPLA to the National Union for Total Independence of Angola (UNITA) during the Angolan civil war. This happened when China sought to counter the influence of the Soviet Union in Angola when the latter also supported the MPLA. This led to the delay in the establishment of diplomatic relations between China and Angola until 1983.

The trade ties between China and Angola have grown since the resumption of diplomatic relations. In 2006, the bilateral trade between the two countries was put at US$11.8 billion. Of that, China exported US$894 million worth of goods to Angola, while Angola exported resources (crude oil) valued at US$10.9 billion to China. By 2010, trade between the two countries was valued at US$24.8 billion. As of 2014, the bilateral trade between the two countries has been put at US$37.7 billion, an amount that is reported to match Angola's combined trade with its next ten biggest trade partners. Chinese investments in Angola are primarily located in the telecommunications, infrastructure and extractive industries (Corkin, 2008).

In telecommunications, Angola's Mundo Startel has signed a framework agreement with Chinese company ZTE Corporation International for the purchase of telecommunications equipment. ZTE Corporation is to invest US$400 million in the Angolan telecommunications industry. Furthermore, Sinopec and Sanangol have formed a joint venture (Sonangol-Sinopec International) to undertake oil exploration. Sonangol will own 45 percent of the shares in the joint venture (JV) while China's Sinopec will own 55 percent. The JV owns 20 percent of Angola's oil Block 15 and in May 2006 made the largest bid to develop oil blocks 17 and 18, with collective reserves of approximately four billion barrels totalling at least US$2.4 billion, including US$1.1 billion in signature bonuses for each block and US$100 million in social projects (Corkin, 2008).

Chinese investment in Angola has come under fire by IFIs, who see an encroachment into their traditional domain due to the low interest nature of Chinese loans as well as their no-strings-attached and non-interference policy. They see it as flouting international business practices and providing resources to "corrupt" African governments; the Dos Santos government was regarded as one example. The Angolan government's decision to approach the Chinese during their negotiations with the International Monetary Fund (IMF) was because it felt it was within its rights to reject the "conditionalities" of the fund, which it viewed as interventionist (Obi, 2010). Besides, the IFIs were not willing to fund Angola's long-term and large-scale loans because the country has not fulfilled its requirements for transparency and good governance. The Angolans therefore argue that they have no choice but to turn to the Chinese.

Generally, Chinese companies have made in broader terms a huge contribution to Angola's development efforts, from the time when it could not get any funding from the IFIs to rebuild its war-torn economy to its acceptance as a member of the Organization of the Petroleum Exporting Countries (OPEC). Moving forward, the concern for Angola's post-war construction efforts is the lack of an institutional framework and government capacity to monitor and encourage direct investments in terms of local skills development and technology transfers. Furthermore, there is the question of whether enough is being done to cultivate and harness Angola's local private sector (Corkin, 2008). Table 4.1 shows some of the significant Chinese investments in the oil sector in Africa.

Table 4.1 China Oil Sector Investment

Country	Oil Sector Investment
Angola	China gave Angola a US$5 billion loan to undertake post-war rebuilding of its infrastructure. Angola will repay the loan using oil exports to China. Of the Greater Plutonio Project operated by Angola BP, 50% is owned by Sinopec.
Gabon	China signed a technical evaluation agreement with the Gabonese oil ministry in 2004 for three onshore oil fields.
Nigeria	In 1998, CNPC bought two oil blocs in the Niger Delta from the government. It bought a further 4 blocs in 2005. In exchange, China will build a 1000MW-capacity hydroelectric plant in Mambila. CNOOC has also paid US$2.7 billion for a rich oil bloc in Nigeria.
Sudan	In 1997, CNPC's Great Wall Drilling Company agreed to buy a 40% stake in the Greater Nile Petroleum Operating Company. The contract has since been renewed and expanded in the year 2000. CNPC owns an oil field in South Darfur and 41% of a field in Melut Basin. Sinopec is building a pipeline and a tanker terminal in Port-Sudan. Of Sudan's oil output, 60% goes to China.

Source: Compiled by the author.

The second country is Sudan, in which China has invested heavily in the oil sector. When it comes to Chinese investments in Sudan, trade and aid continued; however, there was not sufficient significant business expansion and interest to expand trade and aid beyond the ETC and CSTP agreements. In late 1996, the government of Sudan, through its Ministry of Energy and Mining, called for OMNCs to engage in its oil sector. It was at this time that the Greater Nile Petroleum Operating Company (GNPOC) was established as a consortium, with the State Petroleum Company owning 25 percent of the stake, the China National Petroleum Corporation (CNPC) 40 percent, Petronas Carigali Overseas of Malaysia 30 percent, and the Sudan Petroleum Company (Sudapet) 5 percent. In 1997, the US government imposed sanctions on the government of Sudan. In a strategic move, the government of Sudan sold its shares in the State Petroleum Company to a Canadian firm, Talisman. But due to pressures from non-governmental organizations (NGOs) and stakeholders for divestment on human rights grounds, Tilsman withdrew from business in the early 2000s by selling its shares to the Indian oil company ONGC Videsh (Suliman and Badawi, 2010). Table 4.2 show the Chinese firms involved in Sudan's oil sector. Most of these Chinese firms are SOEs (Suliman and Badawi, 2010).

Oil is not the only resource in which China is interested in its current engagement with Africa. It has an interest in Africa's minerals: bauxite, copper, iron, nickel and uranium, to mention just a few. The third country is Zambia. Most of China's copper from Africa comes from Zambia, where China has invested over US$170 million in the mining sector as well as other related sectors. China is now one of the major players and investors in Zambia's extractive sector, which is the largest contributor to the development and growth of the country's economy. Apart from the Vedanta-owned

Table 4.2 Chinese firms operating in Sudan oil sector

Work Type	Number of Companies	Name of Company
Drilling	2	ZPEP and GWDC
Logging	1	CNLC
Seismic survey	2	ZPEP and BGP
Mud logging	2	ZPEP and CNLC
Catering	1	ZEIGIN SERVICES
Information technology	1	CHINA WISDOM
Construction	3	CHENDONG; DUBEC and CPECC
Pipeline	3	DUBEC; CPECC and CPPE
Well heads and casting bitts	1	CPTDC
Cementing	1	GWDC
Research	2	RIBD and DAJIN
Training	4	CNLC; ZPEP; GWDC; and CPECC

Source: Ministry of Energy presentation on "Sudan–China 50 years of Cooperation," Khartoum, Sudan, 2009.

Konkola Copper Mines (KCM) in Chingola, Equinox-owned Lumwana and First Quantum–owned Kansanshi, the most significant investments are those made by the China Non-Ferrous Metal Mining Company (CNMC), which has invested US$150 million in the Chambishi copper mine. In July 2009, China's Zhongui Mining signed an agreement with Zambia to invest US$3.6 billion in mining activities in the Copperbelt and North-Western provinces, creating about 34,000 jobs. The Jinchuan Group announced on August 5th, 2009, that it will take a 51 percent ownership stake in the formerly Australian-owned Albidon nickel mine, which closed in March 2009 due to low nickel prices; and the Lwanshya Copper Mine (LCM).[2]

The government of Zambia selected CNMC to reopen the Luanshya Copper Mine which was shut by ICM (a Swiss–Israeli joint venture) in January 2009 in the aftermath of the collapse of copper prices. CNMC and a smaller Chinese copper firm signed a deal in 2006 to invest US$220 million to build a 150,000-ton copper smelting plant, which has since been commissioned in the same area. Furthermore, CLM took over the Luanshya mine and has proceeded to build an open pit mine at Mulyashi. The company has projected a production of 41,000 tons of finished copper per month, which is approximately 492,000 tons a year. The estimated life-span of the project is 25–30 years if it operates at its full capacity. Thus it can be observed that the Chinese are interested in natural resources in Africa other than oil. Its direct investment in Zambia has propelled the development of the Zambian copper industry. Even during the crisis in the Zambian copper sector, the Chinese did not pull out. One of their companies, NFCA, even went ahead and acquired the Chambeshi mine in 1998. China also played a considerable role in bolstering the mining sector during the international financial meltdown between 2008 and 2010, when some Western mining companies reduced (or closed) production, resulting in substantial job losses (Ibid, Kabemba).

Furthermore, 37 percent of China's cobalt imports come from the Republic of Congo, the Democratic Republic of Congo (DRC) and South Africa. Also, South Africa is the fourth largest supplier of iron ore to China, while Cameroon, Equatorial Guinea, Gabon, and the Republic of Congo account for 14 percent of China's rough wood imports (Trinh and Voss, 2006). China's interest in Africa's abundant mineral resources has been one of the most important reasons for its foray into Africa, and in the process it has made Africa's traditional partners or former colonial masters unhappy. This is an issue that will be looked at in detail elsewhere in this book.

4.4 Africa's Fertile Agricultural Lands

One aspect of China's foray into Africa that has received little attention is its acquisition of Africa's fertile agricultural lands. For China and other Asian as well as Arab countries, the quest for food security due to the increase in global food crises since 2000 has driven most of these countries to look for fertile lands for cultivation. Another push factor that is accounting for the "Scramble" for Africa's arable land is due to the effects of global warming, finite water supplies and the lack of arable lands in the Middle East, in some Asian countries and in China (*Economist*, 2009a). According to the *Economist*, capital-exporting countries like Saudi Arabia, Kuwait and China have quietly acquired more than 20 million hectares of Africa's farmlands, worth about US$20–30 billion (*Economist*, 2009b), for agricultural production.

Unfortunately, little of the agricultural outputs go to the host countries. Examples include countries like Sudan and Ethiopia who have given most of their arable land for foreign use but are classified as food-deficit countries. Between 3.2 and about 6.2 million people are threatened by hunger and malnutrition in those countries, requiring emergency food assistance, while 70 percent of the food produced in those countries is exported to the land investing countries (*Economist*, 2009b). China, for example is estimated to have more than 30 land deals in Africa. For example, in 2009 in Zambia alone, private Chinese farms numbered 15–24. Some of these farms were previously state owned and some were spin-offs from farms sponsored by China's government. China's State Farm Agribusiness Corporation (CSFAC) had agricultural investments not only in Zambia but also in Tanzania, South Africa, Gabon, Togo, Ghana, Mali, Guinea and Mauritania (Brautigam, 2009). In return for these farmlands, China has promised to provide Africa with technology training and infrastructure development funding of up to about US$5 billion for food and cash crop production (GRAIN, 2008; Doriye, 2010).

As far as the accusation that China is grabbing African agricultural lands is concerned, a recent book by Deborah Brautigam, *Will Africa Feed China*, disputes such an assertion. According to the book, Chinese farm investments in Africa are rather limited, and most of these investments are scattered and are on a relatively small-scale basis. Some of these farms are aimed at selling local crops to local markets. Examples given of such farms are in Zambia. Brautigam argues in the book that the idea that Chinese companies are in some kind of coordinated effort to grab and control agricultural land in Africa to grow food and feed their people back home is baseless. In fact, from a practical point of view, this view is not viable because the cost involved to produce and export this food would be high, and the yields are too low to make such a proposition feasible. Brautigam also tried to dispel some perceptions in the book of what she terms some "rural legends" and "urban myths." These include the perception that large Chinese companies are engaged in "land grab" in Africa. The other is that this "land grab" is state driven. One example she gives is the myth that ZTE, a Chinese telecommunications company, has acquired 3 million hectares of land in the DRC; the reality is that the company acquired 200 hectares of land (Brautigam, 2015).

The reason why this issue is important as far as this book is concerned, and why it is raised in this chapter, is not that Africa should not encourage foreign investment in its agriculture. It should, and it must; however, policy makers need to be careful that at the end of the day, Africa is not left holding the bag when their people are driven off the land and end up in cities looking for jobs that are not there. This is because land in Africa is a strategic asset and should be treated by African governments as so. They also need to protect their local markets from being flooded with produce from these large commercial farms, whether they are Chinese, Arab or Asian farms. If this issue is not well managed, it could end up crowding out Africa's subsistence farmers, and it could be a disaster as it pertains to Africa's food security. It therefore requires the requisite pragmatic policies to be put into place and enforced to ensure that this strategic asset is not lost. For those countries that are food deficient, efforts should be made to ensure that some of the food produced in these countries by these foreign agricultural businesses is sold to the local population at affordable prices. Finally, the fact that the Chinese are invested in African agriculture, whether in small or large farms, points to the fact that they are not only in Africa for its mineral resources. Thus, as part of positioning themselves, African countries and policy makers should consider encouraging JVs between Chinese companies and African ones in the agricultural sector. This will produce win–win outcomes for both partners as it pertains to food security.

Moving forward, because agriculture is an important sector in African economies and an important component of their growth and development strategies, it must be regarded as a priority field that is involved in any cooperation with the Chinese. Rather than splitting hairs about Chinese "grabbing" African lands, African leaders and policy makers should seek help from the Chinese on how to solve its food security challenges. The Chinese have 1.3 billion mouths to feed, and I am sure they have a lot of experiences to share with Africans in this area. Furthermore, the Chinese have seen over 20 million of their compatriots die of starvation during the era of Mao Tse Tung. They have survived it and have been able to build resilience against such an occurrence in the future. The Chinese have so far agreed to help Africa in this regard, and under the China–Africa agricultural cooperation agreement, the major areas the Chinese are willing to help Africans are in infrastructure construction for agriculture, food production, breeding industry, exchange and transfer of practical agricultural techniques, processing and the storage and transport of agricultural products (Information Office of the State Council of the People's Republic of China [PRC], 2010). One observation I have is that while it is laudable for China to agree to help as well as to cooperate with Africans to enhance their agricultural sectors, it is important for African countries to blend or anchor all such technologies and techniques to conform to or suit the African environment and culture, or they will not be sustainable.

4.5 Markets for China's Goods and Services

China's interests in Africa, as mentioned earlier, go beyond just a quest for Africa's resources. They are also driven by China's search for markets for its cheap goods and services. The push factor for such a strategy is the fact that China's economic boom has led to the saturation of its domestic markets with goods and services; hence, there is a need to look outward. Another reason for China's search for new markets is the fact that overcapacity and supply is crippling many sectors of the country's domestic markets. This is because the policies of previous Chinese governments, which emphasised industrialisation where such decisions were not market based, created such an oversupply. Without doing something about the oversupply, it could lead to some of the factories collapsing or some of the state-owned banks being saddled with non-performing loans. But it has also been observed that this is a way for the Chinese to sell some of their cheap products in African markets.

But China's search for new markets is a deliberate policy initiative on the part of the Chinese government. The government's "going out" policy is aimed at getting its companies to establish themselves internationally. This "going out" policy emerged from Deng Xiaoping's Open Door policy, aimed at creating trade and investment abroad. When China entered the WTO, its ten 5-year plans marked the rise of China's own version of its globalisation, called *Zou Chuqu*, which means "go global" (Brautigam, 2009; Shambaugh, 2013). This was a formal directive by the Chinese authorities urging its companies to go global. To encourage that, China's Ministry of Commerce has eased and streamlined the application procedures for local companies to invest abroad (Abdulai, 2007; Hornby and Kan, 2010).

The result is that Chinese consumer goods are making huge inroads in African markets. Those companies that produced high-end products were encouraged to establish their brand names abroad, and those at the low end were encouraged to buy small and medium-sized companies abroad as a way of entering those markets. The idea is to use the African market as a learning curve to be able to enter much more developed markets in Europe and the US in future. Table 4.3 shows some of the big Chinese companies that, in

Table 4.3 Some of the Early Top Chinese Companies that were Asked to Venture Out (By revenue, net income and market capitalisation as of 2003–2004)

Company	Sector	Revenue (US$)	Net income (US$)	Market* capitalisation (US$)
PetroChina	Oil/gas	29.5	5.7	90.7
China Mobile	Mobile telecoms	15.5	4.0	65.4
Sinopec	Oil/gas	39.2	1.9	51.9
CNOOC	Oil/gas	3.2	1.1	16.8
Baosteel	Steel	4.1	0.6	11.1
China Aluminium	Aluminium	2.0	0.2	8.4
Shanghai Auto (SAIC)	Cars	0.6	0.1	4.6
Legend**	PCs	2.6	0.1	2.9
TCL	TVs/electronics	2.7	0.05	2.9
Qingdao Haier	White/brown goods	1.4	0.05	1.0

Source: Annual reports; Bloomberg (cited in the *Economist*, March 20–26, 2004, p. 13).
* February 2004
** Year to March 2003

China's earlier state of emergence, were asked to venture abroad under this "going out" policy. The government gave these companies all the support they needed to enable them go international. Today, the number of Chinese companies that have ventured abroad is double or triple what is shown in Table. 4.3. This is due to the huge success of the "go global" or "going out" policy. Deng's vision and the continuous support and nurturing by the Chinese government of the Chinese companies venturing out have also contributed to the success of this policy.

China's "going-out" policy has thus brought about a situation in which there are a lot of Chinese companies looking for markets for their products in Africa. For example, Chinese products are much cheaper compared to those produced in the West because of the cheap labour costs employed in their production.[3] Consequently, most of these goods are affordable even to the poorest in Africa, who live on less than a US$1 or US$2 a day. In most cases, the goods are more conducive to the African condition because they were made in a developing country that has similar constraints to many areas within Africa. The African market has thus become a lucrative one for Chinese products. There are now over 250,000 Chinese companies operating in Africa. The flip side is that these cheap Chinese goods are killing most of the nascent industries in Africa as the latter cannot compete with Chinese industries in the production of such cheap goods because of their cost of production structure. It should be mentioned that even though China's cheap labour costs have been one of its comparative advantages in its ability to produce goods cheaply; that is changing, however, and China's labour costs are rising. Nevertheless, it is still able to produce some goods cheaper than its competitors.

Chinese firms have also found markets in the service industry and other sectors in Africa. For example, the Chinese are busy reconstructing Africa's dilapidated infrastructure, from roads to railways to ports. It is expanding Africa's telecommunication business led by Huawei Technologies, which has a presence in over 50 African countries. In 2010, Huawei and ZTE are reported to have been active in over 50 African countries, to have established more than 40 telecommunications networks in more than 30 African countries, and to have built national fibre-optic communications networks and e-government networks for more than 20 African countries. Africa now accounts for 12–13 percent of Huawei's revenue (about US$3.5 billion in 2010). For ZTE, the amount is about 11 percent (about US$1 billion in 2010).[4]

It has been observed by trade analysts that China's interest in Africa's markets is also a strategy aimed at indirectly benefiting from EU and US African Growth and Opportunity Act (AGOA) initiatives and Economic Partnership Agreements (EPAs) respectively. These agreements offer African countries concessional rates for some of their exports to their markets. By entering into joint ventures with African companies in sectors that benefit from the AGOA and EPAs, these Chinese companies benefit and to some extent are also able to circumvent WTO restrictions if they are directly exporting to the US and European markets. But the "going out" policy in a way is to help Chinese companies gain invaluable experience working in African countries (a sort of cutting their teeth, so to speak) in preparation to undertake larger projects in a more competitive world market as they plan to venture beyond Africa.

In closing this chapter, it is important to mention that the overall trade between China and Africa has gradually seen an increase. In 2000, it was US$10.6 billion; by 2005, it had risen to US$40 billion, and by 2006 to US$55 billion. In 2007, it was US$73.3 billion, and in 2008 it was US$106.8 billion (Diao, 2009). By 2012 the figure had risen to US$198 billion and by 2013 it had reached US$210 billion (see Figure 4.1). Overall trade between China and Africa, therefore, has seen a growth from a small base of US$10.6 billion to its current huge growth of US$210 billion. This growth is projected to continue as African economies continue to grow. Thus, China is currently Africa's largest trading partner, surpassing the US in 2009.

At the time of writing, China is witnessing volatility in its stock and currency markets. The turmoil has spread to other stock markets around the world. According to the *Financial Times*, the most direct threat comes from the sharp and unexpected depreciation of the Chinese renminbi. A weakening renminbi puts pressure on emerging market currencies to weaken as well. This can help emerging markets with their exports but on the flip side can create difficulties for them in their ability to pay foreign exchange debts (Wheatley, 2016). Some are predicting that this could have an impact on China's trade with Africa moving forward, especially for Africa's commodity exporters. According to the IMF, a 1 percent decline in growth in China's investment in its domestic

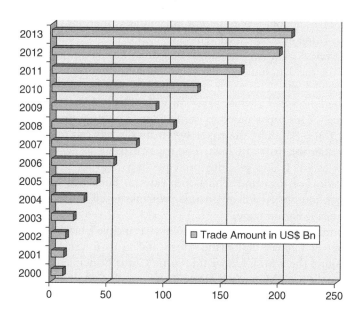

Figure 4.1 Overall Trade between China and Africa (2000–2013).

Source: Compiled by the Author.

economy is equal to a drop of 0.6 percent in export growth from African countries. Because China is the single largest trading partner with Africa, a slowing Chinese economy will definitely have an impact on imports as well as on the infrastructural projects China is undertaking in Africa.

Drawing from this experience, the prediction is that it is unlikely that China's growth will be as commodity intensive as before. Thus, the drop in commodity prices is a signal to African leaders and policy makers that China is shifting away from investment to consumption-led growth. The impact on trade will be significant. So what are African policy makers and leaders doing about this? It is hoped that Africa's new economic and diplomatic partners like Turkey, Brazil and India pick up the slack between the demand for Africa's commodities and current levels of supply (Norbrook, 2015). But this requires a quick re-think and a temporary re-organisation of their policy initiatives to respond to this current volatility faced by the Chinese economy. African leaders should not wait until their backs are against the wall to start looking for solutions. The right time for African leaders and policy makers to act is now, while the Chinese market is under pressure and while the economy is under stress.

4.6 Diplomatic Imperative (One China Principle and One China Policy)

The relationship between China and its so-called "renegade" territory – Taiwan – goes way back to the era of Chiang Kai-Shek's regime, during which it was expelled from mainland China but was recognised by the US as "Free China," while Mao Zedong's regime was isolated as Communist. China has since sought to bring this so-called renegade territory back into its fold as one China. However, a former Taiwanese President, Lee Teng-hui, who was also the leader of the Kuomintang Party, proposed a "two-state theory" as a solution to the debacle. This was not acceptable to China, so in 2000, the authorities in Beijing issued a white paper on "The One-China Principle and the Taiwan Issue." This paper aimed to clarify China's position on the Taiwan issue (Brahm, 2001). Basically, the paper systematically sets out to prove that Taiwan is an inalienable part of China. The paper makes a *de facto* and *de jure* case for such a claim. It also sees this principle as a basis for achieving the peaceful unification of mainland China and Taiwan. Finally, it calls on the international community to adhere to this principle in all its dealings with China diplomatically and in trade.

It is thus worth noting that this "One China Principle" has been one of the cornerstones of China's diplomatic efforts and in its forging of strategic partnerships around the world. Under this "One China Principle," China has successfully brought back Macau and Hong Kong into its fold. It is only the *de facto* independence of Taiwan that stands in the way of it achieving its dream of a single greater China. The "One China Principle" is different from the "One China Policy." The "One China Policy" refers to the policy that all countries seeking diplomatic relations with the PRC must break official relations with

Taiwan known as the Republic of China (ROC) and vice versa. The policy also holds that all countries that recognize the PRC also accept the PRC as the legitimate representative of Taiwan.

Africa is important to China in the entrenching of its "One China Principle" because Taiwan started its own diplomatic campaign for recognition in Africa. From the start, Taiwan was recognised by 30 African countries. At this writing, only Burkina Faso, Swaziland and Sao Tome and Principe have formal ties with Taiwan. Malawi and Gambia were the most recent African countries to sever ties with Taiwan. The benefits so far for Malawi's switching of diplomatic relations from Taiwan to China have been the construction of the Chitipa-Karonga road, the Malawi University of Science and Technology, the Parliament building of Malawi, the National Stadium of Malawi, a five-star hotel, presidential villas and the Malawi Defence Force headquarters, which is yet to be completed. China's strategy is to thwart and frustrate Taiwan's effort in building relations with African countries. By doing that, it is effectively enforcing the existence of "One China." The best way to do this is to enhance its strategic partnerships with African countries in economic and political sectors. China's interest in Africa is also about buttressing not only its "One China Principle" but also its "One China Policy," a diplomatic move to assert its power and bring Taiwan, which it regards as a "renegade province," back into its fold.

4.7 Need for Allies to Advance China's Interest and Garner Support at International Fora

China has realised that in order to counteract US hegemony in an increasingly unipolar world, and indeed US unilateral use of force and the possible impact it could have on its "One-China Principle" as already elaborated on, it needs allies and strategic partners. China tries to do this by supporting initiatives particularly by countries in the south who are seeking reforms in multilateral organisations. China is not oblivious to the fact that 53 of the African countries in the United Nations (U.N.) make up a quarter of its 192 member states. But most important of all, African countries have a significant representation in some of the multilateral organisations, and the Chinese have also observed that these African countries tend to vote in bloc. This is thus of immense importance to China as the support of this bloc can come in handy when China needs it. Supporting these countries and increasing their power on the international stage indirectly helps China when it seeks the votes and support of these African countries at numerous international fora to buttress its diplomatic interests.

China has also realised that by forging strategic alliances with African countries, it can rely on their voting bloc to circumvent sanctions when it comes under attack for some of its policies at home or abroad. The Tiananmen Square crackdown is a case in point; when China was facing international isolation for its violation of human rights, it turned to Africa for support. African countries that held seats on the U.N. Commission on Human Rights frustrated the efforts of some Western countries who wanted to bring about a formal condemnation of China's human rights record, not only after the Tiananmen incident, but also on numerous occasions. The support of China in the U.N. or at international fora is not particularly lost to it because it was African votes at the U.N. which successfully supported its entry to the U.N. in October 1971 (Yu and Longnecker, 1994).

Other areas where China had to rely on diplomatic support from African countries were in recent times, when Africa supported China over the expansion of the U.N. Security Council in 2005 and in the election of a new director-general of the World Health Organization (WHO) in 2006. Over a third of the votes to admit China into the U.N. in 1971 were by African countries. China will be forever grateful to Africa for such a gesture. But neither can it be forgotten that it was 16 African countries that recognised China's full status as a market economy, a crucial marker after its entry into the WTO, helping China to avoid accusations of dumping (Zhang, 2011).

4.8 Africa's Pharmacological Resources

Finally, a little known reason why China is interested in Africa is because of its huge pharmacological resources. The role traditional medicine plays in China cannot be emphasised enough. In 2012, global sales of Chinese herbal medicine alone reached US$83 billion. Besides, the global market for herbal and traditional medicine is projected to reach around US$115 billion by 2020. China realizes that Africa's pharmacological resources are vast because of the continent's biodiversity and the ancient history of its inhabitants and the knowledge of these herbs and herbal medicines that has been passed down from generation to generation. This has caught not only the attention of the Chinese but also that of Western pharmaceutical companies. Most of these traditional medicines have been bio-pirated, and indigenous populations have not benefitted from their commercialisation. For example, the Hoodia gordonii plant, used by the San people of southern Africa to stave off hunger and thirst, saw South Africa's Council for Industrial Research (CSIR) patent the plant's hunger-supressing component (P57) in 1996 and then license it to Phytopharm in the UK, which then licensed it to Pfizer to develop a weight-loss drug. The San people did not benefit from this process. It was only in 2002 that a benefit-sharing agreement with the San people was signed.

This example points to the challenge faced by indigenous traditional medicine. These medicines are usually not covered by intellectual property law, which focuses more on individual or group innovation and disadvantages indigenous knowledge and traditional medicine, which resides within a given locality. The fear is that with China's foray into Africa and the attendant migration that is accompanying this current engagement, it is just a matter of time before Africa loses its traditional pharmacopeia to Chinese bio-piracy. This evidenced by the current challenges faced by the textile industry in Africa, particularly Ghana, due to the pirating of designs by Chinese companies, the printing of cheap counterfeits, and their export to West Africa, where they are dumped on the markets. This is killing the local textile producing companies. It is thus important for African governments to carefully guard their respective biodiversity and pharmacology sectors against any Chinese invasion as well as all foreign invasion.

4.9 Conclusion

China's interest in Africa/foray into the region is not for altruistic reasons; it is definitely aimed at exploiting Africa's rich natural resources. But it is argued in this chapter that this is not the only reason why China is currently engaged with Africa. It is currently engaged with Africa because it is looking for markets in which to sell its manufactured products as well as a way to buttress its "One China Principle" and "One China Policy." Finally, it needs allies to advance its interests and to support it at international fora. Africa's support in realising this strategy is not lost to China. Former Chinese president Jiang Zemin, at a speech before the OAU (AU) appropriately summarises this interest:

> we had a memorable yesterday…we enjoy a splendid today. The flower of Sino-African friendship is blooming with the care and nurturing of the Chinese and African peoples. We will greet a flourishing tomorrow…. China, the biggest developing country in the world, is ready to join hands with Africa, the biggest developing continent in the world, to march into the twenty-first century full of confidence.
>
> (Zemin, 1996)

Thus for African countries to benefit from China's foray into Africa, it is imperative that they understand the reasons why China is interested in Africa to enable them position themselves adequately in their dealings with China.

Notes

1 Response of Mao to Nyerere in 1965, when he asked Mao for help to build the Tazara railway.
2 Claude Kabemba, "Chinese involvement in Zambia," Open Society Initiative for Southern Africa, October 4, 2012. www.osisa.org/books/zambia/chinese-involvement-zambia (accessed 8/2/16).
3 However, at the time of writing, Chinese labour costs are increasing and could affect the cheap cost of their products. For now, China still has this comparative advantage.
4 Andrea Mashall, "China's mighty telecom footprint in Africa," www.newsecurity learning.com/index.php/archive/75-chinas-mighty-telecom-footprint-in-africa (accessed 25/1/16).

5 China's Foray into Africa

The Benefits

5.1 Introduction

To many of the detractors and critics of China's foray into Africa, China is an energy-hungry, opportunistic "dragon," out to colonise and grab Africa's resources just like the West did many decades ago (Taylor, 2006; Lee, 2006). But are such criticisms justifiable? Is China really an "opportunistic hungry dragon" that African countries should be worried about? There are numerous observations on this issue. There are those who argue that the trepidation and anxiety about China's foray and the extension of its footprints in Africa are exaggerated (Le Pere, 2008), while some hold views to the contrary. Even though there are legitimate and, in some instances, justifiable reasons given for such anxiety, such as the numerous contracts China has signed with African countries for their resources, that is just half of the story. These critics have not taken the time to look deep into the benefits that can and are accruing to Africa due to China's foray into the continent.

Africa's developmental challenges have been enormous, and many Africans feel that, to some extent, they have been abandoned, so to speak, by Africa's traditional developmental partners. Such an assertion has been denied by many European leaders. To the latter, China's foray into the continent has filled that gap and brought with it the much needed investment, trade, and debt relief necessary for the continent's growth and development. The benefits to Africa as China entered the region are that China is now a new source of capital and investment, there has been increased trade between China and Africa, China is a new source of aid for African countries, and China has cancelled the debts that many African countries owed China.

Most important of all, China has introduced a new kind of competition in the global demand for Africa's resources. In this respect, Africa's traditional developmental partners are playing catch-up. China's foray into Africa has also made the continent now more attractive to other international investments, as the previous perceived risks in some sectors have disappeared as Chinese companies are already operating in those sectors. The Chinese have even established themselves in some of Africa's inhospitable environments in their quest to extract Africa's natural resources. This has also given China the first mover advantage, and many of the Western companies now have to play catch-up. Let's now look specifically in detail at some of the aforementioned benefits that are accruing to Africa due to China's current engagement and investment in the region.

5.2 China as the Source of New Capital and Investment in Africa

First, China can be regarded as the new investor in Africa. Previous Chinese investments in Africa were mostly based on ideological grounds, and these took place mostly during the period when most African countries attained their independence. Thus, there is nothing much to talk about except for the building of the Tazara railway. But even that was during the Cold War era, and the building of the railway had a political as well as an ideological bent to it. In terms of China's current foray into Africa, significant Chinese invest-ments have entered the region. According to China's Ministry of Commerce, the country's direct investments in Africa from 2000 to 2006 stood at US$6.6 billion. This figure could be higher, because official statistics may not fully capture foreign direct investment (FDI) information about most Chinese enterprises because they rely on retained earnings or informal earning financing arrangements, as is the case with private enterprises. Since 2007, Chinese FDI has increased significantly. For example, the Industrial and Commercial Bank of China's purchase in October 2007 of a 20 percent stake in Standard Bank Group of South Africa alone amounts to about US$5.6 billion. In the ser-vices sector, official Chinese statistics show the sum of "contrasted projects," "labour cooperation," and "design consultation" in Africa, which was less than US$2 billion in 2001 but had risen to US$9.5 billion in 2006 (Wang and Bio-Tchané, 2008). Figure 5.1 shows the specific industries of China's FDI distri-bution in Africa and the sectors to which their overall investments in Africa go.

It is also worth mentioning that to encourage Chinese enterprises to invest in Africa, the Chinese government has set up the China–Africa Fund with an initial capitalisation of US$1 billion. The China–Africa Fund is more like an equity fund that is expected, over time, to provide close to about US$5 billion in financing to Chinese businesses entering or operating in Africa. By the end of 2008, the fund had invested about US$400 million of these monies in 20 projects. By 2012, the fund had financed or co-financed over 60 projects across 30 African coun-tries. The genesis of the fund was announced at the Beijing Forum on China–Africa Cooperation (FOCAC) on November 4, 2006, by former President Hu Jintao. The fund was officially established in June 2007 with US$1 billion of initial funding by the China Development Bank. The China Development Bank was founded in 1994. It operates under the direct jurisdiction of China's State Council. Consequently, debts issued by the China Development Bank are fully guaranteed by the central government of the People's Republic of China.

The fund is focused on investing in industrial development in Africa, the acquisition of stocks in mining interests, and the support of Chinese enter-prises investing in Africa. The fund is mandated to operate in line with market

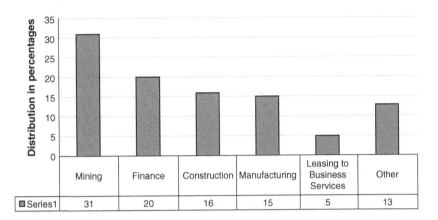

Figure 5.1 Industry Distribution of China's Outbound Foreign Direct Investment (OFDI) in Africa.

Source: Developed by Author with Data from China-Africa Economic and Trade Cooperation 2013 White Paper and the World Resources Institute.

principles. Its investment approaches are in four major ways. The first is through equity investments, the second is in quasi-equity investments and the third is fund investment. This is the case where the fund invests a sizeable proportion of its capital in other funds investing or invested in Africa. The final approach is the provision of management and financial consulting services to Chinese enterprises investing or invested in Africa. The fund's representative offices are in South Africa, Ethiopia, Zambia and Ghana.

Many have described the China–Africa Fund as a sovereign wealth fund. This is not true. This is because most sovereign wealth funds are usually funded directly from the reserves of the central bank of most of the countries establishing them. A case in point for China is that of the China Investment Corporation (CIC), which can be regarded as a sovereign wealth fund. Thus the China–Africa Fund does not fall into this category. It is an equity fund. So why would the Chinese government develop an equity fund like the China–Africa Fund? It is because they see in an emerging Africa an Africa that has rid itself of its troubled past, one that is focused on economic development and democracy with the aim of moving its people out of poverty, an Africa of immense opportunities; and they want to be part of it as well as benefit from it.

The Chinese authorities have also pledged to continue their aid and investment activities in Africa despite the recent global financial crisis (Xinhua News Agency, 2009). It is therefore not surprising that at the Forum on China–Africa Cooperation (FOCAC 2015), held in Johannesburg, South Africa, Chinese President Xi Jinping announced that China will offer US$60 billion to support Africa's industrialization, agricultural modernization, infrastructure, financial services, green development, trade and investment facilitation, poverty reduction and public welfare, public health, people-to-people exchanges, and peace and security over the next 3 years. The amount is a huge increase from the US$20 billion that was pledged by China at FOCAC 2012. The US$60 billion funding support includes US$5 billion of free aid and interest-free loans, US$35 billion of preferential loans and export credit on more favourable terms, US$5 billion of additional capital for the China–Africa Development Fund and the special loan for the development of African small and medium-sized enterprises (SMEs), and a China–Africa production capacity fund with initial capital of US$10 billion.[1]

The only major observation of China's investment in Africa is that it is mostly in the oil and gas or resource sectors (see Table 4.1). The overconcentration of Chinese investment in Africa's resource sector plays into the hands of China's critics, who claim that China is only interested in Africa because of its rich natural resources. Mention should be made that this is now changing as China is increasingly diversifying into road and infrastructure projects, hotels, agriculture and manufacturing. China's building of infrastructure in African countries means that in the end, these countries end up with infrastructure that they never would have had, even if the deals are sometimes raked with alleged corruption. It beats the frittering away of Africa's resources into Swiss bank accounts by Africa's dictators (Rozenberg, 2006). But also it beats the "lecturing" of African countries by Western countries on good governance and democracy without the attendant investments in Africa's infrastructure for its growth and development.

Based on the facts on the ground, China can be regarded as the "new" investor in Africa, differentiating it from its traditional investors – the West. This is evidenced by comments made by former Kenyan prime minister Raila Odinga about the frustrations African leaders face when dealing with the lengthy bureaucratic procedures involved in negotiations with the West and Western institutions when he was in government. Former president Abdoulaye Wade of Senegal concurs with Odinga. He puts forward this perspective best when writing in the *Financial Times* in January 2008. Wade said, "as I like to remind the international business community, a contract that would take five years to discuss, negotiate and sign with the World Bank takes three months when we have dealt with Chinese authorities. I am a firm believer in good governance and the rule of law. But when bureaucracy and senseless red tape impede our ability to act and when poverty persists while international functionaries drag their feet, Africans leaders have an obligation to opt for swifter solutions. I achieved more in my one-hour meeting with President Hu Jintao in an executive suite at my hotel in Berlin during the recent G8 meeting in Heiligendamm than I did during the entire orchestrated meeting of World leaders at the summit – where African leaders were told little more than that G8 nations would respect existing commitments" (Wade, 2008).

Adding to this chorus by African leaders of their admiration for the Chinese is the comment made by Robert Mugabe in his speech at the FOCAC 2015 summit in Johannesburg. Speaking about China and its leadership, specifically Xi Jinping, Mugabe said, "Here is a man representing a country once called poor, a country which was never our colonizer. He is doing to us what we expected those who colonised us yesterday to do. If they have ears to listen, let them hear…we will say he is a God-sent person."[2] Even though such observations by African leaders point to their frustration with the West and Western institutions, it in no way denigrates their relations with the West. What such a frustration points to is that the way the West and multilateral institutions deal with Africa must change with the times or they risk being irrelevant.

At the FOCAC 2015 meeting in Johannesburg, Xi Jinping, in announcing his ten major plans covering next three years, which came with a commitment of US$60 billion, said, "China–Africa relations have reached a stage of growth unmatched in history…let's join hands…and open a new era of China–Africa win-win cooperation and common development."[3] All these examples point to why this author has observed that China is the new source of capital for Africa.

5.3 China Could Introduce a New Era of Banking in Africa

China's foray into Africa is known to be mostly driven by its demand for Africa's rich natural resources to fuel and sustain its growth. The importance of resource security to China's growth and development has driven it to increase trade with some of the top resource-rich countries in Africa, such as Angola, South Africa, Nigeria, Sudan and Zambia, to mention just a few. Most of the acquisitions of these resources are done through joint ventures (JVs) with Chinese and African companies, often government linked. These deals would need bank financing and, in the earlier stages, were done through the China Exim Bank under its trade and project finance arm. But this is changing with China's increased engagement with Africa.

Chinese banks such as the China Development Bank, Export-Import Bank of China, Industrial and Commercial Bank of China, Bank of China and China Construction Bank are now offering their services across Africa. These services include international settlements, trade and financing in areas of financing of services, manufacturing, energy, telecommunications, power, water supply, transportation, agriculture and logistics. Chinese financial institutions have also set up branches and representative offices in Zambia, South Africa and Egypt. Some African banks have also opened branches or representative offices in China. These include Egypt, Morocco, Cameroon, South Africa and Nigeria (Information Office of the State Council of the PRC, 2010). For example, the Bank of China's Johannesburg branch oversaw a 2.7-billion-yuan transaction on November 30, 2015, for a client – Mauritius.

Lately, China has also partnered with some Western banks to finance some projects in Africa, such as China Petrochemical Corporation's (SINOPEC) financing of its JV with the National Fuels Society of Angola (SONANGOL) for offshore block 18; the Chambishi copper mines in Zambia; or the China National Offshore Oil Corporation's (CNOOC) 45 percent stake in an offshore Nigerian oil field. The participation of Chinese banks in such JVs has attracted many Western banks to participate in investing in projects in Africa after initial reticence. The size of Chinese participation has mitigated the risk of such investments, for which Western banks now see value. Previously, most Western banks and investment firms saw such investments as very risky and would not touch them.

Another interesting development is the collaboration between the China Development Bank and the China Exim Bank, which invested US$5 billion in the China–Africa Development Fund. The fund will be deployed to support African countries in agriculture, manufacturing and energy production as well as the development of Chinese businesses in Africa. This has been written about in Section 5.2. The Chinese investment in Standard Bank of South Africa is another way it is changing the nature of banking in Africa. When the Industrial and Commercial Bank of China (ICBC) took a 20 percent stake in Standard Bank of South Africa for US$5.5 billion, the reason was logical enough. The aim was to get Standard Bank to finance ICBC's corporate clients in Africa. Standard Bank was also going to use the funds ICBC invested in it to expand its footprint in Africa beyond its local South African market. The strategy also was for Standard Bank to target Chinese corporate customers in Africa. The bank was also to set up a private equity fund targeting Chinese JVs in Africa as well as other projects on the continent (Meyer, 2008).

ICBC also bought Standard Bank's 60 percent of its London-based business for about US$765 million in 2014. Standard Bank also granted ICBC a 5-year option to acquire an additional 20 percent stake in the unit. Much earlier before this deal, ICBC had acquired 80 percent of Standard Bank's Argentine unit.

The Chinese approach of targeting and acquiring stakes in well-managed, bigger African banks with well-developed institutions and multi-country presence will be the best strategy to exploit their trade ties and investments in Africa. The Chinese investment in the banking sector in Africa and its JVs with Western banks on projects in Africa is changing the risk picture and is encouraging Western banks and institutions to invest in Africa. For example, in 2014, China Development Bank entered into a strategic cooperation agreement with Barclays Bank PLC of the UK and Société Générale to receive banking services to acquire loan assets in Africa. Finally, the mergers and acquisition (M&A) activities, JVs and taking of stakes in African banks by Chinese banks will all contribute to a new era of banking in Africa. It will certainly offer African economies the option of financing capital projects. Chinese banks will now be the "new kids" on the block in African banking, following a long list of Western banks whose presence on the continent started decades ago. African governments and policy makers should take note of this new development and position their economies adequately to benefit from it.

The use of Chinese banks to finance projects in Africa as well as partnering with African banks and in some instances investing in these banks, specifically those with extensive footprints in Africa, is a rather smart move on the part of the Chinese in their foray into Africa. This will eventually transform the banking sector in Africa and introduce a new era of banking in Africa. It might also pave the way for greater Chinese involvement in the African commercial banking sector and could ultimately lead to Chinese banks in the retail banking space on the continent. It has been observed that the investment of Chinese banks in local African banks, like the aforementioned case of Standard Bank of South Africa, the financing by Chinese banks of exports and projects and finally corporate lending is rather important in Africa's current developmental trajectory. This will spur the development of sustainable industry in Africa, as most of the industries in Africa are starved of capital. But for this "new era of banking" to be sustainable and for Africa to benefit from this effort, it is imperative that these Chinese banks' mandate and their banking operations spread beyond a narrow focus on only Chinese-funded projects. These Chinese banks should move beyond their narrow focus of funding Chinese projects in Africa. Moving forward, they should develop a more comprehensive approach in their banking operations on the continent with their increase engagement with Africa.

5.4 Increased Trade between China and Africa

One of the notable benefits of China's foray into Africa is the increase in trade between China and Africa. Today, China ranks as Africa's most important trading partner, followed by the US and ahead of France and Britain. Between 2001 and 2006, two-way trade flows between Africa and China rose on average by more than 40 percent for exports to 35 percent for imports, significantly higher than world trade (14 percent). China's trade with Africa breached the US$100 billion mark in 2008. Trade between China and Africa surged by about 45 percent in 2007 to US$106.8 billion in 2008. Figures from China's General Administration of Customs show that the country's trade deficit with Africa in 2008 was US$5.16 billion. Statistics for that period show that China imported US$56 billion worth of goods and services from Africa, while it exported US$50.8 billion worth of goods to Africa. Figure 5.1 shows exports between the two countries in 2007–2011. (Wang, 2007; Broadman, 2007; Tull, 2006; Diao, 2009).

The statistics show that in 2009, trade between China and Africa slowed because of the global financial crisis. China exported US$43.3 million worth of goods to Africa. In 2010, the figure rose to US$60 million for China and US$67.1 million for Africa. In 2011, Africa exported US$93.2 million worth of goods to China and imported US$93.1 million worth of goods (See Figure 5.2). At the time of writing, because of reduced external demand and lower commodity prices, Chinese imports in the 12 months to October 2015 also saw a contraction of 13 percent compared to the same period in 2014. According to the *Financial Times*, the value of imports from Africa over the same period fell by 32 percent. Countries like Angola, South Africa, Republic of Congo, Zambia and Equatorial Guinea have all seen a steeper contraction in their imports. These countries are also some of the major trading partners of China in Africa. Moreover, for those African countries like Sudan, Angola, Eritrea, Sierra Leone and the Republic of Congo that are more exposed to the Chinese market – that is, the Chinese market accounts for 40 percent of their total exports – the steep contraction in the value of Chinese imports from Africa is largely due to the fact that commodities and crude oil make up more than 85 percent of the total imports.[4] I am of the belief that even though the Chinese economy is slowing down, China's 13th 5-year-plan is seeing the leadership retooling the economy. It will definitely still require Africa's resources to sustain its growth, albeit probably not in as large quantities as previously.

Table 5.1 show the typical imports from Africa by China and by Africa from China. This snapshot is from just the year 2014. What is clear is that most of the exports from Africa to China are composed of raw materials or Africa's natural resources. The snapshot also shows that China's exports to Africa comprise machines, manufactured products, transport equipment and

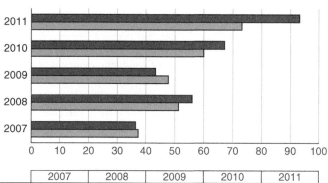

	2007	2008	2009	2010	2011
■ Africa Exports to China	36.4	56	43.3	67.1	93.2
☐ China Exports to Africa	37.3	51.2	47.7	60	73.1

Figure 5.2 China–Africa Trade (Exports) 2007–2011.

Source: Developed by Author based on data from China Customs and National Bureau of Statistics.

Table 5.1 Trade between China and Africa 2014 (Imports in US$m)

China's imports from Africa		Africa's imports from China	
Minerals, fuels, lubricants and related materials	53,470	Machines and transport equipment	42,830
Commodities and transactions, n.e.s.	26,951	Manufactured goods	28,185
Crude materials, inedible, except fuels	17,923	Miscellaneous manufactured articles	18,562
Manufactured goods	14,514	Chemicals and related products, n.e.s.	7,621
		Food and live animals	2,746

Source: UNCTAD.

other miscellaneous manufactured items. Because most of Africa's exports to China are commodities and its imports are manufactured goods and machinery, the value of the imports exceeds the value of the exports, and this is one of the causes of the current trade deficit between China and Africa. This particular issue is important and, as part of positioning themselves, African countries should develop strategies to benefit from this engagement with China. First, African countries should produce much of what they need rather than importing some of the goods they can manufacture in their respective countries. Hence, a practical and workable beneficiation policy should be pursued in the export of goods to China. Secondly, the trade deficits between African countries and China can create current account deficits for these countries, which could lead to lower growth in the export sectors. But it could also reduce the long-term income of these countries. It is thus imperative that a strategic workable industrialization plan be put in place to help African countries to move away from the export of primary produce and the import of manufactured products.

Tables 5.2–5.4 show the two-way trade relationship between China and Africa using data from China's Ministry of Commerce from 2006 to 2008. Table 5.2 shows that 61 percent of total two-way trade in 2008 was concentrated in the top five countries, with the top ten accounting for 79 percent. Table 5.3 shows that in 2008, 79 percent of all exports came from five countries, whiles 93 percent of all exports came from ten countries. Table 5.4 shows the importance of South Africa, Egypt, Nigeria, Algeria and Angola as important markets for China in Africa. The top countries according to these statistics thus account for 55 percent of all exports to China, with the top ten accounting for 75 percent. The situation revealed by this snapshot has not radically changed since China's trade with African countries started increasing. So what is the impact of increased trade between China and Africa? The most important

Table 5.2 Rankings in Total Two-Way Trade

	2006	2007	2008
1	Angola	Angola	Angola
2	South Africa	South Africa	South Africa
3	Sudan	Sudan	Sudan
4	Egypt	Egypt	Nigeria
5	Nigeria	Nigeria	Egypt
6	Congo-Brazzaville	Algeria	Congo-Brazzaville
7	Equatorial Guinea	Congo-Brazzaville	Libya
8	Libya	Morocco	Algeria
9	Algeria	Libya	Morocco
10	Morocco	Benin	Equatorial Guinea
Top 5 as a % of overall	56%	58%	61%
Top 10 as a % of overall	78%	78%	79%

Source: China's Ministry of Commerce.

Table 5.3 Rankings of African Exporters to China

	2006	2007	2008
1	Angola	Angola	Angola
2	South Africa	South Africa	South Africa
3	Congo-Brazzaville	Sudan	Sudan
4	Equatorial Guinea	Congo-Brazzaville	Congo-Brazzaville
5	Sudan	Equatorial Guinea	Libya
6	Libya	Libya	Equatorial Guinea
7	Gabon	Algeria	Gabon
8	Mauritania	Gabon	DRC
9	DRC	Mauritania	Mauritania
10	Morocco	Nigeria	Algeria
Top 5 as a % of overall	77%	78%	79%
Top 10 as a % of overall	90%	91%	93%

Source: China's Ministry of Commerce.

Table 5.4 Rankings of Exports from China to Africa

	2006	2007	2008
1	South Africa	South Africa	South Africa
2	Egypt	Egypt	Nigeria
3	Nigeria	Nigeria	Egypt
4	Algeria	Algeria	Algeria
5	Morocco	Morocco	Morocco
6	Benin	Benin	Morocco
7	Sudan	Sudan	Benin
8	Angola	Togo	Sudan
9	Ghana	Angola	Ghana
10	Libya	Ghana	Libya
Top 5 as a % of overall	57%	55%	55%
Top 10 as a % of overall	76%	75%	75%

Source: China's Ministry of Commerce.

impact is that Africa has experienced a higher rate of economic growth in the last decade, partly due to China's demand for Africa's resources. Consequently, African markets have become more promising as a larger number of African consumers are able to afford the kinds of products that Chinese companies can produce (Broadman, 2007).

Furthermore, the products and services that Chinese companies offer are considerably cheaper than those of their European counterparts. This allows for cheaper access by African countries to infrastructure as well as the development of sectors essential for economic growth and development. In fact, according to a report by the World Bank's Africa region, titled *Building Bridges: China's growing role as infrastructure financier for SSA,* (Foster et al., 2008) China's growing infrastructure commitments in Africa are helping to address the huge infrastructure deficits on the continent (SAPA, 2008), an issue dealt with at length in this chapter.

Another important benefit and effect of Africa's trade with China is that African countries are benefiting from cooperation with their Chinese partners to overcome market entry hurdles, especially in areas of technical and quality control standards. This is due to China's experience in successful penetrating and entering Western markets (Jacoby, 2007). This phenomenon is rather limited at the time of this writing.

Furthermore, because the Chinese take the kinds of risks that most of their Western counterparts will not, a lot of Chinese small, medium, and large companies have been able to operate in harsh and inconceivable locations in Africa. In fact, the Chinese in Africa are just about everywhere, so to speak. They run grocery stores, building materials stores, restaurants and corner shops. For example, the Chinese are into chicken farming in Zambia. China has thus transformed the competitive landscape in Africa as it pertains to trade and investments, gradually moving away from Africa's traditional partners (Broadman, 2007).

The negative criticisms of China's trade with Africa are mostly about the fact that Chinese companies are contributing to the atrophy of local African industry as well as the economic de-industrialisation of the continent (Mbeki, 2005). Other criticisms include the flooding of African markets with cheap products, thus killing promising African businesses. Others argue that Chinese companies operating or doing business in Africa underbid local firms as well as fail to hire Africans to work on projects, thus stunting the growth and development of African businesses. These criticisms and many more are elaborated on in detail in Chapter 6 of this book.

Despite all these criticisms, China's investment and trade with Africa so far has contributed to the growth we are seeing in Africa today. The demand for Africa's natural resources alone has contributed to a competitive element in the global demand for these resources, which is good for Africa. For now, it is advisable for African leaders and policy makers to strategize as to how effectively they can manage the trade relations between Africa and China. Furthermore, they need to learn how to deal with the ups and downs in the global demand for their resources, especially from China, as is currently the case at the time of writing.

5.5 New Source of Aid for African Countries

The major goal of most development aid is to support the socio-economic and political development efforts of developing countries. There are diverse views on the effectiveness of development aid and whether it works. Even though that might not be the preoccupation of this section, it is appropriate to give a brief summary of some such views. Economists like Peter Bauer and many others have argued since the 1960s that aid is ineffective (Bauer, 1959). They point to the fact that it creates Dutch Disease – an unbalanced appreciation of the recipient country's currency; it increases consumption and in most cases, as in Africa, it postpones the necessary economic and political reforms required for sustained growth and development. Moyo (2010) echoes the same sentiment in her book *Dead Aid*, which uses a hypothetical scenario of how aid can choke off the export sector in Kenya. Moyo's argument in her book that aid in general, especially to Africa, is bad is rather misplaced. So is her definition of aid as "the sum total of both concessional loans and grants." Grants can understandably be classified as some form of aid, and definitely not all grants can be classified as such. But to classify concessional loans as aid is unfortunate. Loans, whether they are concessionary or not, have to be paid back at some point in the future with interest. They can in no way, in the view of this author, be classified as aid.

Those who believe that aid is necessary and is advantageous and can contribute to growth and development in Africa and indeed in other developing countries argue that aid can bring about stability and in the process prevent "failed states" (Weber, 1947). *Failed states* as used here refers to the case where the basic conditions in a country or state have deteriorated to such an extent that it can be rightly said that the country or state is derelict in its responsibilities as a sovereign government – to provide for and seek the welfare of its people. It is the case where the normal day-to-day activities of the state have broken down and no longer function. As a result, decay sets in, with the country or state facing the possibility of collapse. Aid can also bring about the reduction of poverty and in some cases can avert humanitarian catastrophes. Some have even pointed to the Marshall Plan to show that aid works and is therefore necessary and can contribute to the growth and development of developing countries in general (Behrman, 2008; Hogan, 1989). In the foregoing view, the importance of China's aid to Africa cannot be emphasised enough. Thus, the announcement by former Chinese president Hu Jintao at the Beijing FOCAC summit in November 2008 that China will:

- Double the 2006 levels of annual assistance to African countries by 2009
- Offer US$3 billion of preferential loans and US$2 billion of preferential buyer's credits
- Set up a China–Africa fund with $5 billion in funds to encourage and support Chinese investments in Africa
- Help build a conference centre for the Africa Union to support its efforts to strengthen the continent through unity and integration
- Cancel all interest-free government loans that matured at the end of 2005 owed by nations that have diplomatic ties with China (US$1.5 billion)
- Extend zero-tariff treatment from currently 190 to 440 exports from Africa's least developed countries (LDCs).[5]

All these point to the fact that China is indeed a new source of much needed aid to African countries for contributing to their growth efforts. Indeed, subsequent pronouncements by Chinese leadership to this effect, for example the recent pronouncements of Chinese aid to Africa by Xi Jinping made at FOCAC 2015 in Johannesburg, South Africa, are all a testimony to this fact. Let's now look at some Chinese assistance to some African countries to drive home this point.

During the last decade, China has been investing heavily in Africa's natural resources, developing mines and oil wells and running related construction companies. Figure 5.3 offers a look at the top ten recipients of Chinese assistance in Africa, the total amounts received and what share of Chinese commitments each of the top ten countries in Africa received.

Figure 5.3 shows the top ten Chinese projects undertaken in Africa between 2004 and 2010 in billions of US dollars. The biggest was a concessionary loan of US$5.49 billion to Ghana, followed by a US$5.38 billion infrastructure for an oil deal and then a US$4.04 billion support to Mauritania for oil exploration and for the development of an iron-ore mine. The rest of the projects were between US$1 billion and US$3 billion. What is unique about this new development aid to Africa from China is that it is unconditional. Many critics of China argue that this will undermine efforts to create democratic and accountable administrations in Africa. Others argue that this will drive African countries that have just benefitted from debt relief back into debt due to China's granting these countries cheap loans (McGreal, 2007). This argument assumes that China has not played any role in Africa's debt relief. Actually, China has contributed to the debt relief of many African countries as elaborated on in Section 5.6. Much as the debt load of African countries should be of concern, my view is that what should be of most concern is what the money is used for. If it is used for infrastructure, education and other projects that will contribute to the long-term development of these countries, I am for it. Previous aid and loans were used by African countries for arms and other worthless projects that did not contribute much to the continent's growth and development.

Those who subscribe to the argument that the granting of cheap loans to African countries by the Chinese will put Africa back in debt point to the Democratic Republic of the Congo (DRC) as a case in point. In 2008, the DRC agreed to a US$9 billion investment deal in its infrastructure with China's Exim Bank. Under the conditions of this deal, China offered to build roads and rail infrastructure across the DRC in exchange for rights over mineral deposits containing more than 10 million metric tons of copper and 600,000 tons of cobalt. However, the International Monetary Fund (IMF) intervened, fearing that the deal, unless revised, would put the DRC more into debt and threaten the delay of debt forgiveness of the country to the tune of US$10 billion. In 2009, the size of the deal between China and the DRC was reduced to US$6 billion, and the minerals extraction guarantee was excluded from the deal (Doriye, 2010).

Others like Curtis (2008) see the China–DRC deal – and indeed the overall Chinese foray into the DRC – as having the possibility of benefitting some Congolese elite but also of perpetuating harmful practices and networks that were established by European and American forerunners. Chinese money, it is

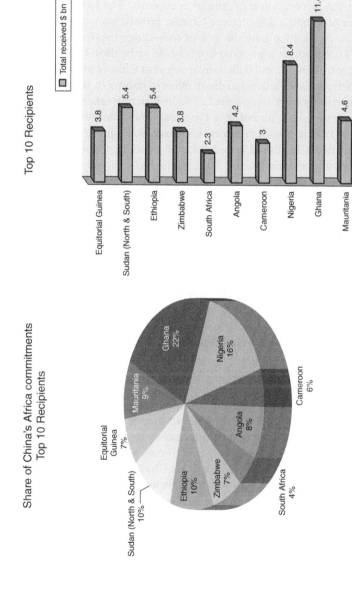

Share of China's Africa commitments
Top 10 Recipients

Top 10 Recipients

Figure 5.3 Top Recipients of Chinese Assistance to Africa.

Source: Developed by Author based on Aid/Data from Center for Global Development.

further argued, may contribute to the resilience of the links between external capital and a disregard for the population in the DRC.

There is a further argument that, because China's aid to Africa is mostly state driven, there is a greater chance of it increasing corruption and graft. There is also the concern that Chinese aid may bring about "Dutch Disease," as it could adversely affect the diversification of African economies. The fact that there is a minimal transfer of technical skills in these Chinese projects is another concern for these critics. The example of how the lack of technology transfers impacted the survival of the Tazara railway is an example often held up by these critics to support the case of lack of technology and skills transfer as part of Chinese projects in Africa. Some have observed that China did make an effort to transfer technology when it built the Tazara railway by training a total of 1200 African workers in technology and railway management. A further 200 Tanzanians and Zambians were sent for further studies in 1972 at Northern Jiatong University in Beijing (Monson, 2009).

Others argue that China's aid is tied aid. For example, China's Ministry of Commerce's grants and zero-interest loans are tied to Chinese companies and goods. It is observed that foreign aid project tenders are posted publicly, but companies eligible to bid on them must be on a list of pre-qualified Chinese firms. Furthermore, China's Exim bank's concessional aid guidelines stipulate that only Chinese companies that are the exporters or contractors qualify for such aid. It also states that inputs for Exim bank–financed concessional aid projects should be procured from China (Brautigam, 2009). A good example is the 70 percent of oil-back infrastructure that was to be built in Angola, which was reserved for Chinese companies because the credit was offered by China's Exim bank. But there is nothing new about tying aid to economic and political interest of countries. For far too long, many Western countries have tied their aid to their interests around the world. According to a 2006 report by the Organisation for Economic Co-operation and Development (OECD), 41.7 percent of official development assistance is untied (OECD, 2006). Thus the Chinese are actually learning from how Western countries used their aid programmes to attain their political and economic interests in the countries in which they deployed them. Hence they are, in the view of this author, doing nothing different by tying their aid to projects they undertake in Africa.

Despite all these criticisms that Chinese aid to Africa may do more harm than good (McGreal, 2007), what is very clear about China's aid to Africa is that it is making a huge difference in the growth and development of African countries. The building of schools, hospitals and infrastructure using Chinese aid are cases in point. It can therefore be said that Chinese aid to Africa is sincere and to some extent altruistic, so to speak, because it is offered without any political pre-conditions attached or interference in the internal affairs of recipient countries in Africa, as has been the case with aid from Western donors. Former president Abdoulaye Wade of Senegal, commenting about Chinese aid to Africa said,

> as I like to remind the international business community, a contract that
> would take five years to discuss, negotiate and sign with the World Bank

has taken three months when we have dealt with Chinese authorities. I am a firm believer in good governance and the rule of law. But when bureaucracy and senseless red tape impede our ability to act, and when poverty persists while international functionaries drag their feet, African leaders have an obligation to opt for swifter solutions.

(Wade, 2008)

The Chinese, in the view of Wade, are offering those swifter solutions, hence their increasing appeal as a preferred development partner by African countries.

China has so far conducted more than 800 aid projects, including 137 for agriculture and 133 for infrastructure, 19 schools, 38 hospitals and a 760,000-seat stadium in Tanzania, and it has sent nearly 16,000 people in medical teams accumulatively. Also, within the framework of FOCAC, China has written off 10.9 billion RMB Yuan in debts of African countries as well as trained over 15,000 personnel of various kinds.[6] This is making Africa's traditional aid donors uncomfortable, pushing them to reconsider their aid policies toward Africa. Table 5.5 below shows completed Chinese aid projects in Africa since 2009.

Table 5.5 gives a snapshot of some of the aid programmes of China in Africa. This does not include the recent US$100 million military assistance to the African Union to support its standby force as well as the African Crisis Response Force. Mention should also be made of the deployment of the Chinese helicopter unit to Africa. All this Chinese aid to Africa cannot be viewed in isolation. It is linked to some of the issues already discussed in this book, like China's eagerness to recapture its past pre-eminence as it pertains

Table 5.5 Chinese US$ Bn to Top 10 African Projects

Billion-dollar Projects		
Country	*Support facility*	*Amount received*
Ghana, 2010	Concessionary loan	US$5.49 billion
Ghana, 2009	Loan for oil and road projects	US$3.00 billion
Nigeria, 2006	Infrastructure in exchange for preferential oil right bidding	US$5.38 billion
Mauritania, 2006	Oil exploration, sewage systems, iron mine, road	US$4.04 billion
Equatorial Guinea, 2006	Oil-backed loan	US$2.69 billion
Ethiopia, 2009	Loan for dam construction	US$2.25 billion
South Africa, 2011	Financial cooperation agreement	US$2.25 billion
Angola, 2004	National Rehabilitation Project	US$1.51 billion
Angola, 2009	Agriculture development	
Madagascar, 2008	Hydroelectric construction	US$1.42 billion
Sudan, 2007	Railway construction	US$1.38 billion
Zimbabwe, 2004	Power plant construction	US$1.01 billion

Source: Aid/Data Center for Global Development.

to its image internationally. But above all, it is to create opportunities for Chinese exports. For example, China's tying of aid to its investment and development assistance to Africa does help promote Chinese exports as well as service contracts in the region. Service contracts signed by China in Africa are alone worth about US$70.8 billion. So the Chinese are not oblivious to what they are doing in Africa. They know they can benefit severally from the aid they give to African countries. The concern, for this author, is to what useful ends African leaders will use this Chinese aid and how effectively some of these resources will be applied to contribute to the sustainable growth and development efforts of the continent. At the end of the day, if this aid is effectively used, then it will spell a win–win situation for the Chinese as well as the Africans.

5.6 Cancellation of African Debts Owed to China

Another benefit of China's foray into Africa is that it resulted in the cancellation of Africa's debt owed to China. The enormous debt some African countries accumulated during the Cold War era became a major obstacle to the continent's growth and development efforts. There are numerous arguments for debt relief, and some of these include economic arguments that too much debt exerts an unnecessary drag on the economic performance of poor countries. Hence, debt relief can contribute to the improvement of the economic efficiency, growth and development of African countries. Another argument in favour of debt relief is a moral one. The argument is often the case that poor countries, most of which are in Africa, should not be allowed to devote most of their scarce resources to servicing the debts they owe to rich countries. Finally, it is also argued that debt relief can bring about the realisation of much-needed additional resources to support the Millennium Development Goals (MDGs).

Those who are against debt relief argue that it is a blank cheque for African governments to go on another spending spree and then wait for another round of debt relief. But they also claim that it is unfair to those African countries that managed their resources well and never got into debt. Others fear that the savings from debt relief will not actually go to the poor who need it most. Hence, the much talked-about concept of the trickle-down effect that debt relief will have on the poor will be non-existent. Rather, they will see the savings from debt relief going to support the lifestyles of bureaucrats and the rich in African societies.

It is against this background that China's cancellation of African debt features. It started with the first China–Africa Forum, held in Beijing in 2000. At this event, the Chinese authorities under the leadership of former president Jiang Zemin cancelled more than US$1 billion of debt owed by poor African countries. During the second China–Africa Trade Summit, held in Addis Ababa, Ethiopia, in 2003, China again wrote off US$1.27 billion in debt owed by 31 African countries (Efande, 2003). Also, at the opening of the Beijing Summit of the Forum on China–African Cooperation, former president Hu Jintao cancelled African debt in the form of all interest-free government loans of heavily indebted and the least developed African countries with diplomatic ties with China. This applied to all interest-free loans that matured at the end of 2005.

There was fear on the part of many African leaders that the 2009 global financial crisis would impact on aid from China and consequently debt relief. This did not happen. China continued with aid to Africa despite the crisis. In a December 2008 meeting between President Jose Eduardo dos Santos of Angola and former Chinese premier Wen Jiabao, in Beijing, the premier stated that China would not reduce its assistance to Africa despite the financial crisis. He noted that "we will implement the follow-up actions agreed upon during the Beijing Summit of the Forum on China–Africa Cooperation (FOCAC) in 2006."[7] Indeed, they did follow through with their agreements (Tables 5.5, 5.6).

What is very interesting about China's debt-relief efforts were that its public pledges were consciously couched as debt relief for "highly indebted" and the "least developed" developing countries. However, it did not follow all the rules of the Heavily Indebted Poor Countries (HIPC) debt relief regime. China cancelled the debts of poor countries unconditionally and did not require benefiting countries to prove their ability to manage their economies or come up with elaborate strategies on how they were going to use the cancelled debt for poverty reduction in their respective countries (Brautigam, 2009). This thus presents a different approach to debt relief by the Chinese, and they made good on their pledge, as opposed to the West and indeed most multilateral institutions to which Africa was indebted. The G8 meeting in Gleneagles is a case in point.

For example, when Western countries plus Russia (G8) met in Gleneagles in 2005, they pledged to increase Official Development Assistance (ODA) to Africa to the tune of US$20 billion a year by 2010. The G8 also committed to cancel 100 percent of the outstanding debt of eligible HIPCs in Africa to the IMF, the International Development Agency (IDA) and the African Development Fund. At this writing (2016), a decade or so later, most of the G8 countries have not made good on their pledges. According to OECD, out of the US$25 billion pledged, only US$11 billion has been delivered (Elliot, 2015). Africans tend to see this action on the part of the West as a lack of interest in the continent's development efforts, and indeed most of these countries have come to the conclusion that some of these European countries do not keep their promises. Is it therefore any surprise that African countries tend to

Table 5.6 Chinese-aided completed projects in Africa 2009

Total	Agricultural projects	Schools	Hospitals	Sports venues	Conference centres	Industrial projects	Others
884	142	71	54	53	62	145	357

Source: Ministry of Commerce of the People's Republic of China.

see the Chinese now as more attractive than Westerners and the Chinese as the people interested in their development? This is because the Chinese deliver on their commitments, and the facts are there to prove it.

On the balance, I think the cancellation of the debts of poor African countries and indeed the efforts being made to enhance the living conditions of their people is in order. That said, I support some of the concerns of some of the Western countries and the IFIs about the efficient use of the savings from debt relief. This is in ensuring that the benefits resulting from debt cancellations of African countries is effectively used for poverty alleviation or investment in projects that contribute to sustainable livelihoods. If therefore there are "conditionalities" to this effect, I support them. But a word of clarification here is in order. I will support what I call *smart conditionalities*, if there is any word like that. By *smart conditionalities* I mean conditionalities that combat corruption in the use of savings from debt relief as well as maximize the efficient and effective use of resources realized from debt relief for poverty alleviation. If these smart conditionalities are going to deter the misuse of these savings by some by some African leaders, then I am for them.

5.7 Conclusion

The benefits of China's foray into Africa are numerous. In this chapter, effort has been made to outline some of the major benefits. China is indeed now a new source of much-needed capital and investment in Africa's growth and development efforts. Increased trade between Africa and China is one of the benefits, and there is the potential for more growth in trade despite the current downturn in China. China is also a new source of aid to Africa, and the uniqueness of China's aid to Africa is that it is unconditional and most of the aid is untied. The aid is not also used as a political tool, and the Chinese do not interfere in Africa's internal affairs. This has exposed China to a lot of Western criticism. Some of these criticisms are elaborated on in this chapter. Most important of all, China has cancelled debt owed to it by African countries. Most of this debt, which was accrued during the era of the Cold War, would allow African countries to grow again. It should be mentioned that the West has also written off some of Africa's debt. The hope is that African leaders will effectively use these benefits flowing from China's foray into Africa to improve the living conditions of the poor in their respective countries and to further the development efforts of their countries. In this case, frankly, it is up to Africa and its leaders to take advantage of this opportunity.

Notes

1 FOCAC, "Xi announces 10 major China-Africa cooperation plans for coming 3 years," www.focac.org/eng/zfgx/dfzc/t1322068.htm (accessed 26/1/16).
2 Robert Mugabe's Speech at 2015 FOCAC Summit in Johannesburg. "Robert Mugabe: China is doing everything that Africa's colonizers should have done," Quartz Africa,

www.qz.com/565860/robert-mugabe-china-is-doing-everything-that-Africans-colonizers-should-have-done.
3 Ibid, "Xi announces 10 major China–Africa cooperation plans for coming 3 years."
4 Valentina Romei, "China and Africa: trade relationship evolves," Financial Times, December 3, 2015. http://www.ft.com/cms/s/0/c53e7f68-9844-11e5-9228-87e603d-47bdc.html#axzz4HfpihNR6 (accessed 27/1/16).
5 "China-Africa economic, trade cooperation," The 2007 Annual Meetings of the African Development Bank Group, http://adb_english.people.com.cn/81811/5687470.html.
6 "China-Africa economic, trade cooperation," The 2007 Annual Meetings of the African Development Bank Group. http://adb_english.people.com.cn/81811/5687470.html.
7 "China Not to Reduce Assistance to Africa Despite Financial Crisis," Ministry of Foreign Affairs of the Republic of China, http://www.focac.org/eng/zxxx/t528005.htm.

6 China's Foray into Africa

The Criticisms

6.1 Introduction

The view that China's foray into Africa is only to grab its resources and that China is the "new colonialist" is contrary to the view, held by many in Africa, that Chinese companies are a force for peace and prosperity. It is without a doubt that China's foray into Africa would have its detractors. Some of these criticisms are legitimate and others are a reaction to the arrival of a formidable competitor on the African economic/political scene by Africa's traditional partners who have always regarded Africa as "*la chasse gardée*" (hunting ground) and taken it for granted. But this observation and criticism of China is also made by indigenous African entrepreneurs and businesses who, for far too long, had been complacent due to the lack of any formidable competition in their backyards. Most of these indigenous African businesses were comfortable until competition finally arrived in the form of Chinese business to jolt them from their slumber.

In fact, most of those who criticise China today as it currently engages Africa have conveniently forgotten that the continent became the step-child of the international trading system, a mere footnote or worse, unmentioned in discussions of global commerce. In fact, Africa's share of global trade has been around 3 percent since 2012. The negative reportage on Africa and the picture painted in the foreign media of the continent as a basket case made it difficult to attract long-term investments into the continent. China's foray into Africa has changed all of that (French, 2004).

This chapter will look at some of these criticisms of China's current engagement with Africa. So what are some of these criticisms? They range from allegations that China is the "new colonialist" to the claim that its foray into Africa will lead the continent to chalk up trade imbalances with China and hence increase its debt load again. Other criticisms include that China undermines good governance and turns a blind eye to human rights abuses in its dealings with some African leaders that are autocrats in some of the African countries that it invests in. Examples include Sudan, Zimbabwe and Equatorial Guinea. And finally, there are claims that Chinese projects undertaken in Africa lack the transfer of technology and skills. This, the critics observe, is important for the sustainable growth and development efforts of African countries. Some of these criticisms are true and some are not. This chapter will look critically at some of these criticisms in detail.

6.2 China, the "New Colonialist?"

One of the criticisms is that China is now the "new colonialist" in Africa. In a 2008 interview with George Soros in Senegal by *Reuters*, Soros referred to India and China as "the new colonialist." According to Soros, "there's a certain irony of the old colonialists recognizing their past mistakes and trying to correct them, and the new colonialist then repeating those mistakes," (Flynn, 2008). The *Economist* (2008) also ran a cover story on China titled "New Colonialist," detailing its huge appetite for acquiring global resources. Some critics acknowledge China's interest in Africa's natural resources but hold the view that its behaviour is no different from that of Africa's previous colonial masters, whose only interest in Africa was to pillage its natural resources. Adam Hochschild's book *King Leopold's Ghost: A Story of Greed, Terror and Heroism in Colonial Africa* is one of the books that critically look at how King Leopold of Belgium pillaged Congo, which he regarded as his personal property. The assertion that China's foray into Africa is because it wants to satisfy its appetite for resources to feed its fast growth is not totally true; it is disingenuous, as already elaborated on elsewhere in this book, and hence I will not belabour the issue. China's current engagement with Africa goes beyond the demand for Africa's natural resources.

Actually, the overall Chinese outward foreign direct investment (FDI) is mostly concentrated in Asia. Africa accounts for a negligible proportion of 2.5 percent of the overall total. This figure challenges the perception that China is colonising Africa (Draper et al., 2010). Africa has always been a source of raw materials for the West as well. For example, in 2006, China purchased only 9 percent of Africa's oil, while the US purchased 33 percent and Europe 36 percent (Aning and Lecoutre, 2007). But China is not only relying on Africa to meet its resource needs. It has signed deals with countries in Latin America and the Middle East to secure the requisite resources needed for its fast-growing economy. This criticism, which is mostly levelled by the West, could be an expression of its concern about losing its influence and grip on Africa's resources (Tull, 2008). Responding to this criticism in support of China, former President Wade of Senegal said,

> if opening up more free markets is a goal that the West prizes and extols as a path to progress then why is Europe fretting about China's growing economic role in Africa? The expansion of free markets has indeed been a boon to Africa and one I applaud...China is doing a much better job of responding to market demands in Africa than Western capitalists.

> (Wade, 2008)

Ngozi Okonjo-Iweala, a former managing director of the World Bank and former finance minister of Nigeria, adds,

> African countries are clear that when it comes to economic growth and transformation, China has much to offer that is relevant to present-day Africa (*African needs*). China knows what it means to be poor and has evolved a successful wealth creation formula that it is willing to share with African countries...for that reason, China should be left alone to forge its unique partnership with African countries and the West must simply learn to compete.
>
> (Okonjo-Iweala, 2006)

In fact, one can argue that China is not in the philanthropy business and that China's foray into Africa should not be based on philanthropy; and it is not. Yet, it can be observed that it may be one of the best hopes for the continent of escaping from decades of poverty. African countries have seen significant growth in their economies due to a much better management of their economies, debt relief, and higher capital inflows, as well as to higher commodity prices driven by Chinese demand (Pilling, 2009). It should also be mentioned that the recent wave of African countries moving toward democratisation is also contributing to the current growth of most of these countries.

The Chinese do not see themselves as a "threat" to Africa or as the "new colonialist," as their critics uphold, and they refute this charge. Premier Li Keqiang, in his visit to Africa in April 2014, refutes the charge of China as the "Neo-Colonialist" in Africa. China's foreign minister Wang Yi, also speaking in Kenya in 2015, refuted such a claim when he said

> In China's exchanges and cooperation with Africa, we want to see mutual benefit and win–win results. I want to make clear one point, that is, China will never follow the track of Western colonialists and all cooperation with Africa will never come at the expense of the ecology, environment or long-term interests of Africa.[1]

The Chinese argue that their relationship with Africa is guided by the principles of sincerity, friendship, equality, mutual benefit and common development. They also argue that they are committed to promoting sustainable development in Africa (Stamp, 2006). The Chinese premise their relationship with Africa as based on "South–South Cooperation," and they perceive themselves as the "blood brothers" of Africans in their mutual suffering as "victims" of Western imperialism. In a white paper published by the Chinese authorities (*White paper on China–Africa Economic and Trade Cooperation*) in August 2013, they argue that they see their trade and economic relations with Africa improving lives and livelihoods and contributing to Africa's economic development.

Even though the arguments are clear that China is not the "new colonialist," it will be foolhardy for African countries to let their guard down in their current engagement with China by accepting hook, line and sinker that their current engagement with Africa is all about friendship and "South–South cooperation." Much as all such platitudes are important, African countries in these modern times must be vigilant with their engagement with the West, the Chinese or indeed with any country engaging with Africa. Martin Luther King, Jr., writing about the need to be vigilant, observed,

> One of the great liabilities of history is that all too many people fail to remain awake through great periods of social change…today, our very survival depends on our ability to stay awake, to adjust to new ideas, to remain vigilant and to face the challenge of change."
>
> (King Jr., 1967)

African countries need to remain awake in their current engagement and negotiations with China and in critically analysing Chinese investment in the continent and how that meshes with Africa's needs. It is only through vigilance that Africa can craft win–win outcomes for its sustainable growth and development with any country that engages it for its resources or otherwise.

6.3 Increase in Africa's Trade Imbalance

Another criticism of China's foray into Africa is that it will lead to an increase in Africa's trade imbalance with China and hence increase the debt load of most African countries, most of whom have just benefitted from debt relief. Hilary Benn, the former UK Secretary for International Development in Gordon Brown's administration, echoed these sentiments when he visited Malawi in February 2007. Benn said,

> If countries are borrowing to the extent that their debt becomes unsustainable then that undermines all the work that has been done in trying to tackle unsustainable debt. The issue for debt is not debt per se, it's can you afford it?
>
> (McGreal, 2007)

The former President of the World Bank, Paul Wolfowitz, also referred to China's increased lending to Africa as problematic. For example, by the end of 2007, China had approved about $23.9 billion in loans to African countries for numerous projects, ranging from infrastructure to dams to the building of schools and hospitals.

At the time of writing, Africa's trade deficit with China is rising, and as China's economy slows down, it is observed that this deficit could even go higher. This is because China will import less from Africa but will try to export more to African countries. This is happening at a time when the US Federal Reserve is also beginning to hike interest rates. Consequently, dollar-denominated debts of African countries would also rise. They could become unmanageable and problematic. The impact on the growth and development efforts of most of these African countries if that happens cannot be emphasised enough.

The Chinese government has acknowledged its trade imbalance with African countries and has pledged to work hard to eradicate it. Speaking at the University of Pretoria in South Africa on February 7, 2007, former president Hu Jintao said, "China takes the concerns about the imbalance in the structure of China–Africa trade and the scope of Chinese investment seriously...we have taken and will continue to take, effective steps to address these concerns."[2] Another way China plans to address its trade imbalance with Africa is to encourage its companies to increase their investments in Africa and provide technical and management training to help African countries develop processing and manufacturing industries to enhance the competitiveness of its exports. The Chinese have also proposed to give those African countries with which it is running trade deficits access to low-cost capital goods from China in favour of their respective national infrastructure investments.

Finally, the Chinese have proposed to encourage more African products to enter the Chinese market. The Chinese Ministry of Commerce hosted an African Commodities Exposition in Xiamen in 2008. The authorities have also increased from 140 to 190 the number of export items from Africa that will attract zero tariffs. If all the efforts are effectively implemented and monitored, it will go a long way to reducing the trade imbalance between Africa and China. However, it cannot be emphasised enough that, no matter how much the Chinese or any country trading with Africa tries to reduce their trade deficits with African countries, the issue of trade imbalance will not go away until African countries first diversify their economies. They also need to enhance their manufacturing sectors as well as increase the value-adds on their primary products before they are exported. This is their responsibility, and no one is going to do that for them.

6.4 China's Activities Undermine Good Governance and Human Rights Abuses in Africa

Another criticism of China's foray into Africa is that its activities undermine good governance and human rights abuses on the continent. Critics point to China's no-strings-attached lending policy as one that supports repressive regimes on the continent, hence hindering good governance. These critics further observe that China's actions permit African countries to circumvent the conditions that come with assistance from Western and international finance institutions. For example, Chris Smith, a member of the US Congress House Sub-Committee on Africa, warned that

> China is playing an increasingly influential role on the continent of Africa and there is concern that the Chinese intend to aid and abet African dictators to gain a stranglehold on precious African natural resources, and undo

much of the progress that has been made on democracy and governance in the last 15 years.

(Fisher–Thompson, 2005; Srinivasan, 2008)

These critics point to the Chinese aid given to Robert Mugabe's Zimbabwe, Teodoro Obiang Nguema Mbasogo's Equatorial Guinea and Omar Bashir's Sudan as cases in point. According to human rights advocates, these leaders are some of the worst human rights violators in Africa. Some of these believe that without Chinese support of these African dictators, those like Mugabe will not last.

Others point to how China broke a U.N. arms embargo by continuously supplying arms to Sudan, a key player in the Darfur conflict, during which human rights abuses were carried out by the Janjaweed militias with the support of Sudan's armed forces. A U.N. report that confirmed its supply of arms to Sudan was suppressed by China at the U.N. (Buckley, 2010). It is reported that between 1996 and 2003, China sold about US$100 million worth of arms to Sudan. These included jets and helicopter gunships. It has written off Sudan's debts and has also provided interest-free loans to President Omar al-Bashir, for whose arrest the International Criminal Court has issued a warrant on charges of war crimes and crimes against humanity in Darfur. The Darfur conflict was eventually solved when pressure was put on China by non–government organizations (NGOs) and human rights groups and other Western countries on their intent to boycott the 2008 Olympic Games, which were to be held in Beijing. There were further efforts to brand the games as the "Genocide Olympics," which the Chinese leaders abhorred. Eventually, China had to cave in and work with the international community to solve the Darfur issue (Srinivasan, 2008; Prunier, 2008; Flint and de Waal, 2008).

China is also accused of breaking an EU and US arms embargo in 2004 against Zimbabwe when it sold fighter aircraft and military vehicles to the tune of US$200 million to that country (Brookes and Ji-Hye, 2006). When Zimbabwe faced economic sanctions and international isolation for its human rights abuses, it announced in 2005 a "Look East" policy, turning to Asia, and specifically to China, for trade, investments and loans. Thus, China, in exchange for mining concessions, invested in building roads and in farming. It is providing Zimbabwe with farming equipment, the generation of electricity, the provision of planes for Air Zimbabwe, buses, light arms, the building of a weapons factory and the provision of 12 jet fighters and 100 military vehicles to the Zimbabwean army. China has also supplied tanks, artillery, armoured vehicles and anti-aircraft batteries to Zimbabwe (Brown and Chandra, 2008). The Chinese are still supporting Robert Mugabe's regime and have not criticised his human rights violations in that country. In fact, Mugabe was awarded the 2015 Confucius Peace Prize by the Chinese. The peace prize is one of the top awards in China. Some see such an act on the part of the Chinese as glorifying dictatorship and dictators who are known to have violated the human rights of their people.

The instability in the DRC has also put China on the frontline for criticism. It is also reported by Amnesty International that 17 percent of small arms collected by peacekeepers in the Congo were of Chinese design. It is alleged that, even after the U.N. arms embargo in the country in July 2003, China still found a way of supplying armed groups and militias in Kivu province and in Ituri. In September 2006, Chinese-made assault rifles were found in Bunia in the DRC (Curtis, 2008). Thus, China's arms sales to Africa continue to fuel conflict in the region as well as human rights abuses.

Besides, it is observed that the state-led business model practised by China in Africa could be problematic because most of these state-linked firms have rather poor standards of corporate governance; this could prove disastrous for most weak states in Africa, where the rule of law does not exist. It could thus be an invitation for a rapacious government (Kurlantzick, 2006). The Chinese responded to these criticisms by saying that human rights, from their perspective, are relative, and hence each country should be allowed their own definition of human rights and the timetable to reach them. They add that "non-interference in domestic affairs," or in the internal affairs of African countries, is a central part of their foreign policy (Hanson, 2008).[3] The former deputy Chinese foreign minister, Zhou Wenzhong, using Sudan as an example, comments thus: "Business is business. We try to separate politics from business...the internal situation in Sudan is an internal affair, we are not in a position to impose upon them" (French, 2004b).

The Chinese have also maintained that human rights are a Western creation and are inappropriate for China, indeed Asia. They point to what they call Asian values, which holds that Asian countries value community and family over individual rights. Furthermore, the Chinese claim that civil and political rights should not be given primacy over economic, social and cultural rights. They therefore agree that their commitment was to promote economic, social and cultural rights in countries they deal with (Brown and Chandra, 2008). This has informed their approach to investment and business in Africa.

They also point to former president Jiang Zemin's declaration of 1996, which states the cornerstones of China's Africa policy as "sincere friendship, equality, unity and co-operation, common development and looking to the future" (Holslag, 2006). With this as the cornerstone of their foreign policy, the Chinese seem to point to the fact that they are friends of Africa and are sincerely interested in seeing Africa develop.

As an observer, without taking sides, what is really interesting about this criticism of China is that what the Chinese are doing is no different from the way other countries pursue their foreign policy interests. For example, during the era of the Cold War, US foreign policy towards Africa often ignored principles of basic democracy and development. It focused parochially on containing communism in Africa by offering military and financial support to brutal and undemocratic dictators like the late Mobutu Sese Seko and the late Samuel Doe of Liberia in exchange for political support and military bases (Adebajo, 2007).

In fact, former US officials like the late Jean Kirkpatrick, a former US Ambassador to the UN, had professed the US government's preference during the Reagan era for moderate autocrats or despotic and tyrannical right-wing regimes in developing countries friendly to US interests (Kirkpatrick, 1979). Furthermore, the US supports governments in countries like Pakistan, Egypt and Saudi Arabia for strategic reasons. Yet these countries have some of the worst human rights records. The recent uprising in 2011 popularly known as "the Arab Spring," which saw the toppling from power of the autocratic rule of President Hosni Mubarak and Zine El Abidine Ben Ali of Tunisia, are cases in point. The Chinese are not oblivious to these double standards. One can therefore view their comment that "human rights are relative" from this angle. Indeed, the Chinese are fast learners; they are quickly adapting to the observation of Henry Kissinger, a former US Secretary of State, who once remarked that "America does not have permanent friends, but permanent interests" (Kissinger, 1979 [2011]).

6.5 Lack of Technology and Skills Transfers in Chinese Projects in Africa

Another criticism of China's investments in Africa is that there is the lack of transfer of technology or skills to those respective African countries in which they are undertaking projects (Botequilla, 2006). Consequently, this has an impact on value creation and employment and, to some extent, the sustainability of the projects once the Chinese have left. The fate of the Tazara railway after the Chinese left due to the lack of technology and skills transfer is a case in point. The critics also argue that most of China's projects, especially those that have an aid component, eventually evolve into trade projects where the labour, often cheap, is imported from China, including all the raw materials. No forward–backward linkages are built in the various economies they operate in, and thus they do not in any way contribute to the growth of the economy in general. The country also loses taxes as most of the inputs and labour are brought into the country under an agreement favourable to the Chinese.

So what is technology transfer? Basically, the term as used in this chapter refers to a process whereby technology developed in one country or place is transferred to another place legally through set-down processes or agreements by the owner of said technology. For the purpose of this chapter, technology transfers will also encompass *know-how* and *know-what*. The transferring of this know-how and know-what from one country to another is what technology transfer entails. Wikipedia defines technology transfer as a process of transferring skills, knowledge, technologies, methods of manufacturing, samples of manufacturing and facilities among governments or universities and other institutions to ensure that scientific and technological developments are accessible to a wider range of users who can then further develop and exploit the technology into new products, processes, applications, materials or services (https://en.wikipedia.org/wiki/Teachnology_transfer).

The importance of the transfers of technology to Africa's economic development cannot be emphasised enough. Mansfield (1975) points out that one of the fundamental processes that influence the economic performance of nations and firms is technology transfer. He adds, "technology transfer is at the heart of economic growth for both developed and developing countries." Transfers of technology can enhance productivity in all aspects of Africa's economic sectors. The process of technology transfer can be attained through licensing agreements, joint ventures (JVs), partnerships, spin-offs and through technical assistance. This section is concerned with the lack of the transfer of technology in most Chinese projects undertaken in Africa. It has been observed that in most of the projects undertaken by China since its foray into Africa, the transfer of technology has been minimal or nil. It is one of the major critiques of Chinese investments in Africa but an issue that is critical and important to Africa's sustainable development.

So why is there minimal or a lack of technology transfer in most Chinese projects undertaken in Africa? From the observation of this author, there is the lack of insistence on the part of most African governments and policy makers to have as part of their agreements between their respective countries and the Chinese governments the requisite technology transfer and skills development component in projects undertaken or to be undertaken. This is probably because they approach the negotiations of these projects with a "beggar mentality." But what do I mean by a "beggar mentality"? It is the case where most African countries or policy makers think or feel that by China willing to finance and undertake a certain project in their country, the Chinese are somehow doing them a favour. This could be because most of these African leaders have approached Western, bilateral and multilateral sources for funding to undertake some of these projects with no luck, except for the lectures they receive from these Western sources on human rights and the conditionalities that will come with their funding if they were to consider granting it. In desperation, most of them turn to the Chinese.

These African leaders are therefore more than relieved when they approach the Chinese and the latter agree to fund the project at a low interest rate and even to undertake the project with no conditionalities. The Chinese, in the process, will even promise these African leaders that they can finish the project on time and under budget, and they usually do. These leaders thank their stars for such good fortune and go away quietly so as not to scatter the deal with any extra demands like technology and skills transfer. Efforts by Tanzania and Zambia to secure funding to build the Tazara railway and the challenges they faced is a testimony to this observation. This lack of assertiveness on the part of African leaders and policy makers in their demand for technology and skills transfers in Chinese projects is one of the reasons for the lack of technology transfer as part of the agreements.

Another reason why there could be minimal or a lack of technology transfer in Chinese projects undertaken in Africa may be due to the lack of foresight and political will on the part of many African leaders and policy makers. It is always the duty of any leadership when they are in power to have a vision of developing their respective countries and leaving them better than they met them for the next generation and for posterity. Would that be easy? Definitely not. But independence-era African leaders like Kwame Nkrumah of Ghana, for example, have done just that. His achievements are too many to mention here. If subsequent Ghanaian leaders had continued where he left off, Ghana would have been an upper-middle to an advanced middle-upper-level developing country today. The role technology transfer and skills development can play as well as contribute to the growth and development of these African countries is not therefore lost on these African leaders. The lack of a clear vision and the lack of the desire to leave a positive legacy as it pertains to this issue, as well as the lack of insistence that it should be part of the agreements with their Chinese counterparts on the projects they undertake in Africa, can be viewed from this angle.

Furthermore, one cannot escape the fact that one of the major challenges Africa is facing that is impeding its development is corruption. Much has been written about this issue (Mbaku, 2010; Guest, 2010; Wrong, 2010; Hope and Chikulo, 1999), hence we will not belabour this issue in this book. Yet it cannot be emphasised enough that corruption and kickbacks have been the bane of most capital projects in Africa. The 10–20 percent kickbacks that get piled onto the cost of projects, leading to the huge inflation of the costs of these projects, can influence the lack of insistence on technology and skills transfers on most of these capital projects. Even the insistence on quality delivery of the projects is also an issue due to corruption, as contractors cut corners due to the magnitude of the bribes they have to pay. Chinese projects undertaken in Africa are not immune to this malady. One can therefore surmise that some African leaders and policy makers would and do benefit from such kickbacks. Thus their preoccupation in their negotiations and approval of these projects is focused on the quantum in the amount of money or other benefits they can get from the project rather than their insistence that technology transfers and skills development be part of the contract, which would benefit their country as a whole. By some of these unscrupulous leaders placing their individual needs above national interests, the country suffers.

Finally, the lack of technology and skills transfers in Chinese projects undertaken in Africa could be the result of a fear on the part of Chinese firms of losing their intellectual property rights (IPR) or their competitive advantage or repeat business to undertake similar projects in the African country involved. The Chinese have also been accused of IPR infringements and violations by many developed countries. If such accusations are true, then the Chinese might just be looking at whether this could happen to them in Africa. Hence that could be why they are cautious. But if it is so, it goes against the Chinese pledge of their preparedness to share their experience and knowledge with Africans and help them in their development. African leaders and policy makers who are sincerely interested in the development of their respective countries and the sustainability of Chinese projects when they eventually leave will question this rhetoric.

So what are the responses of the Chinese to these criticisms? The Chinese argue that they are just taking advantage of their low overheads and cheap materials and technologies as well as their sources of cheap labour to maximise their productivity on projects they are undertaking in Africa. The Chinese have indeed seen this as an important issue; thus, the government issued a white paper on "China's Africa Policy." Some of the areas the paper stresses are the possibilities for deeper bilateral cooperation in technical knowledge development, where the focus of China will be to encourage the use of an appropriate level of technologies in African countries; provide technology training in agriculture and processing sectors; send experts, teachers and technologist to African countries; and bring their experience in telecoms, road construction and power networks to African countries (Broadman, 2007). They also promise to deepen bilateral cooperation with African countries in issues relating to technology transfer. But such pronouncements on the part of the Chinese government are fine. They can only be realised when African governments are truly committed to working with their Chinese counterparts to see it happen.

This process should therefore start with the capacity of governments in Africa to enforce local skills development and technology transfer as part of current or future Chinese projects. African governments should insist on local skills development and technology transfer during the negotiations of the contracts and during the signing of these contracts. To ignore these important steps and to later lament the "lack of skills development and lack of technology transfers" is rather irresponsible. Moving forward, it should be one of the most important issues when they negotiate with Chinese governments – indeed all governments – on projects to be undertaken in their respective countries to ensure that technology transfer and skills development are part of the negotiated and signed contracts.

However, it is equally imperative that the Chinese understand that if they want a sustainable relationship with the locals in Africa for their businesses to prosper, they must also take the first step to help in local skills development and the transfer of the appropriate technologies on projects they have worked on. It spells win–win for both the Africans and the Chinese. But it is good business if Chinese projects and machinery are sustainable when they leave. It could lead to the importing of parts for said machinery by the local technicians who are using the machinery. It could equally lead to their acquiring advance versions of the same machine when old ones are obsolete. Equally, Chinese projects that are sustainable long after the Chinese have left will solidify the cordial relations between China and the respective countries in which such projects are undertaken.

It is the firm belief of this author that, despite all these issues about technology transfer raised in this section, engaging in empty talk and promises on both sides will not contribute to technology transfer unless African countries insist on it and the Chinese deliver on it. There must be a deliberate and concerted effort on the part of African countries in their negotiations with the Chinese to ensure that they benefit from China's current investment in Africa. China has attained its current growth and development status because, in its earlier state of development, it required that all Western companies undertaking huge projects in the country agree to transfer the technology to the Chinese. It has contributed in a way to their growth and advancement in technology today. African countries should take a leaf from China's book in terms of its experience. At the end of the day, it will result in a win–win proposition for both the Chinese and Africans if they work together on the issue of technology transfers to African countries. An African proverb encapsulates this view better: "If you want to go fast, go alone. If you want to go far, go together" (Abdulai, 2000).

6.6 Chinese Abuse Labour Rights of their African Workers

Another important criticism of China's foray into Africa is that Chinese businesses and companies operating in Africa abuse the labour rights of their African workers. For example, a November 2011 Human Rights Watch report condemned Chinese mining companies operating in Zambia for routinely flouting laws designed to protect workers' safety and right to organise. The report detailed persistent abuses at Chinese-run mines, poor health and safety conditions, and regular 12-hour and 18-hour shifts of arduous labour, a violation of Zambian law. Human Rights Watch at that time urged the late president, Michael Sata, to stamp out the abuse of workers in this sector when he had just been newly elected (Reuters, 2011).

Also, when Michael Sata was the political opponent of the late President Mwanawasa of Zambia, he achieved great popularity in the September 2006 presidential elections with the campaign promise to expel Chinese living in Zambia if he was to win the elections (Corkin, 2007). Sata, whose nickname was "King Cobra," made some of his emotional remarks when in October 2006 in Zambia's capital, Lusaka, rioters attacked Chinese and their businesses after mine workers in a Chinese-owned mine were fired on by police for protesting about poor working conditions. Sata accused the Chinese enterprises in his country of exploiting its workers through the payment of low wages and unsatisfactory working conditions in a clear violation of their human rights (Ndulo, 2008). Sata was not successful in his first presidential bid, but in a way this incident pointed to the growing negative sentiments towards the Chinese in some African countries, specifically the abuse of the labour rights of African workers by Chinese businesses.

Michael Sata eventually won the elections held on September 22, 2011. Sata's approach to dealing with the Chinese in Zambia, a group he once rallied against, changed when he got into power. He suddenly went soft on the Chinese. One is therefore reminded of the saying by Abraham Lincoln, the sixteenth president of the United States, that "nearly all men can stand adversity, but if you want to test a person's character, give them power"(Fehrenbacher, 1989). Sata backtracked on his promises and some of his utterances. When he faced criticism for going against his promise, he is reported to have said that he had engaged the Chinese and they had adjusted before he had to introduce any new law to force them to do so. Sata also added that he had told the Chinese that "when you are in Rome, do as the Romans do. When we are in China, we do as the Chinese do" (Ware, 2012). Sata further added that he understood and appreciated the dilemma of the Chinese in Zambia and that if the Chinese were breaking the law and the government of day was turning a blind eye, then the Chinese should not be blamed. Sata added that, whether the person has been corrupt or ignorant, that would change under his rule.

But it is not only Zambian workers who have complained of labour rights abuses. Zimbabwean workers have equally complained of alleged abuses at the hands of their Chinese bosses. For example, the Chinese, who are building a US$98 million military college for Zimbabwe (the building of the college is now completed) have been accused of abusing the workers on the project. It is also alleged by the National Mine Workers Union of Zimbabwe that workers at Chinese-owned mines in the country were often forced to work long hours for low pay in inadequate protective clothing (Moyo, 2011). In one incident, riot police had to be called in after mine workers in a Zimbabwean chrome mine took their Chinese boss, Zheng Nihai, hostage for failure to pay them including arrears in wages to the tune of US$174,000 (*The Times* of London, 2011).

Another example of Chinese labour abuse is in Nigeria. The poor working conditions of Nigerians working in Chinese-owned factories have come under criticism. There are cases where workers processing metal ores were without essential masks. There are also cases where Chinese-owned factories pump poisonous effluents into rivers and emit gases into the air. The major cause for such behaviour on the part of Chinese companies operating in Africa is that there is a lack of institutional regulatory frameworks to monitor and enforce them. Equally, there are no punitive measures that will serve as a deterrent to Chinese companies damaging the environment. Where Chinese companies are caught violating labour laws, they quickly pay bribes and are let off the hook. Thus, law enforcement agencies in Africa are also part of the problem in this equation. The laws may be on the books but they are never enforced, and where they are enforced, it is poorly done.

Other examples of unfair labour practices by Chinese companies operating in Africa include cases of sexual harassment in Namibia and Kenya. Also in Malawi, all female workers on Chinese projects are treated as "casuals," thus denying them some of the benefits enjoyed by their male counterparts. Chinese companies have also been found to violate women's right to paid maternity leave in most of their projects in Africa – even if such rights were enshrined in national labour legislation, as is the case in Angola. It was also found that Chinese employers tended to terminate the employment of female workers in their businesses or on their projects once the women were found to be pregnant. These cases constituted violations of basic international workers' rights as well as locally enshrined rights (Leong, 2009).

In South Africa and Namibia, Chinese companies violated the provisions of affirmative action legislation, locally known as "employment equity." Chinese employers seemed ignorant about these legal provisions, which aim to promote the employment and promotion of women, people with disabilities and those citizens who were disadvantaged during the Apartheid era. It is not certain whether Chinese companies know that a plea of ignorance of the prevailing labour and human rights laws in the African countries in which they operate is not an excuse. Chinese companies also tend to employ African workers for basic tasks at very low pay while importing Chinese managers and supervisors for higher paid positions. Most of the excuses they give for such actions, such as language and cultural differences between them and Africans, are rather flimsy. In Zambia, there was a clear case of discrimination as local managers earned substantially less than their Chinese counterparts – even when carrying out similar tasks at the same company. The same trend was observed in Kenya (Leong, 2009).

Overall, it is imperative for the Chinese government to begin to do something about its image and the perception Africans have about them and their treatment of workers in Africa. All efforts must also be made to build better working relations and conditions for African workers in Chinese businesses, construction projects and mines in Africa. At the end of the day, the blaming of Chinese companies alone is not enough. African leaders and policy makers should stand up and be counted on this issue. They must say enough is enough and enforce the requisite legislation that the Chinese are violating. Where there is no legislation, it must be developed, enacted into law and enforced. This is the only way that labour abuses, not only those by Chinese companies but by all foreign companies operating in these countries, will stop. The only sustainable solution to this issue is when African governments work together with their Chinese counterparts to solve this issue, as it is in their mutual interest.

6.7 Africans are Losing Jobs to Chinese

One of the significant features of China's current engagement with Africa is the use of imported Chinese labour and resources in their factories and mines and on their projects across the continent. This is creating a growing negative sentiment amongst Africans, who are complaining that they are losing jobs to Chinese. For example, Chinese workers are hired in factories in Mauritius to the exclusion of locals and indeed on most of the Chinese projects around the continent. China has a population of 1.3 billion people, and many of these people are unemployed. One way the Chinese government have decided to lessen this unemployment burden is to send some of these people to work on Chinese projects in Africa. Throughout the continent, Chinese citizens can be found working on numerous projects in various African countries. The current outcry from Africans is creating a gradual change in this Chinese attitude, albeit slowly.

Chinese corporations see it differently. To them, it is an exemption from existing wage and labour legislation as it is the case with powerful trade union movements, especially in South Africa. The Chinese argue that, with imported

Chinese labour, the workers can easily be fired and sent home. In some cases, some of these Chinese are brought to Africa as part of the aid package and usually end up in staying behind as support staff to Chinese companies to bid for local projects. But for the Chinese to try to circumvent existing labour laws in African countries by bringing in their own workers from China weakens the existing laws in the country and should not be tolerated. In the view of this author, the Chinese cannot just violate the labour laws of African countries with impunity without help from some of the respective people in authority in the country or without connivance with some of the officials in the country.

The Chinese further argue that in some African countries there is a shortage of skills and that sometimes there is a pressure on them to complete a job quickly, which leaves them no choice under those circumstances than to bring in Chinese labour. Furthermore, they argue that the difficulty in their communicating with locals, as most Chinese do not speak English, French or Portuguese, makes it difficult to hire locals. Such is not the case with imported Chinese labour (Brautigam, 2009). Others see this as a lame excuse on the part of the Chinese. They say it could be the case for some limited number of Chinese but that cannot be the case for the huge number of Chinese imported to do manual work, which Africans can do, especially with the huge unemployment witnessed in most African countries.

Much as this criticism is legitimate, one can contend that the problem does not lie solely with the Chinese. The problem equally lies with the respective African countries and their governments. They are the ones who control the issuance of work permits and who are in charge of policies that have to do with creating jobs for their people and alleviating poverty. They must be the ones that should legislate and enforce the requisite labour laws that will protect the interests of their people (Boyle, 2007). They must also ensure that Chinese investments create employment as well as spill-over effects for their people. For Africans and their policy makers to then cry foul without doing anything about it is wrong. It should be mentioned in passing that some African countries like Angola and the DRC require that 70 percent and 80 percent, respectively, of staff and workers on Chinese projects in the countries are locals. But in Africa, as it is usually the case, it is one thing for governments to come up with policies and another to effectively implement and enforce them. If such policies are effectively implemented and enforced, they will go a long way to easing the unemployment situation in some of these African countries.

Furthermore, little is done by African leaders and policy makers to require that Chinese companies operating in the various African countries harness the development of local companies or small and medium-sized enterprises (SMEs). SMEs can be one of the solutions to the unemployment challenges that African countries are facing. For example, SMEs account for about 52 percent of all US workers, according to statistics by the US Small Business Administration. The observation can be made that Chinese companies are actually mirroring what is on the ground. They are looking at how the labour laws are enforced in the various African countries. Where enforcement is weak, they capitalize on it. Thus, if there is to be a change, then African countries must demand enforcement and have the requisite laws and regulations in place, which should be effectively enforced to protect their people. SMEs in their respective countries must be engaged on Chinese projects as sub-contractors, and indeed on all JV projects between Chinese and African governments. In fact, it should be mandatory that local SMEs be engaged as sub-contractors on such JV projects. This shouldn't be difficult for African leaders and policy makers to achieve where there is the political will.

Another issue that has led to the loss of African jobs to Chinese in certain manufacturing industries like textiles is the 1974 Multi-Fibre Agreement (MFA). The genesis of this problem can be traced back to the setting-up of the MFA by Canada, the US and European countries as a way of protecting their local clothing and textile industries from foreign exports into their markets by capping the amount of these exports into their respective countries. This imposition of quotas was the norm until the World Trade Organisation (WTO) set up the Agreement on Textiles and Clothing in 1994. This agreement introduced the phased removal of all quotas on textiles entering any country for ten years from 1994. Thus, the quotas were to fall away in 2005.

Meanwhile, in 2001, China, which was the biggest textile producer in the world, joined the WTO. When the MFA restrictions ended, the competition in textile and garment exports increased as countries like China entered the picture. It also ended a decade-long agreement with European countries that allowed the poor countries in Africa and elsewhere to export their textiles to these countries. Not only do African countries now have to compete with China in the export of textiles to European and US markets, they also have to contend with protecting their markets from the influx of cheap textiles from China. They are losing that battle too. With China's foray into Africa, most African countries are seeing their markets flooded with cheap, poor quality Chinese textiles, which is putting most of these African textile companies out of business and making many Africans unemployed.

For example, in South Africa, the flooding of the market with cheap imported textiles from China, both legally and illegally, has seen the overall number of workers in the sector nationally drop from 210,000 to 100,000 between 2002 and 2010 (Booysen, 2015). In Ghana, cheap Chinese textiles imported into the country have flooded local markets, making it difficult for local textile manufacturers like Akosombo Textiles to survive. Textile manufacturers in Ghana are also complaining about the malicious copying of some of their designs by Chinese companies and the flooding of the Ghanaian market with counterfeit textiles. Ghana's textile industry at its peak used to employ over 30,000 workers until the 1990s. Today, the industry employs about 3000 workers, a paltry number compared to earlier times. The problem, textile manufacturers say, is counterfeit cloth made in massive quantities in China and smuggled into Ghana. It is reported that about 60 percent of textiles in the Ghanaian market are counterfeits, which sell at half the price of the authentic Ghanaian ones.[4] This is also making it difficult for Ghanian manufacturers to make a profit from their designs (Mwanza, 2015). At the time of writing, the government of Ghana is working hard to revamp and resuscitate Juapong Textiles and Volta Star Textiles in an effort to create jobs for a growing youthful population without jobs.

Finally, in Kenya, China is flooding the market with cheap, poor quality textiles, driving a lot of Kenyan textile manufacturing companies out of business and creating unemployment. These companies cannot invest in the further development of local designs.[5] Even in cases where Chinese have acquired some of these local textile industries, they still end up in bringing in more Chinese labour to work in these factories. The Kenyan government has responded to help Kenyan textile companies with the removal of taxes and has improved on its incentives to the industry. For example, the government has removed taxes on all cotton ginning and textile manufacturing machinery. This is to encourage the import of modern equipment to enable the industry to compete effectively. The government has also dropped the taxes on all goods and services to cotton ginning factories. It has also improved incentives to lure Kenya's textile industries to move into its export processing zones (EPZs). Time will tell if such measures will be able to save the Kenyan textile industry.

Despite this author's admonition of most African governments for the poor efforts on their part to enforce the requisite laws that require Chinese companies working on projects in their respective countries to employ more Africans on such projects or offer them the requisite training where it is lacking, Chinese companies cannot be totally absolved from their responsibility to employ African workers on their projects or train them. It is imperative that if Chinese businesses operating in Africa are to be sustainable, they need to develop good relationships with local Africans in the environments in which they operate. They must take the first steps to help with local skills development, rather than giving excuses that there is the lack of skills to work on their projects. The development of local African skills by Chinese companies and businesses in Africa will spell out a win–win situation for both the Chinese and the Africans. Having said that, it is important to stress that for Chinese companies, there will be no incentive from a business standpoint to incur extra costs to train Africans. They will only comply if they are compelled to do so. Hence, the requisite laws must be put in place and enforced by African countries if this problem is to be rectified.

6.8 Chinese Disrespect of Africans: Ignorance or Racism?

One important aspect of China's foray into Africa that has come under increased criticism is how Chinese migrants or those Chinese who are working for Chinese companies in Africa treat their African employees. There have been numerous complaints by Africans concerning how they are disrespected and poorly treated by their Chinese employers, as adequately elaborated in Section 6.6. Equally a problem is how these migrants disrespect Africans in general. Just recently in Nairobi, Kenya, a Chinese restaurant located in an area called

Kilimani was shut down after it emerged that it did not admit black African patrons of the restaurant after 5pm. The management of the restaurant claimed that the "no Africans after 5pm" policy was based on their belief that Africans pose a security threat to the restaurants' Chinese patrons. But this Chinese restaurant incident is not the only one of its kind; most of these incidents are swept under the carpet in the name of "China–Africa" relations. Numerous insensitive remarks have also been made by some Chinese migrant workers in Africa towards Africans, and this needs serious attention from Africans as well as Chinese leaders before the issue gets out of hand. African leaders must make it clear that racism in any of its forms will not be tolerated. In the case of the Chinese restaurant incident in Kenya, the restaurant was later closed down by the Kenyan authorities. But this is not an isolated incident of Chinese disrespect of their African hosts.

Howard French, in his book *China's Second Continent*, gives examples of how, in a Chinese hotel in Liberia, they do not have towels or do not give them out to Blacks because the Chinese patrons of that hotel would not use towels that were used or might have been used by Black people. In Mozambique, French recalls how a Chinese settler talked disparagingly about Blacks:

> I'd never dealt with African people before, at first just coming in contact with them made me feel uncomfortable, their skin is so black…I didn't think they were so clever, not so intelligent…and I was looking for an opportunity based on my own capabilities…so we have to find backward countries, poor countries that we can lead.
>
> (French, 2014)

In Liberia, French met another Chinese migrant who disparaged the Liberian government thus, "there are villagers in China who have more talent for government than the people who are running this country." He added, "you couldn't find ten competent people here" (French, 2014). Such insensitive comments based on ignorance, which could be regarded by some as racist, are inimical to China–Africa relations. They can cause irreparable damage to current Sino–African engagement if not handled with care. In Namibia, French recounts how some Chinese migrants, even newcomers to the country, arrogantly boss their African employees around. In fact, insensitively, one of these migrants even remarked that "ninety percent of Africans are thieves" (French, 2014).

Finally, others have observed that Chinese migrants' insensitivity comes out of the way they perceive or are informed by their kin of what Black people are like. Mohan (2013), writing in a chapter in the book *The Rise of the Global South*, said that whether Chinese migrants are recent ones or those who are already established, they harbour views and cultural assumptions about "Black" people that cast locals as unsuitable for higher level roles. Thus they tend to limit African workers to menial tasks. Mohan also observed that Chinese businessmen in Ghana complained about how too much culture is impeding Ghanaian productivity, a complaint that can be traced to their observation of their Ghanaian employees, who like to attend funerals or their clan events frequently. Hence, they regard these employees as unreliable and lacking the ability to plan ahead, and some Chinese even conclude that they are "lazy," "money grabbing" and "untrustworthy." This insensitivity and disrespect of Chinese migrants towards their African host can have a devastating impact on Chinese–African relations as well as investments. But it is also clear that some of these Chinese migrants are commenting on the deep-seated culture of an African people that speaks to the humanism and *Ubuntu* culture of Africans, especially the way of paying respect to the departed. But above all, what these migrant Chinese do not understand is that this is also a form of socialization for the Ghanaians as well as representing networking opportunities for business.

There have been instances in some African countries where there have been violent stand-offs, resulting in the looting of Chinese shops and, in some cases, the deaths of some Chinese migrants. From research, this author has found that most of these Chinese migrants, close to about 90 percent of them, are poorly educated or are uneducated. Most of these migrants are also from rural China and come to Africa to work and send money back to family members at home. They do not go through any cultural training or sensitivity programmes before they leave their respective villages. Thus they do not have any idea or true knowledge of who an African is. They therefore fill such a gap with their biases and perceptions of what they believe or are told an African(s) is supposed to be like. Some of these perceptions and beliefs can probably be traced back to the negative depiction of Africans in movies they have seen.

From this narrative, it is becoming increasingly important that as more and more Chinese migrate to work and live in Africa (currently it is estimated that about a million Chinese work and live in Africa), that the Chinese Embassies in the respective African countries give their nationals cross-cultural and sensitivity training. The Confucius Institutes, set up in African countries to teach Africans the Chinese language and culture, could play a dual role of giving sensitivity and cross-cultural training to these Chinese migrants in collaboration with the ministries of culture in various African countries. It should be seen by both African countries and China that the ability to solve this issue will require a collaborative effort on their part. To see it as a "China only" problem will be missing a good opportunity to find a lasting solution to the problem.

But the reverse is the case with African migrants in China. They tend to face serious hostilities and limited opportunities, they can't even open bank accounts in China, and there is no legal path to citizenship. A new immigration law called the "Exit–Entry Administrative Law" now requires most Africans on short visas to China to go back to their home countries to renew their visas rather than across the border in Macau or Hong Kong as they did before. One would surmise that were the Chinese migrants in Africa to face this same plight, their governments would do all they could to prevail on their African counterparts to ease the pressure on their citizens. Even though the observation here is not condoning any form of illegal immigration on the part of African migrants in China, African governments should also intercede on behalf of their nationals if they are treated unfairly by Chinese authorities.

In these discussions on the way Chinese disrespect their African hosts in this section of the book, it will be difficult to forget the hostilities towards African students in the 1980s in China, especially in Nanjing, which resulted in African students protesting the racist way they were treated by the Chinese police. This author was a student in the US at that time and was rather disgusted with the images on television and in the papers of how these African students were treated. There were counter protests by Chinese students calling African students all kinds of racist and ugly names. The anti-African protest even spread to other Chinese cities. All these racist incidences cannot be viewed in isolation, as some policy makers in China want Africans to believe. Those affected by these racist incidences have observed that it is in a way a deep-seated aspect of the Chinese culture as it pertains to the way they see Africans.

Chinese migrants to Africa have thus brought a warped sense of who and what an African is to Africa. This speaks to the way they treat Africans. They should do well to put such outlook of Africans in check as they come to live and work with Africans or else it could cause them a lot of grief and lead to poor relations between them and their African neighbours and hosts. Chinese policy makers and authorities should address this issue with all the seriousness that it deserves as it could have a serious impact on Sino-African relations moving forward and on Chinese investments in Africa. This might seem like a sensitive issue that neither African nor Chinese governments are willing to deal with at this period in their relations. They cannot keep being like the proverbial ostrich burying its head in the sand. The earlier they address this issue, the better it will be for them moving forward as it pertains to their investment and trade relations. Just maybe, the Chinese authorities are beginning to look at this issue with concern, if the comments of Chinese premier Li Keqiang as it pertains to these issues during his recent visit to Africa are anything to go by. When commenting about China–Africa relations, especially China's recent engagement with the continent, he said the relationship was experiencing "growing pains."[6] This is in reference to the numerous challenges that their citizens are facing in China's current engagement with Africa.

6.9 Conclusion

The criticisms of China's current engagement with Africa include the fact that many see China as the "new colonialist," coming into Africa to pillage the continent like its past colonial masters. Other criticisms include the increasing trade imbalance between China and Africa, which many suggest should be addressed in order to offer a win–win for Sino-Africa trade. The other criticisms are mostly by the West and Western organisations and concern how China's activities and investments in Africa undermine good governance and human rights. This is because of China's policy of non-interference in its dealings with Africa, which goes to support dictators on the continent. Other criticisms include the lack of technology transfer in Chinese projects undertaken in Africa. This is because technology transfer in Chinese projects can contribute to the sustainable development on the continent. Others criticize Chinese companies for abusing the labour rights of their African employees and claim that Africans are losing jobs to Chinese because of the importation of Chinese workers to work on projects, ignoring the employment and upskilling of African workers. Finally, the issue of Chinese disrespect or racism towards their African hosts was looked at in this chapter. It should be acknowledged that there are no relationships at the human or government levels that do not have faults or problems. Mentioning these problems is meant to afford African governments and the Chinese government the opportunity to work on finding lasting solutions to these problems so as to strengthen their cooperation. Chinese premier Li Keqiang's acknowledgement recently that the China–Africa relationship is witnessing "growing pains" is a testimony to what this chapter has elaborated on so far. Now the heavy lifting begins. Africans and their Chinese counterparts now need to work together to ameliorate these "growing pains."

Notes

1 David Smith, "China denies building empire in Africa," *The Guardian*, 12 January 2015, www.theguardian.com/global-development/2015/jan/12/china-denies-building-empire-africa-colonialism (accessed 2/21/16).
2 Hill, Matthew (2007), "Hu Jintao pledges action to reduce China-SA trade imbalance." http://www.polity.org.za/article/hu-jintao-pledges-action-to-reduce-chinasa-trade-imbalance-2007-02-07.
3 Hanson, Stephanie (2008), "China, Africa and Oil," Council on Foreign Relations, http://www.cfr.org/china/china-africa-oil/p10586.
4 Yepoka Yeebo, "Chinese Counterfeits leave Ghanaian Textiles Hanging by a Thread," *The Christian Science Monitor*, May 31, 2015. http://www.csmonitor.com/World/Africa/2015/0531/Chinese-counterfeits-leave-Ghanaian-textiles-hanging-by-a-thread (accessed 2/21/16).
5 Mohammed Yusuf, "Chinese Imports Threatens Kenya's Textile Industry," *VOA*, July 12, 2013, http://www.voanews.com/a/chinese-imports-threaten-kenyas-textile-workers-merchants/1700819.html.
6 Reuters, "China premier says Sino-Africa disputes just 'growing pains'," May 4, 2014. http://www.reuters.com/article/us-china-africa-idUSBREA4300L20140504 (accessed 2/21/16).

7 Africa and Millions of Chinese Migrants

7.1 Introduction

The entry of China into the World Trade Organisation (WTO) as elaborated on in Chapter 3 of this book also marked the beginning of China's version of its globalization, called *Zou Chuqu*, meaning "go global" (Brautigam, 2009). This "go global" policy by the Chinese government evolved from Deng Xiaoping's "Open Door" policies. It is a deliberate initiative aimed at getting Chinese companies to establish themselves internationally, creating trade and investment as well as jobs for Chinese. The immediate focus of the policy was on Africa, a continent neglected by the West, as observed by Chinese leadership. The Chinese leaders were also aware of Africa's rich natural resources, which they need for their own growth.

Many ordinary Chinese citizens were not oblivious to this policy. Some of their friends, who were sent to Africa to work for Chinese companies in construction, mining, the oil and gas sectors and trading, to name but a few, returned home with the news that Africa was the new nirvana, with numerous opportunities. Some of these workers decided to stay on in Africa after the end of their contracts. This new and important phenomenon, which is a direct result of China's investment and growing relations with Africa, has been least talked and written about. Howard French is one of the few people that have written about this issue. His take on this situation is in the form of a travelogue across Africa in his book *China's Second Continent: How a Million Migrants are building a New Empire in Africa*.

In this book, French writes that

> one of the most important and unpredictable factors in China's relationship with Africa, however, has been oddly omitted from most of these discussions: China's export, in effect, large numbers of its own people who are settling in as migrants and long term residents in far flung and hither to unfamiliar parts of the continent. By common estimate, Africa has received a million or so of these Chinese new comers in the space of a mere decade, during which time they have rapidly penetrated every conceivable walk of life: farmers, entrepreneurs building small and medium sized factories

and practitioners of the full range of trades, doctors, teachers, smugglers, prostitutes.

(French, 2014)

Others who have written about this issue are Giles Mohan et al. In their book *Chinese Migrants and Africa's Development*, the authors looked at the motivations for and relationships involved in Chinese migration to Africa. The book further looks at the perceptions and linkages of Chinese migrants to their African "host." But why is the issue of Chinese migrants to Africa important? According to French (2014),

> history teaches us that very often reality is more meaningfully shaped by deeds of countless smaller actors, most of them for all intents and purposes anonymous. In this vein, each of China's new immigrants to Africa is an architect helping to shape this momentous new relationship. They accomplish this, in part, by helping build networks that loop back to the home country, channeling goods and products and capital via informal circuits that very often escape official control or even accounting.

There is still more that needs to be written about this phenomenon because it is a new and rather important piece of the China–Africa engagement narrative. Nevertheless, at this juncture of the current engagement, this issue and the potential benefits and challenges that could arise in the future as the number of Chinese migrants increase, have not been much talked about; it is therefore an important issue to examine in this book.

7.2 Why are Chinese Migrating to Africa?

The kind of Chinese migration to Africa that this book is concerned with is the most recent kind. However, it is important to distinguish in passing the Chinese ancestors who came to Africa, specifically South Africa, in the early twentieth century. It is reported that most of these Chinese migrants started arriving in large numbers in South Africa in the 1880s to seek their fortunes in the diamond and gold mines. Some of the Chinese–South Africans' ancestors came as indentured miners recruited by the British. It is reported that 63,000 of these Chinese miners were contracted by the British between 1904 and 1910. The arrival of Taiwanese in South Africa in the 1980s increased the Chinese population of South Africa to around 20,000. After the end of apartheid, from around 1994, large numbers of Chinese from mainland China began moving into South Africa. Today, South Africa has the largest Chinese population in Africa, roughly put at about 350,000.

Recent Chinese migration to Africa today is spread throughout the various African countries. The question is then asked, what are the reasons for the recent migration of Chinese to Africa?

Before one answers such a question, it is important to note that there are three categories of Chinese migrants in Africa. The first category comprises temporary contracted workers who come to Africa to work on large Chinese projects and stay from anywhere from 1 year to 3 years before leaving. The second category are transit migrants who use African countries as temporary bases or breaks in their journeys, or as stepping-stones to get to North America or western Europe. In their temporary bases, they gather funds and documentation for the next stage of their journey. While waiting, they engage in petty trading to keep themselves solvent (Ndulo, 2008). The third category is that of migrant entrepreneurs. These migrant entrepreneurs were, in most cases, not entrepreneurs back home. It is always after coming to Africa that they usually set themselves up in the retail or wholesale trade of Chinese-made goods. This is usually because of their lack of fluency in the local languages, the low capital required for such start-ups, and the ease of entry into some of the sectors in the respective countries in which they settle in; but most important of all, it is because of their linkages to Chinese manufacturers and contacts back home (Park, 2009).

One of the major reasons why Chinese have recently come to Africa is their search for opportunities. The term *opportunities* is used here to denote better living conditions or better livelihoods. Those in all three categories see opportunities in Africa. Those who come as contract workers do so either because their job prospects are limited back home or because they can make more money in Africa. Those who become entrepreneurs do so because the capital requirements are smaller to set up in Africa than for the same enterprise back home and also because of their networks with Chinese suppliers back home, who can offer them merchandise to sell on credit.

For some recent Chinese migrants to Africa, the reasons why they came to Africa include because of hardship and poor living conditions back home. About 55 percent, more than half of the populations of China, live in rural areas. Most of the population that live in the northwest and western regions of China have a low standard of living and are generally regarded by some of their compatriots back home as backward or primitive. Issues of overcrowding and China's population pressure and environmental pollution are some of the reasons why they come. Other migrants have mentioned the issues of the lack of freedom, human rights violations and the inability to realize their dreams of a better life back home as some of the reasons for their migration. Above all, the easing of Chinese governments' traveling and migration laws has also contributed to this outward migration phenomenon.

However, one of the most absurd and even strange reasons this author has come across so far as to why Chinese are migrating to Africa is that it is a means to aid African countries with vast lands that are suffering from a dearth of population. The Chinese surmise that parts of Africa are seriously underpopulated and are in need of people to regenerate their populations, most of which have been decimated by AIDS. Migration offers an opportunity to some of these Chinese peasants to come and work the spare lands, as most of them do not have land back home (Lary, 2012). First, this simplistic reason for Chinese migration to Africa is due to a lack of knowledge; even though Africa may have vast lands, not all the lands are fertile, and indeed some of the land is desert. There have therefore been fights amongst different ethnic groups in Africa for the cultivation of fertile lands. There are even fights between African nomads and landowners in some African countries over grazing rights. Furthermore, the idea that HIV/AIDS have decimated the populations in African countries is due to lack of knowledge about the issue. Yes, HIV/AIDS have seriously affected some African countries, but they have not decimated the populations as is the understanding of these would-be Chinese migrants.

7.3 Impact on and Reactions from Africans

The migration of Chinese to Africa has both negative and positive impacts. One of the negative consequences is a growing anti-Chinese sentiment on the part of some Africans and in some African countries. This has often led to attacks on Chinese and their businesses. Some of the common reasons behind this anti-Chinese sentiment are the view held by some Africans that China is exporting labour to Africa in large numbers, which to some extent is true, as elaborated in this book. This rising anti-Chinese sentiment is also because of the view on the part of some Africans that Chinese are taking over African jobs. This is seen against a background of the high unemployment levels some of these African countries are experiencing. Other causes are the arguments that China is dumping its cheap goods on African markets, killing local industries, an issue elaborated on in this chapter. Another impact of recent Chinese migration to Africa is the dispossessing of powerless landholders of their land, flouting local laws, fuelling corruption and most of all, empowering awful governments (French, 2014).

There is also the argument that the Chinese are destroying the environment, particularly in gold-mining regions of Africa. For example, in Ghana, numerous Chinese illegal migrants were deported for engaging in illegal gold mining in the country, popularly known in Ghana as *Galamsay*. The *Galamsay* phenomenon in Ghana actually started when the government of Ghana put into place legislation to allow artisanal gold mining for Ghanaian locals using the requisite artisanal tools. For foreigners or foreign concerns, the law makes provision for only industrial exploitation of raw materials. The Chinese migrants saw a laxity in the enforcement of the laws and corruption on the part of some of the local and national government officials as well as on the part of some of the greedy local traditional chiefs; the migrants exploited it through bribery and corruption and invaded the *Galamsay* sector. At its peak, it was reported that over 50,000 illegal miners had left China for Ghana since 2005. Most of these Chinese are reported to have entered Ghana with tourist visas via neighbouring countries and ended up as illegal gold miners. These illegal gold miners violated Ghanaian laws with impunity, polluted the waters and environment where they operated and even carried heavy weapons to protect the lands they mined.

This illegal gold mining by the Chinese in Ghana has caused widespread environmental degradation; the use of toxic chemicals; clashes between locals and Chinese miners, which could have a negative impact on social cohesion in those communities; loss of tax revenues to the government; and a possible diplomatic headache for the government of Ghana, to mention just a few issues. This could also be a national security issue if not handled well, as it could affect the stability of the country. The Ghanaian authorities have started to crack down on those engaged in *Galamsay*, and in the process, thousands of Chinese nationals have since been deported. In one crackdown alone, 1577 illegal foreign Chinese miners were arrested, and while most of those Chinese illegal miners arrested since the crackdown have asked for voluntary repatriation, some were forcibly repatriated after being found guilty by due process of law. At the time of writing, five Chinese and their three Ghanaian accomplices were arrested for invading a forest reserve (Apamprama Forest Reserve) in the Ashanti region of Ghana, where they were using excavators for illegal gold mining in the forest.

One of the major fallouts between China and Ghana due to the latter's repatriation of thousands of illegal Chinese gold miners was China's refusal to let Ghana access a US$3 billion loan facility for infrastructural and other development programmes that had been ear-marked for the money. Chinese authorities deny any such claims and say their refusal to let Ghana access the facility has no link to the deportation of illegal Chinese miners. Despite such denials, the timing of such an action on the part of the Chinese authorities is obvious; it was a way for them to send an indirect message to the Ghanaian authorities about their unhappiness over the way their citizens were being treated. The thorny issue of Chinese illegal gold miners is one of the issues that prompted Chinese premier Li Keqiang to talk about the "growing pains" in China–Africa relations. But one cannot totally blame the illegal Chinese miners for the challenges faced by Ghana in this sector. It is the laxity in the enforcement of mining laws and the requisite legal frameworks, corruption on the part of both national and local government structures in the country and indeed greed on the part of local chiefs and community leaders, some of who collude with these illegal miners, for which they are paid pittance but end up destroying the environment. The country's environmental protection agency does not have the requisite resources to prosecute the culprits, whether they are foreigners or Ghanaians; these laws are flouted with impunity.

The other negative impact of recent Chinese migration to Africa is the anger and outrage expressed on the part of African traders in some African countries that the governments of their respective countries have allowed Chinese traders to establish themselves in local markets in sectors of the retail trade carved out solely for the locals. In Zambia, Chinese traders have established themselves in the Kamwala market, and some of them have even engaged in selling live poultry, a preserve of the local Zambians. Some of these Chinese traders are even targets of violent protests by locals in some of these countries. In Ethiopia and Nigeria, Chinese oil facilities have been attacked by militias (Powell, 2007). In South Africa, during the recent xenophobic attacks in April 2015, scores of shops owned by Chinese nationals in South Africa were looted. The Chinese embassy in South Africa complained to the South African police and the country's authorities. Some of the African governments are beginning to do something about it, albeit not enough. For example, in Malawi, the government introduced a law banning foreign traders, a euphemism for Chinese traders operating in major urban areas of the country. In Tanzania, the government has banned Chinese traders from operating in Dar es Salaam's main market (Bowman, 2012).

In Nigeria, immigration officers arrested 45 Chinese for illegally engaging in textile trade and planned to deport them. These Chinese were caught trading in a local textile market in Kano, a city in the northern part of Nigeria, where textile retail activities by foreigners were prohibited (Gosh, 2012). Many of these Chinese nationals have been arrested in Nigeria but released by corrupt officials, who often let them go if they pay a bribe. This further exacerbates the issue, as the Chinese traders are aware that they can break the law and get away with it by paying a bribe.

In Lesotho, many Chinese and Indian private business people have set up shops selling everything from clothing and hardware to groceries, competing with the local Basotho traders. These locals are complaining bitterly of the Chinese influx and how they are crowding them out. They further complain that those of their compatriots left in the retail trade are struggling to make a living or a profit. Because the Lesotho government is keen to attract investment from China to help it battle poverty and high unemployment in the country, it has turned a blind eye to the disgruntlement of the Basotho traders (England, 2013). This is sad, because when the Chinese finally leave – and one day they will, if the economic conditions turn bad – the government will be left with a poor and demoralized people who are a risk to the stability of the country. It is therefore imperative for policy makers to have a medium- to long-term plan as to how to deal with this issue.

But there are also those Africans who see Chinese migration to Africa as a positive thing. According to GU (2009), Chinese migrant entrepreneurs in Africa are contributing to the local economy of their respective countries by providing an important source of additional investment capital at a time when aid alone is unable to meet Africa's perceived shortfall; they also offer employment opportunities to locals, small as that may be. This goes a long way to contribute to the alleviation of poverty and the generation of significant multiplier effects through the local economy. This they do through local sourcing and the provision of local management expertise, engaging in technology transfer and inculcating production, management, distribution and marketing skills and innovation knowledge. Although some of these benefits can be said to be true in the case of a handful of Chinese businesses in Africa, this will particularly apply to mostly medium to large scale companies operated by Chinese migrant entrepreneurs. Some of these benefits, as observed by GU (2009), do not hold true for the Chinese subsistence traders who have come to Africa to eke out a living or seek livelihoods better than those to be found in their impoverished villages back home; nor are they true for those who are using Africa as a transit point into Europe. For these kinds of subsistence traders, their impact on the economy of their host countries may be insignificant or even non-existent.

Others, like Mohan and Lampert (2013), see Chinese migration to Africa as a good thing, particularly for those African firms and entrepreneurs who employ Chinese labour, expertise and technologies, because their affordability helps their companies grow. Some African entrepreneurs who have procured machinery from Chinese companies have hired some of these Chinese technicians to come and install and train their local counterparts in maintaining and repairing the machines. African entrepreneurs employing Chinese technicians have gone on to induce further migration of Chinese to Africa. The observation is that it will only be a good thing if these Chinese technicians are made aware that they have to transfer their skills to their local counterparts.

A less researched factor that induces Chinese migration to Africa is the linkage between Chinese *triads* or criminal elements and those in Africa. Some of these triads or criminal elements are either Chinese migrants that are already African citizens, as is the case for many Chinese in South Africa; or recent Chinese migrants who have secured their resident permits in their respective African countries. They engage in all kinds of illegal activities, ranging from prostitution to gambling, smuggling, money laundering and loan-sharking, to mention just few. A study undertaken by the World Bank in 2011, titled *Ill-gotten Money and the Economy: Experiences from Malawi and Namibia*, gives examples of these activities by some of these criminal elements in Malawi and Namibia, but they cannot be discounted for other African countries as well. Investigations by the South African Police Service have also led to the arrest of some of these elements in the country. Most recently in Kenya, the government arrested 77 Chinese cyber criminals operating from upmarket homes in Nairobi. It is alleged that the group was preparing to raid the country's communication infrastructure, and the equipment they had was also capable of infiltrating bank accounts, Kenya's M-Pesa mobile banking systems and ATM machines.[1]

Another example is the case where Angolan police, in collaboration with Chinese authorities, caught and repatriated criminal Chinese nationals in Angola who targeted the wealthy members of the Chinese community in Angola, particularly those who live in Cabinda province. These criminals belong to a gang called the "Lightning Terror" gang. The gang engaged in kidnapping for ransom, robbery, blackmail, human trafficking and forcing women into prostitution. Their modus operandi is the use of extreme brutality and torture on their victims. This includes beating and burning of victims and burying some of the victims alive.[2]

Much as some of these issues are raised as it pertains to the challenges posed by Chinese migration to Africa, African leaders and policy makers should not panic and undertake any knee-jerk reactions to some of the complaints and agitations from their citizens on Chinese migration into their respective countries. They need to undertake the requisite research into the issue, understand its positive and negative impacts and come up with informed polices and laws to deal with the issue effectively. Having said that, it is important to caution

African leaders and policy makers that they cannot engage in a "wait-and-see" attitude to the issue, as the repercussions, if not handled with care, could be disastrous for the respective governments as well as their relations with the Chinese government. Another way to approach solving this issue is to work with the Chinese government as a partner in this effort. The Chinese are equally interested in removing any obstacle that will affect their relations with African countries, as further elaborated on in Section 7.4.

7.4 Reaction from Chinese and African Governments

Recent migration of Chinese to Africa, as elaborated on in this chapter, has both benefits and challenges. If it is not managed well, it could have a negative impact on the overall benefits of China's current engagement with African countries. For now, the Chinese authorities are aware of the attacks on some of their nationals in some of these African countries, but for the greater interest of the Chinese state, regard these attacks as isolated incidents. The authorities' further proffer that most of these Chinese migrants are private individuals who came to Africa of their own accord and thus are responsible for their own conduct and behaviour in the respective African countries they live in. They are also responsible for obeying the prevailing laws in the countries they reside in. The Chinese authorities are also careful to make sure that the Chinese migrant issue does not affect its African strategy. That said, it is clear at the time of writing that the authorities do not have a specific strategy in place to deal with this issue. For now, the Chinese authorities are preoccupied with plans for bigger projects in Africa as well as repositioning their economy, not with migrants, most of who came to Africa of their own volition.

According to Mohan and Tan-Mullins (2009), the response of African governments to recent Chinese migration to African countries is varied. In some African countries and localities, the Chinese are welcome and in some localities and at certain times, they are resented and are not welcome. In some cases, they are met with violence. Cases in point are Nigeria, Zambia, Uganda and Malawi. Some of these countries, like Malawi and Uganda, are forced to tighten and enforce their migration laws. Apart from the reaction by countries like Zambia, Malawi and Uganda to this creeping Chinese migration, the rest of Africa's governments are taking a "wait-and-see" attitude to the issue. I think that most of the African governments will act if it takes on the dimension of the 2015 xenophobic attacks in South Africa. But the question then can be asked, should African governments wait until it reaches such a level? Definitely not; hence they need to be proactive and put into place plans to manage the issue of Chinese migration before it gets out of hand. Inaction on their part is akin to these leaders acting like the proverbial ostrich, hiding their heads in the sand as if the problem will go away. It will not go away, and in fact it will grow if the leaders and policy makers do not do something about it.

Finally, another issue that African policy makers and leaders are not looking at is the "enclave" mentality of Chinese migrants to Africa. The unwillingness of most Chinese migrants to Africa to integrate with the local communities is worrying. Without integration or an effort to that end, some of the challenges where Chinese businesses and workers are attacked will result. The observation here is not aimed at calling for the forced integration of Chinese in African communities. But some form of integration will minimize the friction between them and their African hosts. Chinese migrants who come to work on Chinese projects live in compounds away from their African colleagues. To some extent, this can be accepted. However, what is problematic is the setting up of what are regarded as "China towns" in some countries in Africa. Examples are in South Africa and "Dragon City" in Namibia. These settlements are more of a concentration of only Chinese as well as their shops and restaurants. African countries need to look into how to deal with an increasing Chinese migration to the continent and come up with an effective workable policy that should also take into consideration the development of "China towns" and how that fits into their overall race-relations and development policies.

7.5 What Plans do African Countries Have to Manage Chinese Migration?

At the time of writing, it can be said that most African governments do not have any plan in place to deal with or manage Chinese migration. Most of the plans available now can be best described as reactive. The authorities in the respective countries react when there is an issue that involves Chinese migrants and locals. For example, in Ghana, when several Chinese migrants were engaging in illegal gold mining called *Galamsay*, polluting the rivers and destroying the environment indiscriminately, the response of the government was to quickly arrest them, process them and deport them, but this was after an outcry from civil society organisations and non-governmental organisations and a general outcry from some of the communities in which the illegal mining was undertaken. The destruction of the environment by the Chinese miners, who used bulldozers and other mechanical equipment, polluted rivers and streams with chemicals, deprived the locals of their livelihoods and even mined in forest reserves, was enough to rally the communities in the affected areas against these illegal miners before the Ghanaian government acted.

Other reactive methods can be seen in Malawi, Uganda, and Nigeria, where migrant Chinese caught trading in the preserves of locals are deported or laws are hastily passed to bar them from those areas, as has been the case in Malawi. There has not been a planned, well-thought-out process to deal with this issue. Part of this could be due to the fact that these African leaders and policy makers are focused on encouraging foreign direct investment (FDI) at any cost, and the financing of huge infrastructural projects by China has moved their focus away from minor issues like Chinese migration. It could also be because of the relations between some of the local African elites and Chinese businessmen. The African elites use their local connections to shield these Chinese businessmen from sanctions when existing laws are broken. Yet, it cannot be emphasised enough that unless current Chinese immigration is managed effectively, some of the fallouts from this immigration, through the clashes in some African countries between locals and Chinese migrants, will have an impact on greater Sino–African relations.

Moving forward, civil society organisations such as trade unions, business associations and pressure groups should put the requisite pressure on their respective governments to make sure that Chinese migration to African countries is effectively managed to ensure win–win outcomes for the locals as well as the Chinese migrants to these African countries. Furthermore, African countries should consider reconciling the differences in their national laws that deal with this issue without contravening international laws. In tandem, the enforcement regimes of laws in general in Africa are an issue that governments of the continent should serious focus on. What is the sense of having laws on the books that are seriously flouted without any repercussions for those who break those laws? This is one of the major causes of illegal Chinese migration to Africa and the reason why migrants violate the laws with impunity; they know they can get away with it by paying a bribe. Those law enforcement agents and officers who are caught accepting bribes, encouraging the flouting of laws, should be severely punished.

7.6 Conclusion

The issue of Chinese migration to Africa has been less written about. Yet its potential impact on social relations in the respective African countries in which these Chinese settle cannot be emphasised enough. The potential impact on China–Africa relations going forward cannot be emphasised enough in the face of clashes between Chinese migrants and their African hosts. The chapter started by looking at the reasons why Chinese come to Africa, for example, to work on Chinese government projects as a result of China's "go global" policy, to look for a better life or because China joined the WTO.

The reactions by Africans to this new phenomenon, especially as Chinese migrants enter into retail trade as well as taking jobs away from locals as the Chinese bring their own labour to work on their projects. Rising anti-Chinese sentiments are also seen in places like Ghana, where Chinese migrants are engaged in *Galamsay* (illegal gold mining). There are incidences where they have been attacked in countries like Zambia and in South Africa. Despite the potential impact this could have on China–Africa relations, the inaction or the minimal action taken by African and indeed the Chinese authorities to address this issue is worrying. As of this writing, few African governments have strategies or policies in place to address this issue. China's current investments as well as engagement with Africa have benefitted most African countries and vice versa. As it is often said, small leaks can sink big ships. This small issue of Chinese migrants in Africa, if not handled with care, can have an impact on China–Africa relations and investments moving forward.

Notes

1 BBC, "Kenya breaks 'Chinese-run Cyber-crime network'," December 4, 2014. http://www.bbc.com/news/world-africa-30327412 (accessed 27/1/16).
2 Tom Philips, "Chinese 'gangsters' repatriated from Angola," *The Telegraph*, 20 August 2012, http://www.telegraph.co.uk/news/worldnews/asia/china/9500517/Chinese-gangsters-repatriated-from-Angola.html (accessed 2/12/16).

8 How African Countries Can Position Themselves to Benefit from China's Foray into Africa

8.1 Introduction

The foray of China into Africa, despite its challenges, has been seen by many Africans as an opportunity to forge new strategic partnerships with the Chinese to help in the continent's growth and development efforts. Some Africans particularly have observed that "the Chinese relationship is benefiting us…they are building infrastructure, they are building hospitals, and they are providing loans…they are bringing lots of development, which African countries probably wouldn't get otherwise" (French, 2014). This is also because Africa's traditional relations and partnerships with the West have not helped Africa overcome the structural obstacles of eradicating poverty and reversing its economic marginalisation (Manji and Marks, 2007). Even though there are those who may disagree with the observation of Manji and Marks (2007), that Africa's traditional relation with the West has not helped Africa overcome its structural obstacles; few will disagree with the positive impact that China's foray into Africa has made so far. Thus, some have observed that the emergence of China as an economic and political power and its subsequent foray into Africa should be seen as an opportunity for African countries to "Look East" for a change.

Robert Mugabe, the president of Zimbabwe, a nemesis of the West, puts a different twist on this "Look East" view by saying that "we are looking to the East where the sun rises, and have turned our backs on the West where the sun sets."[1] This author is in total disagreement with Mugabe's "Look East" pronouncement and its connotation. "Looking East," for this author, doesn't necessary mean a total abandonment of the West, which is what Mugabe is proposing. As I see it, *looking East* means African countries repositioning themselves to take advantage of China's current investment in Africa and channelling the benefits of these investments into the growth and development efforts of the continent. African countries can do this without ignoring the other benefits they can get from engagement with the West, such as a market for Africa's exports and a source of investment and aid as well as access to new technologies and methods. Indeed, it is strategically beneficial for African countries to have the flexibility to deal with the West as well as the East. For strategic reasons, African countries should not put all their eggs in one basket, so to speak. Even Western countries are dealing with China; hence it would make no sense for African countries to turn their backs on the West as advocated by Mugabe. That would indeed be short-sighted and an engagement in retrogressive thinking.

At this juncture, it would therefore be appropriate to give some *sub-rosa* reasons why Mugabe made such a statement. Mugabe's comments were made because of the intense pressure he had been under from the West and the imposition of economic sanctions on his regime. This was because of the West's denouncement of Mugabe's autocratic rule and his human rights abuses as well as his land redistribution campaign in Zimbabwe. The impact the sanctions had on Zimbabwe, once a bread basket of Africa, are biting and difficult. Equally, the destructive and self-defeating actions undertaken by Mugabe have destroyed the Zimbabwean economy. At the time of writing, the country is facing a severe drought and thousands are fearful of starvation in the country. The Zimbabwean currency – the Zimbabwean Dollar – collapsed and became worthless. In Zimbabwe today, ironically, it is the US dollar and the South African Rand that are the currencies used despite Mugabe's vilification of the West. The help and support Mugabe got from the Chinese has so far kept him in power and his economy afloat. His "Look East" pronouncement then can be seen from this angle.

One can also surmise that when Mugabe uttered this "Look East" pronouncement, he was influenced by a similar pronouncement by Dr. Mahathir Mohammad, the former prime minister of Malaysia during the 1980s, when Western countries had lost their drive due to economic stagnation. At this time, vibrant economies like Japan, South Korea and Taiwan had emerged. Mahathir therefore thought that Malaysia should emulate the success of these countries in the East. Malaysia's "Look East Policy," which was launched in late 1981, was not to copy or follow Eastern habits blindly or to trade solely with these countries. It was to learn the good values of the East, particularly their work habits, their work ethic, and their technological skills. On this issue, Mahathir said, "we never intended to simply 'ape' everything Japanese; indeed, we are well aware that outright copying would be quite impossible considering the quite different ethnic and historical backgrounds of our countries. Neither did 'Look East' mean that we were going to completely reject positive elements from the West" (Mahathir, 1999). Thus, Mahathir's take on Malaysia's "Look East" policy is different from that of Mugabe. It is this kind of "Look East" policy that this author is advocating for Africa; a "Look East" policy that is pragmatic and forward looking, not backward and myopic as advocated by Mugabe. Indeed, such a "Look East" policy still regards the West as an important partner and player in Africa's socio-economic growth and development.

The anxieties in certain quarters about China's foray into Africa are understandable. But if Africa cares about its growth and development, it must let go of the crippling anxiety and fear that "the Chinese are coming," a rather xenophobic outlook akin to the Chinese Exclusion Act signed into law in the US in 1882.[2] Africa should look to its current strategic partnership with China with faith and adequate planning if it is to benefit from this partnership. Obviously, there are going to be some hiccups and challenges in this relationship, as already elaborated on elsewhere in this book and which Chinese premier Li Keqian has described as "growing pains." But it would be a tragedy if, because of greed and short-sightedness on the part of their leadership and political elites, African countries were to squander the windfall benefits of China's current investment in Africa as seen in the rising demand for Africa's natural resources. If these benefits are squandered in the building of dubious prestige projects like new showcase capitals and gaudy palaces, in conspicuous consumption and in the funnelling of such resources into foreign bank accounts, Africa will have itself to blame (French, 2014). Africa has been down this road before in the era of the Mobutus, the Sani Abachas, the Omar Bongos and the Jean Bedel Bokassas. These so called "big men" of Africa have plundered the resources of their respective countries and spent them on useless and unproductive prestige projects. This has been to the detriment of the development of their people. These and others have been much written about by the late Basil Davidson in his book *The Black Man's Burden: Africa and the Curse of the Nation-State*. These are mistakes Africa cannot afford to repeat.

African governments must therefore first consider what projects they need for their national development and then negotiate with the Chinese on each and every project that is to be implemented in their respective countries to allow for a greater employment of their nationals, allow for the transfers of technology to African countries and insist on the understudy of their processes and techniques by Africans working on Chinese projects. Furthermore, for capacity building efforts, they must insist that their nationals should be sent for training and further studies in Chinese institutions. This will ensure the sustainability of most of these projects when the Chinese have left. But it will also help Africans to develop their own technologies through "learning by doing" or enhance those that are already in place to increase productivity and contribute to their growth and development efforts.

According to Henry Ward Beecher (1813–1887), an American clergyman and abolitionist, "every tomorrow has two handles. We can take hold of it with the handle of anxiety or the handle of faith" (Lloyd, 1887). Africa should choose the latter, believing that if they position themselves well, they will benefit from China's current engagement with Africa. So how are African countries going to position themselves to achieve this goal? This is the most important strategic question governments and policy makers, and indeed the African Union as well as regional organisations on the continent, should be asking. Another important question they should be asking themselves is what they really need or want to benefit from this relationship with China whether they have a plan for that. Definitely, any such plans should go beyond Chinese financial investments in Africa. Much as China's current investments in Africa are important and necessary, there are other benefits that could accrue to Africa as part of this relationship. Finally, African governments and policy makers should also plan and strategize for any eventualities, such as a downturn or slowdown in the Chinese economy and the adverse impact this could have on

African economies and their respective development plans. They should also have in place alternative strategies to mitigate such an occurrence.

A clear and concise answer to these questions by African policy makers and the relevant governments of the day will help African countries come up with workable solutions to help them better position themselves economically, politically and socially to take advantage of China's current foray into Africa. This chapter will look critically at this issue in detail. It will look at whether Chinese capabilities indeed mesh with African needs. The chapter will also look at whether African countries have a strategy in place or an idea of what they need and want from China. This is because China knows exactly what it wants from Africa. The chapter will also look critically at what China "really" wants from Africa apart from its natural resources. It will also look at how African countries can effectively harness the benefits it will realise from China in a sustainable manner to bring about their economic growth and development. The chapter will also consider the fact that Chinese aid and investments in Africa do not come with conditionalities, as they do with Western aid, and the benefits that this entails. The chapter will give reasons why African leaders and policy makers should insist on technology transfer in Chinese projects undertaken in their respective countries and offers some suggestions on how this can be done.

8.2 Do Chinese Capabilities Mesh with Africa's Needs?

The first place for African countries to start in the effort to position themselves to benefit from China's foray into Africa is to do a true needs analysis of what they currently have and what they truly need as a continent, as different regional economic communities (RECs), and as individual countries in their growth and development efforts. These "needs" should be clearly separated from "wants." I am sure that there are very many things that African countries "want" from China, but do these "wants" really contribute to their growth and development, and most important of all, can they afford the "wants"? From the perspective of this author, *wants* are basically things that a person, organisation or country desires, while *needs* are things necessary for the survival or sustenance of a person, organisation or country.

Africa therefore should dwell on what it "needs" from its relationship with China, looking at its environment and capabilities. In this process, Africa should also look critically at what they have in terms of both human and fiscal resources and ask how they can deploy what they have to mesh with China's capabilities in its current engagement with Africa to help it in its economic growth and development efforts. Undertaking such a process will inform African countries what should go into the specific strategies they develop in their dealings with China. And as each region of the continent undertakes this critical analytical process of their needs, they must exchange notes and learn from each other to give them the requisite advantage in their dealings with the Chinese to truly benefit from their investment and foray into Africa. This will also help them to adequately strategize to use their resources effectively to mesh with China's capabilities.

So what does Africa specifically need from its relationship with China? In this chapter, I will spell out these needs and clarify why I think they are necessary to Africa's socio-economic growth and development as it pertains to its current growth and development trajectory. But this process of identifying Africa's needs will also help African policy makers to ascertain the true capabilities of Chinese companies and the projects they are currently engaged in or will be engaged in to help African countries achieve their developmental needs and goals.

One of the important needs of Africa and all African countries is infrastructure. Good infrastructure will help Africa unleash its true potential for its growth and development. The importance of infrastructure such as motorable roads, airports, railroads, manufacturing industries and ports to the growth and development efforts of African countries cannot be emphasised enough. The World Bank and other Western development agencies were major investors in infrastructure projects in Africa and indeed in other developing countries between the early 1940s and the 1960s. It is reported that around that time, about 75 percent of all infrastructural projects in developing countries were funded by the World Bank. This focus of the World Bank later changed, resulting in most of the infrastructure deficit in many African countries today (Michalopoulos, 1989). According to the Africa Infrastructure Diagnostic Study (AICD), it is estimated that Africa needs about US$93 billion a year to adequately address its infrastructure deficit (Foster, 2008).

China's foray into Africa and Africa's huge infrastructure needs have seen China quickly occupying that space. China is constructing roads, hospitals, hydroelectric dams, railways and numerous other infrastructures in different countries around Africa. Over 35 African countries are dealing with China on various infrastructure financing deals. Most of the largest recipients are Nigeria, Angola, Sudan and Ethiopia. Chinese infrastructure commitments in Africa rose from less than US$1 billion per year in 2001–2003 to around US$1.5 billion per year in 2004–2005. By 2006, it had reached US$7 billion before falling back to US$4.5 billion in 2007 (Foster and Briceno-Garmendia, 2010). Most of this financing is channelled through China Export-Import Bank (Eximbank) and this is usually on terms that are marginally concessional. In some of the infrastructure projects financed by China in some African countries, the deals are packaged in such a way that it is linked to natural resource development or extraction from the African country. This is usually known as the "Angola model." In this case, the repayment of the loan for infrastructural development is made in natural resources. This model is used for countries that cannot provide adequate financial guarantees for the infrastructure loans. These loans offer on average an interest rate of 3.6 percent. The grace period is usually 4 years with a maturity period of 12 years (Vines and Campos, 1998).

Another important area in which Africa need China's help is in the development and enhancing of Africa's manufacturing sector. The role of manufacturing in Africa's economic development cannot be emphasised enough. It has been observed that few countries have been able to grow and develop their economies without investing in their respective manufacturing sectors. This then often leads to the industrialisation of these countries. Consequently, the manufacturing sector in Africa, if developed and enhanced, could do the same for the continent's industrialisation. The manufacturing sector would enable Africa add value to its raw materials before they are exported. It would also contribute to the reduction of the huge unemployment situation witnessed in many African countries because of the labour-intensive nature of manufacturing. Above all, manufacturing is less vulnerable to external shocks like commodities. The current downturn in most of African economies at the time of writing because the collapse in the prices of the commodities they export is a case in point.

Unfortunately, Africa's manufacturing sector is faced with numerous challenges. Some of these include the lack of skilled labour, poor infrastructure and the negative image of Africa in the media, which makes it hard to attract long-term capital investments, to mention a few. According to the World Bank, manufacturing accounts for only 13 percent of the gross domestic product (GDP) in Sub-Saharan Africa (SSA), a rather small share; hence, most countries in the region do not regard it as an important source of their export earnings.[3] This is an area in which China can help Africa. Apart from the fact that it has taken the manufacturing route to development, China is shifting from a manufacturing economy to a consumption and services-focused economy because of the rising cost of its labour, which makes it less competitive compared to other countries with large labour forces but lower labour costs. Africa could be well positioned to benefit from the movement of China's manufacturing industries looking for low-cost labour havens. As a country that has been able to attract labour-intensive Chinese manufacturing, Ethiopia is a case in point. As China rebalances its economy, this is an opportune time for African leaders and policy makers to have this conversation with their Chinese counterparts in order to take advantage of this situation.

Another important area in which Africa needs China's help is in revolutionizing its agricultural sector. According to the World Bank, Africa's agricultural sector employs about 60 percent of the continents labour force and accounts for 32 percent of its GDP. In some countries in Africa, agriculture employs about 70–80 percent of the population. The agricultural sector in Africa is also important because it can contribute to the eradication of poverty, hunger, and rapid industrialization; the diversification of the economies; and the creating of jobs, to mention just a few. Furthermore, by the year 2050, Africa's population growth is projected to have reached two billion. This population will need food to feed itself. This will be a challenge, because agricultural growth on the continent has not kept up with population growth so far. It is a challenge African leaders would do well to reflect on and begin finding workable solutions to deal with this looming issue.

The agricultural sector in Africa accounts for most of the jobs, but unfortunately, the production in the sector is low compared to the non-agricultural sector. This thus retards economic growth on the continent. It thus stands to reason that if productivity in the sector is raised, it will contribute to the economic growth of the continent. Therefore, if most of the countries on the continent want to achieve sustainable growth and reduce poverty, as mentioned earlier, they should invest in revolutionizing the agricultural sector. Finally, food insecurity on the continent can undermine the stability and sovereignty of the countries on the continent as evidenced in 2006 and 2008, when international prices of foodstuff rose, affecting most poor and some middle-income countries in Africa. This led to food riots in Burkina Faso, Cameroon, Zimbabwe, Egypt, Tunisia Mozambique, Madagascar and Guinea, to mention a few.

China can help Africa is this respect to revolutionize and transform African agriculture. First, China is the number one country in the world when it comes to farm output. The agricultural sector employs over 300 million people, and it has been able to employ improved farm methods to be able to feed its population. But where China can help Africa's agricultural sector the most is through the provision of investment in the sector and in helping the different countries on the continent to mechanize some of their farms to increase output. The way this can be done is by using the current China–Africa agricultural cooperation initiative. This initiative has seen China help with 142 agricultural projects in Africa. The Chinese have set up 14 agricultural technology demonstration centres in Africa (Information Office of the State Council of the PRC, 2010). All these efforts are laudable. However, this initiative should be broadened; it should also highly consider the exchange or the transfer of appropriate agricultural technology to African countries. These technologies should be in the areas of food production, processing and storage, as most of the food produced on the continent rots for lack of processing and storage facilities after the harvesting season. Finally, the government must also encourage private Chinese companies, as part of their "Going Out" policy, to consider investing in agriculture on the continent. Definitely, the governments must be willing to make it attractive for private Chinese companies to invest in African agriculture.

African countries can do this through the development and the offering of attractive tax and other incentives that will encourage private Chinese companies to be willing to invest in the African agricultural sector. Policies should also be put into place to encourage joint ventures in agriculture between Chinese and African investors. The government should go further to consider enabling measures that will create demand for some of the produce of this sector for industry and for domestic consumption.

Drawing from the analysis so far in this section, it is clear that some of the major needs of African countries are the sustainable development of good infrastructure, agriculture, their manufacturing sectors and their education sectors, to mention just a few. From the experience of many African countries so far, from some of the projects China has undertaken in Africa in the aforementioned areas and from the successful completion and commissioning of these projects, it can be said that China has the capabilities and the financing ability to undertake more of such projects of importance to Africa's growth and development efforts. It can therefore be said that the Chinese capabilities mesh with African needs. Their ability to fund the projects (a huge challenge faced by most African governments), their technological know-how and their ability to deliver the project cheaper and within budget all point to their capability.

In passing, mentioned should be made that others have criticised some of the Chinese projects undertaken in Africa as lacking the desired quality and robustness that they should have. Hence, it is said that most of some of these projects do not last as soon as they are commissioned. The only way to mitigate this is to stress and negotiate a water-tight contract that includes the required lifespan for the project according to international standards. Examples include roads built by Chinese companies. Hence, if the projects do not reach the negotiated lifespan before they break down, the Chinese should be compelled by the terms and conditions of the contract to re-do the projects at their own cost. If African countries do not insist on the quality and durability of most of the Chinese projects undertaken in Africa by these performance contracts, they will have themselves to blame. The question then that needs to be asked is, does Africa as a whole have a clear and concise approach to or strategy to achieve what they want from China?

8.3 Have a Clear and Concise Approach or Strategy towards China

For mutually beneficial and sustainable benefits to evolve from the relationship between Africa and China in the latter's current engagement with Africa, it is incumbent on African countries to have a clear and concise idea of what they really want from China. It starts with a clear knowledge on the part of Africans of what China wants from Africa – how African countries can provide what China wants at an acceptable price or based on the exchange of resources in return for the delivery of what China wants or through mutually beneficial arrangements that result in a win–win outcome for both partners. But this is also informed by what Africans want from China in return. With this knowledge, African countries can therefore develop the strategy that will get them maximum returns on whatever product or resources they exchange. That is one of the reasons why this book started with the history of and detailed information on where China came from, how it got to this point and what African leaders and policy makers can learn from this history to help them in their dealings with China.

As already elaborated on earlier in this book, China knows what it wants from its engagement and partnership with Africa and has the attendant strategies to attain it. This includes its effort to enforce its "One China" policy and principle, a need for Africa's natural resources to meet its increased growth requirements, an export market for its products and services and a need to build political alliances with African countries to further its global ambitions. Africa is equally a testing ground in the preparation of Chinese companies in their effort to go international. To this extent, China has developed a well-thought-out African policy (The Chinese have a Department of African Affairs under the Ministry of Foreign Affairs). In fact, China is constantly reassessing and adapting its policies to the shifting realities of Africa's realpolitik (Aning, 2010). The question is, do African countries know what they want from their partnership or engagement with China? Do they know how to position themselves to benefit from China's foray into Africa? Without that crucial knowledge and strategy, at the end of the day, African countries could be left holding the bag, and the relationship could be one in which Africa would see its resources plundered as it was the case during the era of its colonial masters (see Hoschchild, 2006).

Regrettably, African countries and indeed the African Union (A.U.) at the time of writing do not have what this author will call a clear or coordinated or official "Africa Policy on China" as it pertains to its foray into Africa. The A.U. has not been able to coordinate or foster a continental unified or official policy on how to engage China. Without such an explicit and coordinated African policy or stance in its engagement with China, the continent is faced with an economic, security, environmental and governance risk, which poses a serious threat to its long-term development. It also poses a challenge when African countries have to negotiate with China and thus it puts them at a disadvantage. There will be policy incoherencies as Africa deals with China, and without a unified strategy or policy towards China, Africa as a whole will lose out in the negotiations. China can always use the "divide and conquer" tactic of negotiations in its dealings with African countries to extract maximum value for its interest and for its benefit. African countries should always remember that China is not a charity or non-governmental organisation (NGO), and thus its foray into Africa is not to undertake charity work. Therefore, it cannot be emphasised enough that having a clear and coordinated African strategy towards China is the first place to begin.

But having a clear strategy alone is not enough. This strategy should be based on a new paradigm and the realities of the African condition as it pertains to its efforts at development and its transformation. It should also be based on its current and future needs of its growing population. The strategy should also encompass the "Africa Rising" narrative, which goes beyond GDP growth of African countries, as is commonly accepted as being the case. It should encompass the A.U. Vision 2063 and, where possible, Africans finding African solutions to Africa's developmental challenges and not relying too much on the Chinese or outsiders. This strategy should also take into consideration that the market size and indeed the economies of most African countries are rather weak; hence, the current bilateral engagement with China, which I describe as an "each for himself and God for us all" approach, should change.

This is because it puts the continent at a disadvantage. Thus a regional/continent-wide approach in engaging China will be the best option for Africa. This approach will allow Africa to speak with a unified voice about its growth and development needs as a continent. Second, it will eliminate the "each for himself and God for us all" approach and mentality. This can be achieved by the A.U. defining its China policy and strategy, which should be aligned with Africa's socio-political and economic interests and should incorporate the A.U. Vision 2063. The following are some of the advantages that will accrue to Africa if a unified approach is employed in its dealings with China:

- Common regional framework on industrialisation: directing Chinese expansion into areas of national/sub-regional interest; technology and management skills transfers, and so on;
- Common framework on natural resource exploration and social and environmental responsibilities;
- Common framework on trade, as opposed to bilateral economic partnership agreements (EPAs), which can only help fragment the continent and weaken the capacity of individual African countries to negotiate with China from a strong platform;
- Common regional regulations on investment, which might include requirements for local inputs into Chinese ventures, encouraging the creation of backward and forward linkages to existing or newly stimulated local companies; labour rights; and labour training.[4]

The specifics that will go into these approaches can be formulated at the level of regional economic communities (RECs). This is important because each region may have specific needs, but the coordination of these needs would bring about improved linkages and benefits to the whole continent. Formulated at the RECs level, these needs could then be funnelled through to all levels and developed into an Africa-wide approach to dealing with China. These strategies should also change with the prevailing global conditions as well as that of the African socio-economic and political landscape.

The other way African countries can position themselves to benefit from China's foray into the region is that African leaders must network, share their experiences and compare notes, so to speak, about their dealings with China and Chinese companies operating in their respective countries. They must also talk to each other more, visit each other more and see Chinese projects in each other's countries. They should also learn to negotiate more as a block rather than the current individual negotiations each country engages in with China. They should insist, as China did in its early stages of transformation and growth, that foreign companies entering their markets should do so through joint ventures with local companies and that technology and skills transfers should be part of such negotiations.

In the process of writing this book, I have interacted with colleagues and friends formally and informally across the continent on this issue of having a clear, unified and coordinated policy towards China. I have asked some of my friends and colleagues whether such an approach was necessary and whether it can be achieved. Some colleagues agreed with me that such an approach was possible and indeed necessary if Africa was not to repeat what happened during the colonial era. However, some colleagues, even though they see the rationale of such an approach as necessary, do not believe that it is possible and can be achieved. Some of those who subscribe to the latter view observed that African countries have competing interest at the RECs level as well as the continental and international level, making it hard for them to shelve their competing interests and rally around a unified policy and strategy towards China, and that hence the proposition would not work.

As an example to buttress this point, one of my friends pointed to the race to select a new World Trade Organisation (WTO) secretary-general to replace the departing Pascal Lamy. He mentioned that Alan Kwadwo Kyerematen, Ghana's former trade minister, had the experience and the qualifications for the job and was supported by the African Union as the preferred African candidate. The presupposition was that all African countries would rally around his candidacy for Africa if he was to stand a chance of winning. Many were sure that he had a very good chance of being the next WTO head, which would be a source of pride to Africa. While preparations were going on to seek international support for Alan's candidacy, suddenly Kenya fielded their candidate – Amina C. Mohamed, Kenya's ambassador to the WTO at that time – to also contest for the position. Thus, even though Africa stood an excellent chance of occupying the position this time around by being represented by two candidates, it lost its shine, and both were eliminated in the first round of the selection process. This is a case of competing interests amongst African countries. Obviously, there may be those who may have an alternative view to this issue. Nevertheless, the observation of the lack of unity and competing interests among African countries has been made. These friends further point to the challenge of integrating Africa as one of the reasons why they think it will be impossible for Africa to develop or pursue a unified policy towards China.

Others observe that the numerous conflicts on the continent as well as insurgent Islamic terrorist attacks by Boko Haram in Nigeria, Al-Shabab in Somalia, and Al-Qaeda in the Maghreb and their recent attacks on hotels in Mali and Burkina Faso, to mention a few, have tended to force more of the limited resources of African countries to where these conflicts and insurgents predominate. They spend most of their resources to fight these insurgencies. Some of the countries do not even pay their dues to the RECs or the A.U. and thus cannot fund these African organisations. Currently, over 50 percent of the operating budget of the A.U. is funded by external donors who have their own interests. These interests may be different from the interests of the A.U. and the African people. It thus makes it difficult for the A.U. to formulate a unified policy towards China.

Numerous observations have been made by colleagues as to why the proposition of Africa developing a unified strategy and policy towards China will not work. The final observation I would like to give here is their observation that the RECs and the A.U., and indeed most African organisations, suffer from what they term "implementation deficit." African governments and institutions like the RECs and the A.U. engage in numerous meetings, conferences and workshops to deliberate on African challenges and problems. When they come up with workable solutions, these are often not implemented. Thus they engage in what I term *NATO* (No Action Talk Only). Because of these observations and many more, they believe that the proposition will not work.

Despite these observations to the contrary, if Africa is to benefit from China's current investment and engagement with Africa and to use such investment as a springboard to achieve its economic growth and development, it is important that it develop and have in place a clear, unified policy and strategy to deal with China. As often said in Africa, if one wants to go far, one must go in a group or go together with a team. If Africans are to benefit from the Chinese foray into Africa, they must go together as a team as well as work together as a team in their dealings with the Chinese. Kwame Nkrumah's call for African unity in his famous speech before African leaders in Addis Ababa, Ethiopia, on the 24th of May 1963, when he said, "Africa must unite or perish" (Nkrumah, 1963), should be the watch-word for African leaders and policy makers in their dealings with China.

8.4 Have an Informed Knowledge of What China "Really" Wants from Africa

The commonly held notion is that China is only interested in Africa's rich natural resources and can thus be regarded as the "new colonialist," as written about elsewhere in this book. It is also written about in Chapter 4 of this book that China is interested in having Africa's support of its "One China" policy as well as being able to rely on Africa's support on issues at international fora, especially at the United Nations (UN). Also in Chapter 4, it has been outlined that China has seen Africa as a market for its finished goods and services. For example, the Exim bank of China has a policy that 60 percent of the input of all the projects it finances in Africa must come from China. But China's "going out" policy has also resulted in some of the Chinese companies selling their goods and service in Africa, using Africa as a learning ground to enter other international markets like the US and Europe.

Despite these known reasons why China is interested in its current engagements with Africa, much more intense research and critical thinking and analysis has not gone into the inquiry of what it "really" is that China wants from Africa. This is because what China really wants from Africa goes beyond the accepted observation that China is interested in Africa's raw materials. The constant utterance by China as it becomes a global power is that it is pursuing a path of "peaceful rise," one that accommodates other developing countries in seeking mutual growth. Yet some of the most recent literature dealing with the rise of China, such as *China's New Empire*; *When China Rules the World*, points to a kind of "hegemonic" aspiration on the part of China. Whether this observation by the literature is true or not is a topic for other writers to explore. What the issue is, as far as this book is concerned, is whether – deducing from the literature pointing to this "probabilistic" aspiration – China's foray into Africa is one of its strategies to use Africa to further its hegemonic aspirations? This is because Western countries have done so in the past. In fact, during the

Cold War era, Africa was caught between hegemonic ambitions and a struggle between East and West. China could be learning from the West and the East (the former Soviet Union) in this respect.

So what is a hegemon? It is the political, economic or military predominance or control of one state over others. According to the *Oxford Advanced Leaner's Dictionary*, it is "leadership or dominance, especially by one state or social group over others" (Hornby et al., 2010). Lake (1993) observes that *hegemony* refers to leadership or primacy in an international system and that a hegemon is a state that possesses sufficient capability to fulfil such a leadership role. So what are some of the characteristics of a hegemon? First, it must have the capability to enforce the rules of the system. Secondly, it must possess the will to do so, and thirdly, it must be committed to a system that is perceived as mutually beneficial to the major states. It also has the following attributes: First, it should be a large growing economy; second, it should have dominance in a leading technological or economic sector; and finally, it should have political power backed by a projective military. But it should be able to provide a leadership role directly related to its values and accepted by other states in its sphere of influence, and it should be willing to act to maintain and expand its role and position in what it determines to be its sphere of influence (Schoeman, 2007).

So based on this understanding and based on the analysis in this book as it pertains to China's current engagement with Africa, does this point to a rising hegemon? This section will use some of the characteristics of a hegemon to help in this analysis. First, one of the characteristics of a hegemon is that it shows the propensity to control and dominate other states in its region. Since the focus is on Africa, and Africa is not in the Asian region, and despite China's diverse engagement in Africa, it is difficult to say that China's current engagement with Africa points to any such ambitions. Secondly, a hegemon is characterised as having power in the domains of politics, economics and the military. In this sense, China has some power, but it is not as dominant as the US or the EU. Even though China has impressive military and weapons assets as well as being a recognised nuclear power, it still does not command the status of the US (Schoeman, 2007). Hence it cannot be regarded as a hegemon as per this characteristic.

Another characteristic of a hegemon is that it provides certain public goods and other benefits to its allies or other members of the system. Some of these goods can include the creation of openness in the international trade system or the provision of international military security. China's provision of such benefits to Africa is rather on a much smaller scale than that which is usually associated with a "genuine" hegemon (Schoeman, 2007). Hence, China is not a hegemon as per this characteristic either. The final characteristic of a hegemon that will be looked at here has to do with the fact that a hegemon will act to maintain and expand its influence in areas it considers as its sphere of influence. Again, as it pertains to Africa, there is no evidence so far that China has acted in such a way that it has prevented other external actors interested in Africa from dealing with Africa. India, the US and the EU are all still dealing with

Africa. So as it also pertains to this characteristic, China is not a hegemon. This analysis shows that the concern that China wants to use its foray into Africa to prop up its hegemonic ambition does not hold.

However, it has been observed that China's rise and its increased involvement with Africa has prompted some countries like the US and some European countries to view China as a potential hegemon (Mearsheimer, 2006; Schoeman, 2007). But this has still not answered the question of what China "really" wants from Africa. However, what this analysis has done is to point to the fact that if China does not want to use Africa to foster its hegemonic ambitions, then what does it "really, really" want from Africa? To deduce this will require a look at where China came from, that is, its history and what it went through, specifically the period of intervention and imperialism and China's Century of Humiliation, amongst others.

This author is of the view that China's increased investment and involvement in Africa is because, as mentioned in Chapter 2 of this book, it wants to recover its past pre-eminence. The China of yesterday was an innovative country with inventions like gunpowder, paper, printing technologies and the compass, to mention a few. It was a nation of renowned philosophers and explorers like Zheng He. China's ambition to recapture its past pre-eminence in the world and the prestige and the psychological significance that comes with it cannot be emphasised enough. The Chinese leadership realises that in the current global environment, Africa is an important continent that can offer China this opportunity, either through supplying China with the raw materials and important resources needed for its growth; political support at international fora, as evidenced by the support of Africa for China to be accepted into the UN; or a market for its finished products, to mention a few. All of these factors can contribute to China redeeming its past greatness. Most important of all, China is not oblivious to the importance of the greater African diaspora, most of whom, no matter where they are, still have affinity in various ways towards Africa. China needs their support in its effort to recover its past eminence.

Another observation by this author as to what China "really, really" wants from Africa can be deduced from the impact of China's Century of Humiliation, or the 100 years of national humiliation known in Chinese as *pinyin: bǎinián guóchǐ*. This has been hard-wired into China's memory, and the resolve of the Chinese that such humiliation will never happen to them again is one of the cornerstones driving most of the country's decisions. The Chinese and indeed China do not like to lose face or what they term *mian-zi* – "saving face." The Chinese will go to any length to save face. They cannot afford in this modern era to be humiliated again as was the case during the 100 years of humiliation. This refers to the period of intervention and imperialism by Western powers and Japan in China between 1839 and 1949. The term arose in 1915 in the atmosphere of rising Chinese nationalism opposing the Twenty-One Demands made by the Japanese government and their acceptance by Yuan Shikai with the *Kuomintang*. The Chinese Communist Party subsequently popularized the characterization as more of a rallying cry of Chinese nationalism (Kaufman, 2010).

Others trace the beginning of this period to the mid-nineteenth century, specifically to the eve of the First Opium War, which was characterised by widespread opium addiction amongst the Chinese populace as well as the political unravelling of the Qing dynasty. Other major events of this Century of Humiliation include the unequal treaties of Whampoa and Aigun, the Taiping Rebellion, the Second Opium War and the sacking of the Old Summer Palace, the suppression of the Boxer uprising by the Eight-Nation Alliance, the Sino–French War, the First Sino–Japanese War and the Second Sino–Japanese War, to mention a few. This has emboldened and formed China's new nationalism because during the aforementioned period, it lost all the wars it fought. As a result of these loses, it was forced to make major concessions in treaties signed during this period (Hayes, 2004). The Chinese have since vowed that they will not go looking for trouble but that if any enemy attacks them as was the case in the Century of Humiliation, they will fight to the finish. This time, they have the resources and the weaponry to back their word. African strategic mineral resources such as uranium, cobalt, tantalum and chromium, to mention a few, are important in this strategy. From this analysis, therefore, the Chinese need Africa.

If these are some of the important and strategic things that this author believes that China "really, really" wants from Africa, how should African countries position themselves to equally benefit from China's use of its current foray and investments in Africa to help it redeem its past greatness? First, African countries must have a clear strategy as to what they need and want from China as elaborated on in Section 8.4. At the end of the day, African countries know what their developmental needs are, and they are the best people to make sure that such needs mesh with Chinese capabilities to deliver on the requisite projects that will contribute to their growth and development. African countries can then build on this knowledge and use it to their benefit in their dealings with China. But this will require a united African strategy and policy towards China.

8.5 Effectively Harness Benefits from China to Africa in a Sustainable Manner

Another important thing to note if African countries are to benefit from China's foray into Africa is to effectively harness in a sustainable manner the benefits this current engagement brings, such as debt relief, investment, infrastructure development, trade and aid coming their way from China. The first important step is to harness these benefits to build and improve on Africa's dilapidated infrastructure. One of the factors that contribute to the high cost of doing business in Africa is its poor infrastructure. According to a study prepared by the World Economic Forum, the World Bank and the African Development Bank, African firms lose as much as 8 percent of sales due to power outages (World Economic Forum, 2007). A case in point is the numerous power outages in Ghana called *Dumsor* or blackouts, which were pronounced in 2015. Transportation delays cost as well, accounting for 3 percent of lost sales in Africa.

Building and upgrading of Africa's infrastructure require huge investments and expertise which most African countries lack but need. Also, Africa's traditional bilateral and multilateral partners allocate a limited amount of their resources for infrastructural development in Africa. Chinese investment and expertise could be directed to building the continent's infrastructure, which would contribute to the improvement of the business environment and the cost of doing business on the continent, subsequently contributing to growth and development in Africa. It is important to point out that some African countries are already harnessing these benefits well to build and improve on their infrastructure. China is already undertaking infrastructure projects in 35 African countries. For example, Angola is using an aid package from China to build major infrastructure destroyed in years of the country's civil war, and Nigeria is working with China to help rehabilitate its rail transport system.

In Ghana, the Chinese have built the Bui hydroelectric dam in the northwestern part of the country. The dam was built by Sinohydro and was financed by China to the tune of US$292 million at an interest rate of 2 percent at 12 years' maturity with a grace period of five years. The Chinese accepted a resource-secured (the sale of cocoa beans) loan from Ghana to finance the building of the dam (Brautigam, 2011). They also built the Atuabo Gas plant in the western region of the country as well as constructing numerous roads in the country. In Nigeria, China is already involved in US$1.7 billion worth of infrastructure projects. During the recent visit of Chinese premier Li Keqiang to Nigeria, China signed a US$1.1 billion infrastructural agreement with the government of Nigeria to build roads, airport terminals in four cities, and a light-rail system in Abuja, Nigeria's capital. Similar infrastructure projects are being undertaken in other African countries. A conscious and concerted effort on the part of African countries to harness these benefits from China will go a long way to positioning African countries to benefit from China's foray into Africa.

China's current investment in Africa is making Africa's traditional allies uncomfortable. This discomfort could be because China's investments and aid to Africa are breaking the choke-hold the West has over trade with Africa, a region it has long regarded as its "sphere of influence." One of the reasons for China's success in its forays into Africa is that it is willing to go, and has gone into, parts of Africa that present them with numerous risks that their Western counterparts will dare not take. They are also willing to settle for slim profit margins and, in the case where their state-owned enterprises (SOEs) are involved, they are willing to make short-term losses in pursuit of their government's long-term strategic interests. According to former Senegalese president Abdoulaye Wade, "China's approach to African needs is admittedly better adapted than the slow and sometimes patronising post-colonial approach of European investors, donors and NGOs. In fact, the Chinese model for stimulating rapid economic development has much to teach Africa" (Wade, 2008).

African leaders and policy makers should understand that despite the benefits that are flowing from China's foray into the region, the Chinese have their own interests. As long as these interests remain, the Chinese will continue to invest in Africa. But there will come a time when these interests change. China, just like every sovereign country, has permanent interests. For example, the recent cooling of the Chinese economy has had an adverse impact on the demand for African commodities. The impact on African economies that mostly rely on commodities cannot be emphasised enough. It is a concerted Chinese policy to transition its economy from investment and manufacturing to consumption and services. This decision was not taken with African economies in mind; it was about the Chinese economy and the welfare of its citizens. African leaders and policy makers should thus maximize the benefits they are enjoying from China's foray into Africa while they last and should even complement them with their own home-grown projects and programmes. At the end of the day, if these opportunities are squandered on prestige projects or on irrelevant pursuits, they will only have themselves to blame, and their people will never forgive them for the missed opportunities.

8.6 China's Aid and Investment have No Conditionalities

Furthermore, China's aid and investment in Africa does not come with the conditionalities and rules of good governance that their Western counterparts usually demand of African countries. China has always upheld that they have a policy of non-interference in the internal affairs of African countries. But of what importance is this and how can it benefit African countries? Because Africa's traditional allies are looking for resources, markets and influence in Africa, just like China, this is going to lead to some form of competition between China and Africa's traditional allies. If African countries position themselves well, they could take advantage of the competition between China and Africa's former allies/colonial masters. It could even influence the kind of conditionalities that come with funding from multilateral agencies targeting Africa, which would lead to economic growth and development. It could also lead to increased prices for Africa's resources as was the case before the pre-2008 global financial crises. African countries stand to benefit from this windfall, and if the resulting resources are used wisely, it could contribute immensely to the growth and development efforts of the continent.

The increased trade and investment between China and Africa is because of the latter's comparative advantage in terms of natural resources. But it is also due to and driven by economic complementarities between Africa and China based on factor endowments. It is the case that Africa has natural resources and unskilled labour, while China has technically skilled labour and more advanced technologies. If African countries position themselves very well, they can build their competitiveness based on Africa's endowed natural resources. This can be done if African countries develop local value-added activities based on their respective natural resources. This will, however, require that African countries put into place stable and sound economic policies. These value-added activities can then be used as a stepping stone to higher value-added activities (Broadman, 2007). But African countries can also take advantage of China's huge domestic market of 1.3 billion people. Because of the complementarities, Africa should strive to position itself to export more of its non-traditional resources like timber, cotton, pineapples and other products to the Chinese market. The processing and adding of value to these resources before they are exported to China will help Africa a lot.

Even though bilateral trade between China and Africa is growing, there is room for more growth. China is currently adopting numerous measures to increase imports from Africa. For example, it does not charge tariffs on imports from some of the less developed countries in Africa. It has also increased from 190 to 440 items that will attract zero tariffs exported from African countries. These measures offer African countries the opportunity to increase their exports to the Chinese market. If they do, the spill-over effects for their respective economies are going to be numerous. But African countries must be willing to take the challenge. China should also be willing to reduce non-tariff barriers on African products entering the Chinese market.

8.7 Insisting on Technology Transfer in Chinese Projects in Africa

If African countries are to really benefit from China's foray into Africa to help transform their respective economies, then they will need to insist that subsequent projects undertaken by Chinese companies, both public and private sector, include the transfer of skills or technology to the locals. First, this will ensure the sustainability of the projects when the Chinese leave and will avoid a situation like the fate of the Tazara Railway years after the Chinese left. It will also lead to the creation of jobs and the enhancing of the skill sets of the locals. It will also lead to positive spill-over benefits like improved productivity through demonstration effects and better quality standards as well as forward–backward linkages. Finally, it could set the stage for African countries to produce their own technological products as well as enhance innovation in their respective countries. So far, African leaders have been rather silent on such insistence.

Here are some ways that African leaders can ensure that technology transfer can be attained in projects undertaken by Chinese in Africa. These include

- Deliberate government policy
- Insistence that technology transfers are part of contracts/licensing agreements
- Joint ventures
- Partnerships
- Technical assistance

Deliberate Government Policy

So far, Chinese projects that have been undertaken in Africa are short on the transfer of technology and skills to Africans in the respective countries in which the projects have been undertaken. The Chinese are in no way going to transfer technology voluntarily. Hence, it is imperative that African governments and policy makers, after careful thought, make it mandatory, consciously and deliberately, that technology and skills transfers are going to be part of all major contracts involving Chinese companies. The government, where necessary, should set targets for the number of Africans that need to be skilled or up-skilled in certain technical areas. It must also make sure through monitoring and evaluation that the requisite skills transfers actually do take place. It should also be made one of the major criteria of the successful completion of the project(s) that the set targets of people to be trained are achieved.

Deliberate government policies to ensure technology transfers to China by foreign companies that were undertaking projects in the country in the early stages of its development efforts is a lesson Africans can learn from the Chinese. It was part of their strategic plan to attain technological know-how during the early stages of their development. They made it a requirement in all foreign direct investments (FDIs) coming into China, especially those funds coming in to fund major projects in transportation, infrastructure and manufacturing, that the requisite technologies were transferred to the Chinese who worked on those projects. They even engaged in reverse engineering in many cases as a compliment to their technology transfer efforts. Further, they sent their people abroad for further studies and to bring back the knowledge to help in the development of the country. African leaders and policy makers will be doing themselves and their people a huge disservice if they do not insist on technology transfer as the Chinese did many decades ago, but equally they must learn from the latter's experience.

Insisting on Technology Transfers in Contracts/Licensing Agreements

Other ways in which African countries can ensure that technologies and skills are transferred from Chinese companies to African ones, or to Africans working on Chinese projects, whether public or private sector projects, is to insist that such transfers be part of the project contracts they sign. In situations where the projects are of a build, operate and transfer (BOT) nature, the part of the contract dealing with technology transfer should be clear and succinct, with specific goals, targets and milestones for the technologies to be transferred. In the case where the technology transfers are in the form of a licencing agreement, African partners must make sure that the licensing scope is very clear and well spelt out, not being so restrictive that they would not be able to deliver on the development and sales of the specific product. They should negotiate to have access to the source code(s) and the right to combine or modify the products to suit the environment and conditions of their respective cultures and countries. In their negotiations with their Chinese partners, they should also have a clause(s) in the contract to indemnify them for any patent or copyright infringement. All these precautions are necessary. There are those who will say that such insistence on the transfer of technologies to African countries will be impossible with the Chinese. That may be true, and there may be specific situations where it may not be possible. But at this present moment, as African leaders have not or do not insist on these transfers, they cannot tell what they can get away with.

Joint Ventures

A joint venture (JV) is the case where one or more people, or different parties with different strengths, come together and enter into a business agreement or form a company to undertake a specific project(s) or a unique business, which is usually for a specific period of time or purpose. Usually, parties to a JV contribute a certain amount of equity to the setting up of the business as well as exercising control over the business. JVs that are for a specific project are usually dissolved when the project is finished. JVs are usually set up for four major reasons:

- To enable the JV partners to gain a faster entry into the marketplace with a product or service;
- To acquire expertise in a specific area or in a specific technology;
- To enable JV partners increase production scale in a particular product or service;
- To enable the JV partners to expand the business by gaining access to distributorship in other markets that either one partner in the JV does not have or that both partners do not have.

In the case of Chinese projects in Africa, the kinds of JV that I would like to stress here are what are known as co-operative agreements. This is the case where one of the JV partners is seeking technical expertise from the other. In this case, the Africans are seeking technical expertise from the Chinese. This is where African leaders and policy makers should insist that it becomes part of the contracts/agreements.

Partnerships

Generally, partnerships entail the coming together of at least two or more people to start a business or a project. The partners share the burden and challenges associated with the business or the project as well as the rewards. The individuals who are parties to the partnership could be from a particular country or from different countries abroad. Governments also may partner with other governments to attain specific goals or a certain end that will be of mutual benefit to the partnering countries. The partnership between countries may be to attain specific national security or national interest goals. The kind of partnerships that this section is concerned with to facilitate technology transfers to Africa should be the reason why African governments partner with Chinese companies to undertake certain projects that will contribute to the national development of African countries or China. Another case is where African companies investing in China, or vice versa, partner with local businesses or individuals to undertake the business either as a requirement of law or because of a need for complementary skills or know how.

In this case, the legalities that entail the transfer of technologies should be clearly spelt out; these include specific issues dealing with intellectual property rights use and violations, the requisite compensations and the requisite time lines involved. According to the World Intellectual Property Organisation (WIPO), the ability of partners to be able to negotiate the transfer of specific technologies depends on the relationship between them. It will also depend on some specific factors, such as

- The complexity and the level of development of the technology that is to be acquired;
- The actual needs of the recipient;
- The technological capacity of the transferee and its ability to use and/or adapt the technology being purchased;
- The relevance, availability and cost effectiveness of alternative technologies;
- The price to be paid (in cash or kind) by the recipient;
- Other proposed terms and conditions for the transfer, such as support offered during and after transfer in absorbing and adapting to the new technology, or rights over improvements or adaptations made by the recipient;
- The negotiating power of both parties (which will, in turn, depend on variables such as size, technological sector, demand for the technology, number of competitors, etc.);
- The type of relationship envisaged between the two parties (e.g. long-term, short-term or one-off purchase of products/services.);
- Issues concerning product liability, indemnity, warranty, and so on;
- Whether technical support and training for use of the new technology and related equipment is required.[5]

So what are some of the factors that could significantly influence the outcome of the negotiations between the parties in achieving a mutually beneficial outcome or agreement in cases dealing with technology transfer? The first has to do with the external context under which the negotiations are been held. This includes the requisite laws prevailing at that time, the competitive context and the demand for the technology, to mention just a few. The second is the characteristics each party brings to the table, that is, the size of the company and its technological capacity and other intervening factors like the company's ability to absorb new technology developed by others. All these increase the said company's negotiating power. Thus, companies who have the capacity to easily manage and effectively integrate new technologies elsewhere may not need assistance from the transferor, unlike those who do not.

Technical Assistance

Technical assistance (TA) is one of the ways through which China can transfer technologies to African countries. TA, according to the World Bank (1991), is basically "the transfer or the adaptation of ideas, knowledge, practices, technologies or skills to foster economic development." The general reasons why some countries offer technical assistance is to support the trade agreements they have with other countries. Furthermore, it is also a way to reduce trade barriers by supporting regional integration efforts. But some countries are genuinely concerned about poverty in certain developing countries in the world and hence use TA to help in poverty alleviation programmes. Finally, TA is used by some countries to bolster historical or long-standing ties between them and countries within a geographical area or based on a common language.

The types of technical assistance programmes vary; some of these include national or regional seminars, long or short-term advisory interventions or attachments from donor to recipient country and training programmes and study missions, to mention just a few. Whichever form a technical assistance programme takes, what is of importance to the recipient country is that at the end of the day, they are successful in contributing to the set goals that were put in place for them to achieve. So what, then, makes a TA programme successful? First, the programmes must be designed with input from the recipients. Equally, it is important that the recipients have some influence on the design of the TA programme that is going to affect them; if they do not have ownership of the programme, it will not be sustainable. Secondly, it is important that the recipients have the requisite absorptive capacity for the TA programme, which means that a thorough needs assessment study should be done. Thirdly, the programme should be designed in such a way that it is flexible enough to be able to adapt to constant changes in the environment as well as the changing needs of the recipients over time. Other ancillary factors include that technical advisors sent to these developing countries should be of top quality and their focus should be on imparting skills and knowledge with a long-term perspective in mind. Above all, the skills and knowledge to be transferred should be tailored to suit the recipients' needs rather than the priorities of the donor (Federal Trade Commission and US Department of Justice, 2009).

From this general analysis of TA, it is clear that most of China's TA programmes will fall under support of their trade agreements on some of the projects they are undertaking in Africa or some of the machinery for the various productive sectors African governments is procuring or has procured from China. However, this does not preclude African countries requesting TA from China to help them in some specific national projects that they feel will have impact on the economic development and growth of their respective countries. It could also be a multilateral effort or project, and the Chinese would be at liberty to bid for the contract. If it happens that a Chinese company should win the contract, African countries could ask for TA as part of the delivery on the project. At the end of the day, whichever agreement is signed between China and the various African countries it is undertaking projects in, TA is one of the ways it can transfer know-how and know-what to Africans. The aforementioned factors that make for a successful TA programme should guide TA programmes from China to Africa, and African leaders and policy makers should use it as a guide in negotiating such programmes coming from the Chinese.

8.8 Conclusion

It is often said that if you do not know where you are going, any road will take you somewhere. But is that somewhere really where you want to go? This is the case with how African countries deal with China's foray into Africa. African countries would have to know exactly what they want out of the relationship if they are to position themselves well to benefit from it. It is thus imperative that the A.U. and other regional organisations in Africa come out with a clear and unified strategy for how they will deal with China. African countries must also harness effectively the benefits from trade with and investment from China. Equally, the aid from China should be used towards poverty eradication. African countries also have the opportunity to learn from China's model of development, which has seen a country where about 20 million people died of hunger during the era of the "Great Leap Forward" develop into an economic powerhouse.

For African countries to be able to do that, it is suggested in this chapter that they should first assess whether the capabilities of the Chinese mesh with their needs. This will enable them to effectively strategize and commit their limited resources to the respective economic development projects and programmes for maximum returns. It is further recommended that African governments and policy makers develop a concise approach and strategy in their dealings with China to be able to achieve win–win outcomes in their current engagement with China. Equally, it is recommended that African leaders and policy makers have a clear idea of what China "really" wants from Africa beyond what is known, such as China's interest in Africa's natural resources, support for its "One China" policy and support at international fora, to mention just a few. Knowing what China "really" wants from Africa apart from the "known-knowns" will enable the continent position itself well to benefit from this current engagement with China.

It is further suggested in this chapter that African leaders and policy makers effectively harness the benefits that will accrue to the continent from China's current investment in Africa. They should equally take advantage of China's non-interference and no-conditionality policies to use the aid and investment in sectors and projects that will contribute to growth and development on the continent. The directing of investment to the infrastructure sector is an example in the right direction. Finally, they should insist on technology transfer and skills training in current and future Chinese projects on the continent to ensure the sustainability of the projects once they have been completed and the Chinese have left.

Notes

1 Swain, Jon (2008), "Africa, China's new frontier," *The Sunday Times*, February 10th, 2008, http://www.thesundaytimes.co.uk/sto/news/world_news/article80075.ece.
2 This was an act signed into law by President Chester Arthur on May 6th, 1882, prohibiting all immigration of Chinese labourers to the US.
3 KPMG (2014), "Manufacturing in Africa: Sector Report," https://www.kpmg.com/Africa/en/IssuesAndInsights/Articles-Publications/General-Industries-Publications/Documents/Manufacturing%20sector%20report%202015.pdf (accessed 28/1/16).
4 Fantu Cheru, "Decoding the evolving China–Africa relations," http://www.cebri.org/midia/documentos/eventos_03_ucla_paper9.pdf.
5 WIPO, "Overview of Contractual Agreements for the transfers of technology," http://www.wipo.int/export/sites/www/sme/en/documents/pdf/technology_transfer.pdf.

9 China's Foray into Africa

Impact on Interests of External Players?

9.1 Introduction

China's foray into Africa is not sitting well with Africa's traditional trading partners and some of its former colonial masters, who have always believed, rather arrogantly, that Africa is their *chasse gardée* (hunting ground). Most of these Western countries and former colonial masters, some believe, are thus lashing out at China out of frustration or in an effort to stop its rapid expansion in its engagement with Africa. For example, in July 2005, US congressman Christopher Smith said, "China is playing an increasingly influential role on the continent of Africa, and there is concern that the Chinese intend to aid and abet African dictators, to gain a stranglehold on precious African natural resources, and undo much of the progress that has been made in democracy and governance in the last 15 years in African nations," (Naidu and Davis, 2006).

Similarly, US secretary of state in the first Obama administration, Hillary Clinton (currently a presidential candidate for the Democratic Party) warned during a June 2011 visit to Africa about a creeping "new Colonialism" in Africa. In Lusaka, Zambia, she said, "we saw that during colonial times, it is easy to come in, take out natural resources, pay off leaders and leave. And you don't leave much behind for the people who are there. We don't want to see a new Colonialism in Africa" (Lee, 2011). Although the former US secretary of state did not directly mention China in her speech, it was obvious that the speech was directed at China. In fact, she also mentioned in Lusaka that US diplomats in Africa have been asked to provide Washington with assessments of Chinese projects in the countries to which they are assigned. The Chinese state media, *Xinhua*, lashed out at Mrs. Clinton about her comments. The paper said that Mrs. Clinton's comments were "cheap shots" and a "plot to sow discord between China and Africa." The paper also added that Mrs. Clinton's trip was part of a hidden agenda, "aimed at least partly at discrediting China's engagement with the continent and curbing China's influence there," (Manson, 2002). It is very clear that the US is not willing to stand by and watch China's influence grow on the continent. According to William Fitzgerald, US deputy assistant secretary for African Affairs, "China's role as the preferred trade and investment partner for most African countries can no longer be ignored" (Langeni, 2010).

The European Union (EU) is equally not sitting idly and watching China to take over in their former colonies. China's increase foray into Africa and its expanding influence on the continent has jolted the EU into action to protect their interests there. In a policy paper published by the EU in 2007, the commission said that it was going to launch an enhanced "partnership of equals" with African countries, ranging from trade to aid, to meet a rise in Chinese influence in its former colonies. The policy paper added, "if the EU wants to remain a privileged partner and make the most of its relations with Africa, it must be willing to reinforce, and in some areas reinvest, in the relationship"; it added, "the nature of the relationship will go beyond the donor–recipient relationship of the past and reflect a political partnership of equals" (Mark, 2007). I would add that the relationship should also move away from the old paternalistic approach whereby the Europeans think they know Africa better than the Africans. Hence, they engage in "lecturing" Africans and their leaders about how to grow their economies, qualifying any support for such efforts with conditionalities. This so called "partnership of equals," in my opinion, should entail listening to Africans more than "lecturing" them all the time.

This brief summary of US and European sentiments concerning China's foray into Africa points to the perceived and the real impact that it will have on the economic and political interests of external players. Let us now look at this issue in detail.

9.2 China's Foray into Africa and the Increased Competition for Africa's Resources

China's current investment in Africa is because of Africa's natural resources. Its number one interest is in Africa's natural resources, of which the continent has plenty, to fuel China's growth. However, China's foray into Africa is also due to other interests, as elaborated on in Chapter 4 of this book. China used to be one of the fastest growing economies in the world, and its economy has been growing between 8 and 9 percent per annum for the last two decades. Even though the economy is slowing down at the time of writing, it still needs resources to sustain its economic growth. China's non-interventionist approach in Africa has allowed it to engage with Africa in trade and investment without getting involved in Africa's internal affairs. African leaders like that. The following comments by President Museveni of Uganda are a testimony to this:

> the Western ruling groups are conceited, full of themselves, ignorant of our conditions, and they make other people's business their business, while the Chinese just deal with you who represent your country, and they represent their own interest and you just do business.
>
> (Taylor et al., 2012)

For example, while the West's aid and loans to Africa for its development efforts often come with conditionalities, China's do not. Some of the main targets or countries that China invests in have been in oil from Sudan, Angola, Equatorial Guinea, Gabon and Nigeria. China also targets platinum from Zimbabwe, copper from Zambia, iron ore from South Africa and tropical timber from Congo-Brazzaville (Farndon, 2007; van de Looy, 2006).

China's foray into Africa has been observed to have heightened the competition for Africa's natural resources. Previously, that was not the case. Africa's traditional trade and investment partners and indeed the international organisations those partners control have in the past treated Africa with disdain. They devised numerous strategies to acquire African resources on the cheap, including the use of numerous conditionalities, sanctions or strict entry requirements for African resources or products into their markets. Their aid is often "tied-aid," and they drag their feet on investing in long-term infrastructure projects that will bring growth and development to the African people. They mostly believe in short-term, less risky investments, because they regard investing in Africa as risky. Thus, with China willing to go to any length to ensure that its resource needs for today and tomorrow are met, it has heightened the stakes in the competition for Africa's natural resources between it and the West. According to Sarah Raine in her book *China's African Challenges*, competition from China has had the effect of increasing the West's attention to its own interest in Africa's resources and how it pursues them – an interest that had to some extent previously been taken for granted.

One can understand the anxiety amongst external players in China's foray into Africa if we look at oil as an example. Like China, the US imports a lot of resources from Africa. For example, in 2007, oil accounted for 80 percent of all US imports from Sub-Saharan Africa. One of the reasons why US interest in African oil has peaked is because of its anxiety about depending on Middle Eastern oil due to the turbulent nature of the region. Hence, to ensure US energy security, access to African oil must be factored into US long-term strategy (Raine, 2009). Let's now look at the impact on the interest of specific external players in China's current engagement with Africa.

9.3 Impact on America Interest in Africa

China's foray into Africa and its increasing influence in the region has not gone down well with Africa's former colonial masters; neither has it gone down well with the Americans. A Pew Research Center survey of six major African countries – Kenya, South Africa, Uganda, Nigeria, Senegal and Ghana in Questions 78 and 79 – asking which country, the US or China, has a great deal or a fair amount of influence on their respective countries, offered the following responses: in Ghana, 65 percent said the US and 58 percent said China; in Senegal, 66 percent said the US and 59 percent said China[1]; in Nigeria, 69 percent said the US and 67 percent said China; in Uganda, 70 percent said the US and 54 percent said China; in South Africa, 77 percent said the US and 71 percent said China; in Kenya, 85 percent said the US and 78 percent said China. The percentages at that time the survey was taken were too close, with China closing in on the US If the same survey was to be undertaken today, China's influence in some of these countries would surpass that of the US This then points to the fact that China's foray into Africa and its attendant investment and aid programmes, which do not come with conditionalities or interference in Africa's internal affairs, unlike those of the US, are some of the reasons accounting for this increase in its influence. Let us look at some of these reasons in detail.

What could be some of the reasons why the US is losing influence in Africa? First, African leaders and policy makers know that, historically, the continent has always remained on the periphery of US foreign affairs. It is usually only when security concerns flare up that will affect US interests on the continent that Africa really matters to the US Furthermore, African countries see US foreign direct investment (FDI) to Africa has mostly hovered around 2 percent of the overall US FDI outflows every year. Even when there are such investments, they come with strings and conditionalities, and they are usually made through the traditional model of using the World Bank and the International Monetary Fund (IMF) in their dispensation. The Chinese, meanwhile, have surpassed the US as they have poured billions of dollars in investments into African infrastructure. They have replaced the US as Africa's largest trading partner. African leaders also like the idea that the Chinese do not interfere in their internal political affairs. The opposite is the case with the US, and previously, the Central Intelligence Agency (CIA) has been involved in the overthrow of some African political leaders, like Kwame Nkrumah and Patrice Lumumba (Stockwell, 1978; Devlin, 2008). Finally, African leaders do not like been preached to about the rule of law, human rights, reforms and corruption by the US any time they need help from the US. All these are some of the reasons contributing to the US losing influence in Africa.

During the era of the Clinton administration, the US commerce secretary, the late Ron Brown, said on the website of the organisation that "the United States would no longer concede the African market to former colonial masters" (Campbell, 2008). If it was not willing to do so to Africa's colonial masters, it was definitely not willing to do so to China. In fact, a former US deputy assistant secretary of state for African affairs, William Fitzgerald, said that, "China's role as a preferred trade and investment partner for most African countries can no longer be ignored" (Langeni, 2010). The US has thus formulated a new strategy to re-engage with Africa to regain lost ground.

Why such a change of heart? After all, wasn't it due to the US–Soviet rivalry during the era of the Cold War that led to numerous wars in Angola, Mozambique, Ethiopia, the former Zaire (DRC) and other parts of Africa, and saw the overthrow of African heads of state who would not side with the American camp? Didn't this rivalry create and support corrupt regimes and leadership in Africa that almost bankrupted their economies? (Chin-Hao, 2008). The change of heart is due to the US national interest. This is informed by concerns about global energy, regional security, counter-terrorism, and public health as well as political influence. For example, in 2012, 13 percent of U.S oil imports came from Sub-Saharan Africa (SSA) and countries such as Nigeria and Angola supplied a bulk of it. But Africa has other minerals that the US is interested in to supply some of its high technology industries – minerals such as uranium, tantalum, and titanium, to mention just a few.

Furthermore, the U.S has also had a change of heart towards Africa because of security concerns and its fight against terrorism. Since the 9/11 attacks on the US; the August 1998 Al Qaeda–linked attacks on the US embassies in Kenya and Tanzania and the subsequent attacks on Israeli tourists in Mombasa, Kenya, in November 2002; and current terrorist attacks in the region, its military engagement with Africa has expanded substantially. The establishment in 2002 of a US base in Djibouti, the Joint Task Force Horn of Africa Command, is a case in point. In 2003, a US$100 million United States–East Africa Counter-Terrorism Initiative (EACTI) was launched to provide training and equipment to states in the region, particularly Kenya and Ethiopia. Also, in 2005, a US$500 million 5-year Trans-Sahara Counter-Terrorism Initiative (TSCTI) was launched to build the capacities of the following African countries: Algeria, Chad, Ghana, Mali, Morocco, Niger, Nigeria, Mauritania and Tunisia. This initiative was to help these countries patrol their respective borders and intercept any terrorist groups intending to cross their borders (Adebajo, 2008).

Other security initiatives put in place were the Gulf of Guinea Maritime Security Initiative, developed in the late 2007; and the ambitious Horn of Africa Counter-Terrorism programme. It was also announced in February 2007 that the US was looking for a location in Africa to establish a new US African Command (AFRICOM) to oversee and coordinate US military-related activities on the continent (Chin-Hao, 2008). This later proposal by the US has been difficult to implement as no African country was willing to accept the offer to host AFRICOM. These few examples illustrate why the US had a change of heart towards Africa, specifically as it pertains to its strategy when it comes to regional security and counter-terrorism concerns.

When it comes to public health, the US has played its part in alleviating the HIV/Aids epidemic in Africa. In a speech in Accra on July 10th, 2009, President Obama, speaking about how the US will help strengthen public health services in Africa, said, "in recent times, enormous progress has been made in parts of Africa. Far more people are living productively with HIV/Aids, and getting the drugs they need. But too many still die from the diseases that shouldn't kill them" (Warren, 2009). Under the George Walker Bush administration, the US made a substantive contribution to the fight against global Aids. Bush set up the President's Emergency Plan for Aids Relief (PEPFAR), which was a US$9 billion, 5-year commitment between 2004 and 2008, targeting 15 of the most heavily affected countries in the world. Of these, 12 were in Africa: Botswana, Cote d'Ivoire, Ethiopia, Kenya, Mozambique, Namibia, Nigeria, Rwanda, South Africa, Tanzania, Uganda and Zambia (Copson, 2007; Adebajo, 2008). America's public health policy towards

Africa should go beyond its support for HIV/Aids to malaria, tuberculosis and mother/child care. Another important area that is equally damaging to the public healthcare system in Africa is the keeping of unsafe drugs off the market. African governments must do their part, but the US must also do its part in keeping unsafe drugs off the African market.

A good example is the polio vaccine. There are two types of the polio vaccine currently used in Africa. The safest, according to experts, is the injectable one, which is made from a killed version of the virus. Unfortunately, this is very expensive. The second type is made from a modified live virus. This second type is administered orally. Now and then, the active virus in the oral polio vaccine can cause polio in children, as it can often mutate into a dangerous new strain (Warren, 2009). The US Food and Drug Administration should remove this vaccine or stop it being shipped to Africa. All these are some of the ways the US can re-engage Africa to re-assert its influence due to the Chinese threat.

China's foray into Africa and its growing influence on the continent will impact US interests in the area of US trade with Africa, the US need for strategic minerals for its high-technology industries, its national security concerns with the rise in terrorism after 9/11 and its security initiatives in Africa, to mention just a few are driving this new engagement. Thus, it is imperative that the US not allow China to counter its influence and interest in Africa without an appropriate response. The appropriateness of the response is yet to be seen. Africans had felt that because President Obama's father is an African, perhaps his administration would have been more understanding of Africa's developmental challenges and condition. There was a general feeling that he would do a lot for Africa. Unfortunately, they were disappointed. Most Africans are hard pressed to point to Obama's achievements in Africa. In fact, his predecessor George Bush is seen by Africans to have done more for Africa than Obama. Hopefully, the next American president will change this picture; if not, the US will continue to lose influence in Africa as the Chinese continue to grow their influence through their investment and aid.

9.4 Impact on European Interest in Africa

The relations between Africa and Europe go away back to era of the slave trade. However, in this book and for the purpose of this chapter, the Berlin Conference of 1884–1885 will be our starting point in terms of African–European relations. It was at the Berlin Conference that the partition of Africa took place, during which the continent was carved out like a quilt, with each European country claiming to own certain African countries. This enabled these European countries to exploit Africa's natural resources for the growth of their economies to the detriment of African ones. Part of Africa's developmental challenges today are due to this partitioning and the owning of African countries by European countries. Colonialism also enabled the colonial masters to introduce a cash crop and a one-crop economy which has bedevilled most African countries today. Most of the exports from these countries are single-crop exports. Another important impact of colonialism is the lack of industrialization of African countries. The colonial masters exported primary products to Europe and imported finished or manufactured goods to the colonies. These kinds of economic relations characterized Africa and it colonial masters. These few examples illustrate the devastating impact of colonialism on Africa.

Fast-forward to the era of the Cold War. During this period, Europe was certain and resolute in making sure that African countries did not fall like dominoes into the Soviet camp. The Europeans were referring to the domino theory that was prominent from the 1950s to the 1980s. The theory speculated that if one country in a region came under the influence of communism, then the surrounding countries would become communist, falling like dominoes into the communist camp. The interest of these European countries was therefore not in building sustainable and prosperous African economies. By the 1980s, according to Tull (2008), the EU restricted its relations with Africa largely to development policies. Throughout the 1980s, Europe discharged its responsibilities to Africa to the Bretton Woods institutions. According to Tull (2008), this was another way for it to support structural adjustment policies towards Africa. The devastating consequence of such policies on the continent cannot be emphasized enough.

In the 1990s, because of the growth in economies and opportunities in Asia and because of the enlargement of the EU to include countries from Eastern Europe, Africa's importance to Europe was mostly lost. Africa was regarded in most European capitals as a "burden," so to speak. What was left of this interest in Africa was directed mostly by European countries "lecturing" Africans and African countries, insisting that they become democratic and that they should respect human rights, yet most of the issues pertaining to Africa's socio-economic development fell of the radar of Europe at that time (Tull, 2008). By the mid-1990s, European policy towards Africa took another turn. This was a time when Africa was plagued by very many conflicts and challenges. The root of most of these conflicts can be traced back to colonialism. It was at this time that the Rwanda genocide occurred. Sadly, the Europeans were also absent during this crucial time when Africa needed them. Africa was left to fend for itself, and perhaps the hope was that the United Nations could supplement Africa's efforts as the Europeans were conveniently absent. In these dark days in Africa, even France, one of the former colonial masters, wanted to disengage from Africa (Kroslak, 2004). Africans have not forgotten this abandonment in their time of need.

With the foray of China into Africa, suddenly Europe has re-discovered and developed a renewed interest in Africa, the same Africa that one of the European magazines once described as the "hopeless continent" (*Economist*, 2000). This "new interest" in Africa by the Europeans is viewed with suspicion by many African countries. They are asking each other, what does Europe want? Certainly, this "re-discovery" of Africa by Europe would not have happened without the arrival of China on the African scene. Thus, in a rush to protect their interest in Africa, in late 2005 the EU adopted an African strategy, which has as its goal to give the EU a comprehensive, integrated and long-term framework for its relations with the African continent (Council of the European Union, 2005). Some have observed that even the recent EU policies toward Africa are more about projecting the international ambitions and interest, values and policies of the E. U. rather than its objectives in Africa (Tull, 2008).

Thus, while the Europeans are dawdling, the Chinese are busy with their engagement and investment in Africa. For example, the Chinese are busy occupying and taking over areas abandoned by Western interests and businesses. These include infrastructure, dams and manufacturing projects in Africa. The Chinese have increased their aid to Africa and have forgiven some African debt, as elaborated on elsewhere in this book. The Chinese are now the largest trading partner with Africa and they are positioning themselves to benefit from Africa's large numbers at the U.N. to bolster their international interest and relevance.

Furthermore, African leaders like the idea of China's non-interference in the internal affairs of their respective countries when it comes to aid or investments. They also like the idea that the Chinese can make quick decisions on funding for African projects, unlike the West, as well as the speed at which they complete those projects. African leaders also tend to resent the paternalistic attitude of Western Countries towards them. This warped idea in the West that it is their responsibility to "change" a "backward Africa" to be like them is much resented in modern-day Africa. The Chinese have no such illusions. No wonder their influence is growing in the region to the detriment of the Europeans.

Thus, whatever renewed interest Europe has in Africa is more of a reflex, triggered in the most part by China's current engagement with Africa. The Chinese are also seriously taking advantage of Europe's own actions and its contradictory policies towards Africa. This has caused some of the challenges Europe is facing vis-à-vis China's foray into Africa. For example, Europe's stated goals, like the eradication of poverty, promoting democracy and human rights and security in Africa, simply do not square with its narrower interests such as propping up its own "security" (in terms of migration) or imposing trade agreements on Africa and maintaining agricultural subsidies, which are hurting African countries and impacting their growth (Tull, 2008). These are all cases in point that work against Europe's influence and interests in Africa.

Thus China's foray into Africa is a welcome relief to African countries vis-à-vis European hypocrisy, as Africans see it. Unless Europe's policies towards Africa move away from such perceived hypocrisy to reflect the realities on the ground in Africa, and unless they become pragmatic enough, Europe stands to lose more ground to China in its current foray into Africa. Moving forward, Europe can change this picture. It needs to re-engage Africa just as the Chinese are doing and invest in Africa in the long term. Trade is another area in which Europe can re-engage Africa. According to Eurostat figures, the whole of EU member states' trade with Africa in 2014, for example, represented less than 4 percent of their total worldwide trade. Increased trade with Africa will go a long way to lifting most of its people out of poverty as well as contributing to its sustainable growth and development. The increased trade between China and Africa is an example, and Europeans can learn a lot from their Chinese counterparts in their re-engagement efforts with African countries.

9.5 Impact on Interest of Asian Countries in Africa

About 50 years ago, in 1955, 29 Asian and African countries met in Indonesia under the invitation of the late Sukarno, a former President of Indonesia. This meeting was called the Bandung Conference as it was held in Bandung. It was an effort on the part of the newly independent African and Asian countries to agree on the non-alignment to the Eastern or Western blocs during the Cold War era. But it was also a collective effort by these countries to develop a way in which to trade with each other. The Chinese delegation was well represented at the Bandung Conference. It was led by the premier and foreign minister Zhou Enlai. The members of his delegation were composed of Vice-Premier Chen Yi, Minister of Foreign Trade Ye Jizhuang, Vice Foreign Minister Zhang Hanfu and Chinese Ambassador to Indonesia Huang Zhen. At the conference, Zhou said,

> there exists common ground among the Asian and African countries the basis of which is that the overwhelming number of Asian and African countries and their peoples have suffered and are still suffering from the calamities of colonialism. All the Asian and African countries gained their independence from colonial rule, whether they are led by the communist or nationalists. We should seek to understand each other and respect each other, sympathize with and support one another and the Five Principles of Peaceful Co-Existence may completely serve as a basis for us to establish relations of friendship and cooperation and good neighborliness.[2]

It is based on these long established relations between Africa and Asia that the recent foray of China into Africa is analysed.

If one takes trade, for example, Thailand's trade with Africa is put at US$11.6 billion, Indonesia's at US$10.7 billion and Singapore's at US$9.5 billion (Hutt, 2014). It is even reported that Malaysia's investment in Africa is put at US$50 billion. So what are some of the impacts on the interests of Asian countries with China's aggressive foray into Africa? According to Gera (2012), China's aggressive foray into African markets with cheap trade credits backed by Chinese government support could have an impact on Asian countries' trade and investment in Africa, particularly, India's trade and investment in Africa. It will dim some of India's age-old traditional ties with African countries. Because of the fact that most of Chinese investments are on quite favourable terms, the recipient nations are obviously more obliged and favourable to Chinese than others (Gera, 2012). The same can be said for the impact on trade between other Association of Southeast Asian Nations (ASEAN) countries and Africa.

Currently, there are over 200 ASEAN companies operating in Africa, and combined they are one of the largest investors in Africa. These companies from ASEANs operating in Africa are mostly in agribusiness, manufacturing, oil and gas and urban development. Most of these companies will not be able to compete with China in sectors that require huge capital like infrastructure projects and will thus have to carve a niche for themselves in order to survive their competition with China in Africa. Olam International, a Singaporean agribusiness company, is a case in point. It has been operating in Africa for 25 years and that is its niche (Hutt, 2014). It has large cashew processing centres in Africa in Nigeria, Mozambique and Tanzania.

Japan and China's relations have been strained for some time now over the refusal of Japan to acknowledge its wartime past to the satisfaction of China. The relations between China and Japan are also frosty over the claims they both lay on some uninhabited rocky islands in the East China Sea, known as Senkaku by the Japanese and Diayu by the Chinese. China's foray into and investment in Africa has seen this rivalry been played out on the continent. The Japanese, for a long time, due to complacency, had in a way ceded their interest in Africa. This has enabled China to build up a huge political and economic capital as well as influence in the region. Japan is now playing catch-up, so to speak. Japanese prime minister Shinz Abe has announced a major shift in his country's strategy towards Africa. Before the prime minister left for a three-nation tour in SSA – the Ivory Coast, Mozambique and Ethiopia – in 2014, Mr. Abe remarked that "Africa is a frontier for Japan's diplomacy" (York, 2014). This visit was the first for any sitting Japanese prime minister in eight years.

Better late than never, Mr. Abe announced US$14 billion in Japanese trade and aid to Africa and has announced a huge Japanese development assistance programme to Africa at the Sixth Tokyo International Conference on African Development (TICAD), held in Nairobi, Kenya, in August 2016. This commitment is viewed by some as a way of countering the recent announcements by Xi Jinping of China at the sixth triennial Forum on China–Africa Cooperation (FOCAC), where he promised US$60 billion in financial support to the whole continent. President Jinping's aid package includes US$35 billion in preferential loans and export credit lines, US$5 billion in grants, US$15 billion to the China–Africa Fund and US$5 billion in loans to small and medium-sized enterprises (SMEs).[3]

Japan has lagged behind in this race and will find it hard to catch up. Most of Japan's engagement with Africa has been as an aid donor. In 2013, it promised US$23 billion to support the private and public sector in Africa for 5 years. Most African countries are beginning to develop a lukewarm attitude towards aid and are more concerned with developing business partnerships, on which the Chinese are more focused in Africa. So why are the Japanese now playing "catch-up" in their renewed engagement with Africa? The first reason is that

Japan is vying to become a permanent member of the U.N. Security Council. Hence its current re-engagement with and aid to African countries is to woo them to consider voting for it for the U.N. Security Council seat. Japan's strategy is also to find a way to help Japanese businesses on the continent. Currently, there are very few Japanese businesses invested in Africa as China is. Japan thus sees Africa as the last major growth market in the world, and its goal is to get its businesses to go in there and offer high-quality products and services as well as high-quality infrastructure and technology as alternatives to Chinese ones.

China's current engagement with Africa has an impact on Asian countries, mostly in the area of trade. Most Asian countries do not have the support of the deep pockets of the Chinese. The fact that China supports its state-owned enterprises (SOEs) with cheap credits and huge capital to undertake infrastructure and other capital intensive projects puts these countries at a disadvantage. Hence, they need to find niche markets in Africa to survive. Japan is also interested in Africa (apart from trade) for the support it can give to its quest for a seat on the U.N. Security Council. China's current engagement with Africa does indeed have an impact on the interests of Asian countries on the continent.

9.6 Impact on the Interests of International Organisations Operating in Africa

China's foray into Africa also has an impact on the interests of international organisations operating in Africa. The first impact concerns the fact that Chinese influence in Africa is superseding that of international organisations in the continent. For example, China's Africa agenda focuses on what is termed *the Beijing Consensus*. Some of the characteristics of this model, according to Zhang (2006), include the replacement of trust in the free market for economic growth with more robust state involvement in the development process, the absence of political liberalisation and the involvement of a strong leading role by the ruling political party in the development process.

According to Zhang, the features of the Beijing Consensus include a down-to-earth strategy for modernisation with a focus on meeting the most pressing needs of the people; thus its focus is that people matter. This focus dovetails well with Africa's communalistic ethos, where people matter. Furthermore, the model believes in constant experimentation, where all changes go through a process of trial and error on a small scale, and when they work, they are applied elsewhere. The model also believes in gradual reform rather than the big bang, shock-therapy, neo-liberal kind. The model works through existing imperfect institutions while gradually reforming them and re-orienting them to serve modernisation. The Beijing Consensus model also believes in a strong developmental state that is capable of shaping national consensus on modernisation and ensuring overall political and macroeconomic stability. Other aspects of the model include selective learning, even from the neoliberal American model; and the correct sequencing of priorities (Zhang, 2006).

Zhang (2006) argues that this model is more appealing to African countries than the Western neo-liberal model (the *Washington Consensus*), which emphasis the IMF-designed Structural Adjustment Programmes. The Washington Consensus model, according to Zhang, is largely ideologically driven, focusing on mass democratization with little regard for local conditions, and the thinking that Western institutions, when introduced to Africa, will automatically take root. The model often imposes liberalisation before safety nets, privatisation before regulatory frameworks are put in place, and democratisation before a culture of political tolerance and rule of law is established. The end results have often been devastating (Zhang, 2006).

Another impact of China's engagement with Africa is that even though its overall aid budget is still less than what the large institutions in the West can provide, China is increasingly in a position to displace multilateral organizations as a source of development aid. This is because of the speed and competence with which the Chinese negotiate and execute their development programmes compared to multilateral organisations. Furthermore, most multilateral aid programmes are bogged down in bureaucracy and persistent delays, and in some cases they are never completed. African countries, therefore, tend to see China's aid and execution of development programmes as appealing. Their aid programmes also do not entail any interference in the internal affairs of these countries and do not come with any conditions. China's aid program in Africa, for example, has already exceeded that of the World Bank (Alden, 2009).

9.7 Conclusion

China's current foray into and engagement with Africa is definitely not going down well with external players who also have interests in Africa. The chapter looked at such an impact on American interests. First, China's influence on the continent is growing tremendously and may overtake that of the US in Africa. It could also impact the US demand for strategic minerals in Africa. This, along with US security interests after the 9/11 attacks, have seen it renew its interests in and engagement with Africa.

China's foray into Africa also has an impact on European interests in the region. Historically, most African countries were former colonies of Europe. Europeans at certain stages in Africa's history directed the running of their colonies from the metropole and, to some extent, they still do today. Thus, there is nostalgia on the part of these former colonial masters to see China enter their former spheres of influence. They also have interests in Africa's natural resources as well as a market for its finished manufactured products. With China's current foray into and investment in Africa, Africans are gravitating more towards China. The impact on European investment, trade and influence in their former colonies cannot be emphasised enough. Europe is now trying to re-engage Africa due to the competition from China.

Asian countries are also impacted due to China's foray into Africa. Even though they are heavily invested in Africa, they find it difficult to compete with the Chinese as the latter have deep pockets and are willing to fund projects at low interest rates that most Asian companies cannot afford. Hence, they lose business to their Chinese counterparts. Most of the current impact of China's foray into Africa as it pertains to Asian countries is in the area of trade. Finally, another impact of China's current engagement with Africa is on international organisations such as the World Bank/IMF operating in Africa. One of the major differences is that the Chinese do not interfere in the internal affairs of African countries and do not attach conditionalities to their aid or investment. The opposite is the case with the World Bank/IMF. African countries thus tend to look to China for aid and investment, ignoring the World Bank/IMF and indeed other international organisations. It thus impacts the latter's mandate and operations.

Notes

1 Kate Simmons, "US, China compete to woo Africa," Pew Research Center, www. pwresearch.org/fact_tank/2014/08/04/u-s-china-compete-to-woo-africa.
2 Ministry of Foreign Affairs of the Peoples Republic of China, "The Asia-African Conference," http://www.fmprc.gov.cn/mfa_eng/ziliao_665539/3602_665543/3604_665547/t18044.shtml (accessed 2/22/16).
3 John Aglionby, "Tokyo takes on Beijing in Africa, claiming quality over speed," *Financial Times*, January 11, 2016, http://www.ft.com/cms/s/2/564df09e-824a-11e5-a01c-8650859a4767.html#axzz4GqLQSGG7 (accessed 18/2/16).

10 China and Africa

The Way Forward and Prospects for the Future

10.1 Introduction

There is an African proverb that says that, "when the blind carry the crippled, they will all go far" (Abdulai, 2000). This proverb depicts the epitome of collaboration, partnership and working together to capitalise on each other's strengths for mutual benefit. The current China–Africa relationship falls into this category. China needs Africa in numerous ways if it is to continuously grow and to further its international ambitions, and Africa can help it in this regard. Africa also needs China for its growth and development efforts, and China is willing and able to help Africa in this regard. China knows that African countries have the natural resources it needs to fuel its growth as these countries are the majority at the United Nations (U.N.) and in other international organisations whose support it will need from time to support its international agenda and positions. This new strategic partnership was defined elegantly by former President Hu Jintao in his address to the Nigerian National Assembly in 2006, when he said, "Africa has rich resources and market potentials, and whereas China has available effective practices and practical know-how it has gained in the course of modernisation."[1] Thus Chinese–African collaboration from Hu's perspective will be a formidable partnership that will provide a win–win situation for both partners.

Similarly, Jiang Zemin, the former Chinese president, speaking at the opening of the first China–Africa Co-operation Forum in Beijing in 2000, said, "China is the largest developing country in the world and Africa is the continent with the largest number of developing countries....China and Africa are faced with both historical opportunities for greater development and unprecedented challenges" (Muekalia, 2004). This thus speaks to a symbiotic relationship as opposed to the exploitative one often touted by China's critics. The tangible results have been the win–win achievements that have accrued to Africa and China so far. So what is the way forward for China and Africa? This way forward is encapsulated in Zhou Enlai's proclamation at the 1955 Bandung conference, *qiu tong cun yi*, meaning seeking communalities and avoiding differences. Africa and China should seek communalities and avoid differences in their current engagement, focusing on win–win propositions.

The following, therefore, are some proposals to guide this way forward for both partners, constantly revisiting the well of renewal, forging stronger partnerships at international fora, increasing cultural exchange, focusing more on trade and investments than on handouts and undertaking other bilateral methods to strengthen the relationship.

10.2 Constantly Visiting the Well of Renewal

First, any relationship needs constant nurturing to grow and succeed, and that between China and Africa is no exception. Hence the leadership of China and Africa must constantly revisit the well of renewal, so to speak, to constantly enhance their relationship in a fast-moving and dynamic global environment where events of kaleidoscopic proportions can put a damper on the relationship. Consequently, the numerous visits by Chinese leaders to Africa and vice versa should be encouraged and maintained. So also should the numerous trade and cooperation meetings. The exchange of students and the sending of Chinese volunteers and peace keepers to Africa are all steps in the right direction in an effort to further enhance this relationship.

Each partner must be vigilant not to take the other for granted. China should be particularly careful not to become smug and develop a patronizing attitude towards Africans, akin to what they have witnessed from their previous colonial masters. In fact, the Chinese must make sure that they do not through their actions, either by omission or commission, subscribe to this notion that they are the "new colonialists." It will create resentment and could affect the relationship between the two. The Chinese authorities should check the "racist" and despicable behaviour of some of their nationals that have settled in Africa in terms of their disrespect for their African hosts in some countries. If left to persist, it could drive a wedge between China and Africa. Mention should be made that the Chinese government is waking up to these criticisms. They are making it clear that their relationship with Africa is about win–win and that they do not have any neo-colonialist tendencies. As regards the behaviour of some Chinese migrants in Africa, the Chinese authorities see it as "growing pains" in terms of the China–Africa relationship and hope to work with African governments to solve it.

Neither should African countries become complacent and expect China to do for Africans what they can do for themselves or abuse the relationship by taking China for granted. Indeed, Africans will lose respect and credibility if they expect China to do everything for them. Any undue reliance on China by Africans can become "a feel-good opium" whose numbing effect can rob Africans of effort and the "can-do" attitude needed for its sustainable growth and development. Africans must apply effort to understanding that whatever projects that are being undertaken on the continent by the Chinese are only a complement to their own independent efforts to grow and develop. The Forum on China–Africa Cooperation (FOCAC) should be continuously enhanced to cooperate with the African Union (A.U.) and other sub-regional organisations on the continent to strengthen collective dialogue and broaden the consensus between the two partners as well expand their common interests and deepen their relations. In this respect, China's support of the A.U. with a US$2 million donation to support the organisation's peace and security efforts is laudable. Furthermore, the US$100 million also earmarked by President Xi Jinping to support the African Standby Force and other peace-keeping operations in Africa at FOCAC 2015, held in South Africa, is equally laudable. All these gestures will go a long way to contributing to the building of a solid China–Africa relationship moving forward.

In terms of enhancing China–Africa relations, this author has made an interesting observation that is worth mentioning. Since the 1990s, Chinese foreign ministers have always paid annual visits to Africa to enhance the relationship between China and Africa. For example, current Chinese foreign minister Wang Yi paid visits to Africa in 2014 and 2015. In 2009, the Chinese foreign minister at that time, Yang Jiechi, visited Uganda, Rwanda, Malawi and South Africa. In 2008, Yang visited South Africa, the Democratic Republic of the Congo (DRC), Burundi and Ethiopia. In 2007, the Chinese foreign minister at that time, Li Zhaoxing, visited Equatorial Guinea, Guinea-Bissau, Chad, Benin, Central African Republic, Eritrea and Mozambique (Zhu, 2010). It has also been observed that Chinese presidents and their premiers also regularly visit Africa. All these visits are to enhance the China–Africa relationship. Such efforts are laudable and should be reciprocated by African leaders.

10.3 Forging Stronger Partnerships at International Fora

Furthermore, since China's entry into the United Nations (U.N.) with the support of votes by African countries in October 1971 and the subsequent support by China for the failed bid by Salim Salim of Tanzania to be the secretary general of the U.N. in 1981, a new partnership to cooperate on international issues and affairs of mutual benefit to China and Africa was born. More than ever, in a constantly changing international environment with its numerous challenges, China and Africa need to forge an even stronger partnership to support each other at international fora on issues pertaining to their development. For example, they must support each other and speak with one voice with other partners from the south to bring about reforms of the Bretton Woods institutions and the U.N. Security Council. China and Africa should also coordinate and support each other in multilateral fields. China, with its position as a permanent member of the U.N. Security Council, should always stand by African countries as well as supporting the proposals and positions of the African Union at international fora. The two partners should also consult and cooperate with each other on issues within the U.N. system and in other international organisations.

Furthermore, China and Africa should work together to alleviate the fear and anxieties on the part of the West of seeing China as a competitor for political, economic and social influence in Africa. China and Africa should also work together to persuade the West, and indeed the international community, to work together with China and Africa on issues of human and economic development pertaining to Africa. By working together, they will benefit by exploiting the growing intersection of mutual interests between them.

Another area that China and Africa need to cooperate more on moving forward is in the area of health. This cooperation should focus on, but should not be limited to, HIV, malaria, reproductive health, human resources and access to vaccines and commodities. It should also focus on south–south cooperation initiatives on health and the sharing of experiences and challenges as well as developing solutions together on health issues. Other areas of cooperation should include sharing best practices on how to guarantee safe medical products, how to ensure adequate capacity in health institutions and strengthening health systems. The 2-day China–Africa Health Cooperation meeting held in Gaborone, Botswana, on 6th and 7th May 2013 to strengthen collaboration in health development and share knowledge and technology is a step in the right direction. The collaborative efforts of China and Africa to improve health conditions in Africa moving forward should be enhanced. The current assistance of China in building hospitals in Africa, sending medical teams to Africa and providing medicines and medical supplies all go a long way to enhancing this relationship.

Finally, China and Africa should consider forging partnerships with non-governmental organisations (NGOs), Western countries and even the US to tackle some of the pressing issues of development in Africa. China and Africa cannot go it alone all the time. Some specific areas for research include better food production and collaboration to deal with epidemics like Ebola, which killed so many people in Liberia, Sierra Leone and Guinea. In the fight against Ebola in West Africa, China should be commended in its efforts to fight the pandemic and its contributions to the post-Ebola construction efforts of countries affected by the virus. Apart from making donations directly to the countries affected, China also donated to the U.N., the A.U., the World Health Organisation (WHO) and other international organisations that came together to fight the virus. China was the first country to provide aid to Ebola-hit countries, and by November 2014, China had offered humanitarian assistance to the tune of US$113.77 million to the affected countries. It also sent four rounds of thousands of medical personnel to the Ebola-hit countries.

For example, China donated a P3-level biolab to Sierra Leone, provided food aid to Ebola-hit Liberia, trained 10,000 Ebola medical staff for West Africa and also sent medical workers to Ebola-hit countries. Its medical workers are still helping in the post-Ebola reconstruction efforts in countries like Sierra Leone. What is actually notable is that Chinese foreign minister Wang Yi made a formal visit to Sierra Leone, Liberia and Guinea, three of the countries that were heavily affected by Ebola. During the visit, the foreign minister listened to suggested ways that China could help the affected countries in its post-Ebola construction efforts. It is hoped that China and Africa can forge partnerships to fight future pandemics like the Ebola virus in Africa, should they arise.

10.4 Increase Cultural Exchanges

In addition, China and Africa need to expand their partnership beyond the political and economic sphere. There needs to be an increase in cultural interaction between the two. Moving forward, China and Africa should engage in cultural exchanges to share their vibrant and splendid cultures. Cultural exchanges should be promoted between organisations and institutions in China and Africa. China and Africa have a lot to offer each other culturally. Africa is the cradle of mankind, and China is the home to ancient civilisations, as elaborated on in Chapter 2 of this book. Together, their contribution to human civilisation cannot be emphasised enough. This cultural interaction can be achieved through sports meets and exchange of artists as well as through cooperation between Chinese and African cultural institutions and media organisations, student exchanges and working visits, to mention a few. At the time of writing, China has started a new programme to court African journalists to help tell the "China Success" story to Africa and the world. It has thus put into place programmes that will bring African journalists to China for periods ranging from two weeks to ten months, during which they will be exposed to everything about China. This programme is called *The China–Africa Press Exchange Workshop for Senior Journalists*. In the latter part of 2015, 13 journalists from Ghana and Nigeria were in China under the aegis of this programme. (Kale-Dery, 2014).

It is also important to also mention that the Chinese should increase the funding in its African Human Resources Development Fund, not only to offer more training to Africans in Chinese institutions but also to send Chinese experts to Africa to give short courses and vice versa. This is a great way to increase mutual understanding and build strong bonds of friendship between the two. But it is equally important to encourage Chinese citizens living in Africa to be the cultural bridge between their native land and their adopted countries. It is reported that there are currently about one million Chinese living as migrants or permanently in various African countries (French, 2014). Living in harmony with their African brothers and sisters should be one of the pillars of this cultural interaction. The "Ugly Chinese" syndrome exhibited by some Chinese nationals living or working in Africa must stop. The numerous reports of some Chinese nationals in Africa disrespecting Africans, an issue also written about in Section 6.7 of this book, the maltreatment of their African workers and their flouting of local laws must stop. The development of a "China Town" mentality, where Chinese migrants carve out sections of the countries they live in around the world to form Chinese-only communities, thereby refusing to integrate, would not help them in Africa. The excuses for this behaviour by Chinese migrants, pinning it on language difficulties and cultural differences between them and their African hosts, is rather lame. In fact, living in Chinese-only communities will make it difficult for them to integrate into the communities of the respective countries they live in. The various Chinese embassies in Africa should educate their nationals about the negative effects and consequences of their actions and inaction.

Another way of increasing cultural understanding between China and Africa is through the establishment of China's Confucius Institutes across the continent. The aim of these institutes is to teach Mandarin in Africa countries, to promote Chinese culture and to foster exchange programmes between Africans and Chinese. There are currently about 38 Confucius Institutes spread throughout Africa. Through these Confucius Institutes, Africans will learn the Chinese culture and be able to relate to Chinese migrants and tourists as they will also understand the culture of these Chinese, which is based on Confucianism (Lee, 2012). The ability of Africans to speak Mandarin will be a plus. This will also benefit China as it will contribute to its soft power engagement with Africa. Through some of these Confucius Institutes, some African students might even decide to study in China under Chinese-sponsored scholarships or they could go to China and self-fund their education. This could also lead to future employees of Chinese companies in Africa being able to speak Mandarin with their employers. But this would also go a long way to contributing to a reduction in conflict as Chinese and Africans begin to work and live together on the continent. The ability to be able to communicate and understand each other's cultures will be indispensable to this effort.

10.5 Focus More on Trade and Investments, Not Hand-Outs

To add to this, the adage that "if you give a man a fish, you feed him for a day; but if you teach a man how to fish, you feed him for a lifetime" represents a sound idea. Africa appreciates Chinese aid and debt-relief efforts, which have run into billions of yuan. Such efforts on the part of the Chinese government have helped a lot of poor African countries in their growth and development efforts. But in all honesty, Africa cannot develop by relying on aid alone. Aid should be regarded as a stop-gap measure or to be used in the case of natural disasters. Much as this author thinks that aid is an important component in Africa's growth and development effort, it should not become a "crutch." Rather, African governments should provide an environment conducive to attracting the requisite investments to bring about economic growth and development. Moving forward, the China–Africa relationship should focus more on trade and investment, not hand-outs. It is very clear that both China and Africa can benefit from their different endowments of capital, labour and natural resources as well as technology to forge win–win outcomes for them.

The theory of comparative advantage posits that gains from trade will be achieved when countries import what they have limited quantities of and export more of what they have in abundance. Trade, therefore, is the vent for surplus (Gillis et al., 1996). However, in practice in most cases, this is usually not the case. But the point here is to stress the importance of trade between countries. The trade between China and Africa has grown tremendously, as elaborated on in Chapter 5 of this book. In a short time, it has hit the $100 billion level. Yet this comprises about 3 percent of China's trade with Africa. The room for growth is tremendous, and every effort should be made by the two partners to expand two-way trade between China and Africa. Greater access to the Chinese market should be accorded to African products. Hence the proposed reduction in tariffs, that is, the zero-tariff treatment that will apply to some commodities from Africa, is a step in the right direction. However, it cannot be emphasised enough that African exports to China still face numerous non-tariff barriers. This does not augur well for the relationship and should be addressed by the Chinese authorities as soon as possible.

Increased investment in China and Africa is on the increase and should be encouraged. The formation of the China–Africa Business Conference will go a long way to promote mutual understanding between Chinese and African entrepreneurs and hopefully will become a catalyst to boost investment on both sides. China should also implement the cooperation initiatives reached at the editions of the Forum on China–Africa Cooperation (FOCAC) held in 2007 and 2015. As it pertains to joint ventures between China and Africa, these should be encouraged to transfer technologies to African countries. China should help African countries create low-cost manufacturing industries, and these industries should benefit from China's technology transfer efforts. China should also consider locating some of its sunset industries to some of the African countries, particularly those countries that lack natural resources. The relocation of some Chinese industries to resource-poor Ethiopia is a step in the right direction. African countries and China should both facilitate the ease of investment in their respective economies as well as the avoidance of double taxation.

Finally, African countries should engage the China Council for the Promotion of International Trade (CCPIT) to set up, as soon as possible, a China–Africa chamber of industry and commerce to further facilitate trade and investment in the continent. But a word of caution needs to be made here for the benefit of African countries. As African countries open up their economies to China, they should take a leaf out of the book of Deng Xiaoping in his approach to opening up China to the world. He said, "we must cross the water by feeling the stones" (Xiaoping, 1984), meaning China should open up its economy gradually to the world and should be cautious and vigilant in the process. African countries should learn from Deng's wise counsel, for it will do them a lot of good as they begin their engagement with China and as trade and investment begins to grow. Africa should open up its economy to China gradually.

In parallel, it is imperative that African countries and their respective leaders get to know China very well. This includes where it came from, its culture and its policies and how it attained development as a poor country, moving most of its people out of poverty in quite a short time. It is equally important for African countries to understand the Chinese psyche and how they approach things. It will go a long way to contributing to how they deal with the Chinese. This book has sought to do so in the first three chapters. This knowledge will help African leaders appreciate more China's investment in their respective economies and effectively leverage these investments in their respective countries to enhance their sustainable growth and development efforts.

10.6 Other Bilateral Measures to Strengthen Relations

Another observation as to the way forward for China–Africa relations is to move beyond trade and investments. This relationship should deal with some of the areas that can bring direct benefits to the people of China and Africa. A white paper issued by the Chinese government in 2003 captures these other measures beautifully. The paper proposes the enhancement of high-level visits to foster dialogue, deepen friendship and promote mutual understanding and trust between Chinese and African leaders.

The paper also proposes and calls for the exchange between legislative bodies, specifically legislatures from the National People's Congress (NPC) and the parliamentarians of African countries and the Pan-African Parliament, to deepen understanding and cooperation. Furthermore, it calls for exchanges between political parties in China and African countries based on the principles of independence, equality, mutual respect and non-interference in each other's internal affairs. The paper also calls for the establishment of consultative mechanisms between the Chinese foreign ministry and those of African countries in trade and economic affairs, science and technology and other consultations to increase understanding and friendship between China and Africa. In addition, cooperation in international affairs and exchanges between local governments are some of the bilateral measures China has proposed. Others include people-to-people exchanges and co-operation in areas of non-traditional security, such as terrorism, small-arms smuggling, drug trafficking and transnational economic crimes, to mention just a few (Ministry of the Foreign Affairs of the PRC, 2003). All these aforementioned measures proposed in the white paper will, if implemented, greatly enhance the relations between Africa and China moving forward.

But a note of caution needs to be sounded to African leaders as they engage China in its new current foray into Africa. They must ensure that this new foray does not repeat centuries of underdevelopment and exploitation that the continent went through under Western colonisation. Therefore, African countries must approach any investment opportunity or plan presented by China with a critical eye, and they must analyse the plan and the benefits that it proposes to bring to their respective economies as well as the possible negative impacts. Plans must then be put into place to mitigate these negative impacts. Rushing to sign investment deals for the sake of it or because some of these African officials stand to benefit from some kick-backs is rather myopic. In fact, the greater good of the people should be paramount in signing these deals. Hence, without any critical evaluations of these investments, years down the road, Africans will be left holding the bag.

The way forward therefore for Africa is to develop a short, medium and long-term strategy in their dealings with China. In the short term, it is sug-gested that the progressive forces in Africa engage with China to hasten the breaking of the West's stranglehold on Africa in some respects. China's foray into Africa is already beginning to serve as an alternative to Western investment and influence. In the medium term, it is suggested that the popular democratic forces must strengthen African co-operation leading, to the union of the governments of Africa. The unity of Africa, as put forward by Kwame Nkrumah and other independence-era leaders in Africa, cannot be overemphasised in this regard. This will be the period when it will be essential to break the disarticulation between the financial and productive sectors of African economies. In the long term, Africa must zealously guard their independence, because it is a fact that all big powers, in the final analysis, seek to act as hegemons. China is no different in this regard (Campbell, 2008). China has denied severally any plans on its part to be a hegemon. Even though the analysis in this book so far points to the fact that such is not the case, Africans cannot be complacent in this regard.

It is also suggested in certain circles that the development of a continental charter of rights governing investment in Africa is one of the ways to avoid the proxy wars that could result because of the "new" scramble for Africa's resources. Such a charter, it is argued, will have to be negotiated at the A.U. level and could supersede bilateral agreements, which will force all external powers to accord specific set of practices investments and engagements with Africa (Habib, 2007). The perceived challenge will be to enforce compliance, taking into consideration the administrative capacity, resource constraints and weakness of the A.U. I also think that another challenge is the different agendas and competing interests of African countries, which will make it difficult to agree on the form and the shape of this charter. But when all is said and done, Africans must understand, in no uncertain terms, that nobody, no matter how concerned and caring they are about the African condition – indeed no matter how much they like Africa – can like Africans more than Africans themselves. Africans must therefore employ effort, hard work and foresight in any relationship or partnership in its efforts to develop. The current engagement of China in Africa is no exception.

10.7 Conclusion

At the 2015 FOCAC meeting in Johannesburg, South Africa, Angolan president Jose Eduardo dos Santos said, "China is now a vital partner for development of our continent. To confirm this, just keep in mind that since 2013 China has become the largest trading partner of Africa and has increased by more than 44 percent of its direct investment in the continent." President dos Santos's comments point to the importance of the current China–Africa engagement, which is well written about in this book. But all relations sustain and grow only if they are well nurtured. The China–Africa relationship is no exception to this rule. Thus, moving forward, it is imperative that China and Africa consistently work to renew the bond of friendship that is the bedrock of this relationship, and neither side should take the other for granted. At an international level, the two partners should work together to be able to successfully deal with most of the issues that play to their interests or are against their interests. The two should also increase cultural exchanges to foster a better understanding of each other's cultures and way of doing things. This is becoming more and more important as China increasingly engages Africa, and many Chinese migrants are moving to Africa and some calling Africa home. The same can be said about some African migrants to China and indeed some Africans working and living in China.

Furthermore, African countries are grateful to China for the increasing amount of aid it is receiving from the country. However, for this relationship to be sustainable and for Africa to really grow and develop, the focus of Chinese aid to Africa should be more on enhancing trade between the two. Chinese is now Africa's largest trading partner. Through trade, African can lift most of its people out of abject poverty. Investment, not handouts, should be another focus in the China–Africa engagement moving forward. This investment should be in infrastructure, agriculture and manufacturing. These are the sectors in which China's investment in Africa can have a huge impact on the transformation of the continent. But at the end of the day, this partnership will work only if African leaders and policy makers know what they need and want from China. China already knows what it wants from Africa. African leaders and policy makers should strategise and position themselves well to benefit from this engagement. It will also require effort, hard work and commitment from a visionary set of African leaders whose focus is on working to develop the continent with the support of China.

Note

1   "China's Hu urges more African ties," BBC News, http://news.bbc.co.uk/2/hi/africa/4949688.stm.

Conclusion

China and Africa: Looking Backward to Move Forward

I set out in this book to look at Chinese investments in and China's foray into Africa and the attendant benefits that these investments have brought to a continent long neglected and regarded as hopeless and incapable of development (Economist, 2000). The premise on which this book stands is that Chinese investment and indeed its foray into Africa have, overall, benefitted Africa and indeed have contributed to the "Africa rising" narrative. China's demand for Africa's natural resources has contributed to the growth of most of the resource-rich African countries. Unlike those who do not believe in the "Africa rising" narrative, this author believes that the narrative is true, despite the fact that China's economy is slowing down and the impact this is having on the growth and development efforts of African countries. This slowdown, in my opinion, is going to be temporary.

But then again, Chinese investments in Africa have not been all about profits alone or the demand for Africa's natural resources. They are also about the support of China's diplomatic initiatives and interests as China becomes an economic and political power to be reckoned with in the world. It is also about China looking for markets for its goods and services among, other things. Thus, I believe that even though the Chinese economy is slowing down, China will still invest in Africa. China needs Africa at this point in its growth trajectory and vice versa. China, at the very least, will still need Africa's strategic minerals.

The book then argues that because of Chinese investment in and China's current engagement with Africa, it has contributed immensely to Africa's growth and will continue to do so. It is thus imperative that African countries position themselves well to benefit from these investments. This positioning starts with African countries and policy makers knowing China's history, where it is today and what it went through to get to where it is today. Thus, the early chapters in the book about Mao Tse Tung and his "Great Leap Forward," his "Cultural Revolution," and the impact of these initiatives on China; and the era of Deng Xiaoping and his "opening-up" policy, which set the stage for the growth and development of today's China, are steps in that direction.

For African leaders and policy makers to be able to position themselves well to benefit from China's foray into Africa, it is equally important for them to understand some of the factors that contributed to China's awakening and its current growth and development. Some of these factors include China's desire to reclaim its past pre-eminence, the lessons learnt from Mao's failed policies by subsequent Chinese leadership, China's entry into the World Trade Organisation (WTO) and, above all, Deng's visionary and pragmatic leadership. It is also important to mention the importance of continuity as it pertains to the transition of power from one Chinese leader to the other. What is also important is that each leader continues where others left off and even adds more to the continuous growth efforts of the country. Once they are out of power, they stay out of the way of the subsequent leaders and support them behind the scenes for the success of the decisions and strategies that they put into place.

The knowledge of where China came from and what it went through to get to this point is important, but, for African leaders and policy makers to position themselves and their respective countries to benefit from the Chinese investment in and foray into Africa, it is equally important to know why China is interested in Africa. To afford for a win–win outcome and indeed for Africa not to repeat the mistakes of its colonial past, this knowledge is important. The book identifies some of these interests, which include China's need for Africa's natural resources to fuel its growth, a market for China's manufactured goods and services and to bolster its diplomatic and other international initiatives.

If, as mentioned in the beginning of this concluding chapter, China's investment and foray into Africa have benefitted Africa, it is important to list some of these benefits. The first is that China has become a new source of capital and investment for Africa. Not only are the Chinese providing the requisite capital to undertake the numerous infrastructure projects that Africa seriously needs, they are also able to build these projects on time and within budget. China's foray into and investments in Africa have increased trade between China and Africa. Currently, China is Africa's largest trading partner. China is also a new source of aid for African countries. China has built schools, stadia and hospitals and even made a gift of US$200 million to Africa for the African Union building. It has cancelled most of the debts owed to it by African countries.

But China's current foray into Africa, its investment and engagement in Africa are not without criticisms. The first criticism is that China is the "new colonialist" and that its foray into Africa is to pillage Africa's natural resources as Africa's former colonial masters did. Other criticisms include the fact China's investment activities in Africa undermine good governance and foster human rights abuses because of its no-conditionality and non-interference policy approach in the aid and low-interest loans it gives to Africa countries. This investment and approach to aid disbursements by China in Africa is different from the approach taken by the West, which puts up conditionalities as prerequisites to those African countries that will benefit from their investments and aid. This situation has resulted in the Chinese gaining more influence in Africa compared to the West.

China is also criticised for the lack of technology and skills transfers in the projects it undertakes in Africa. The view is that without technology transfers, most of these will not be sustainable when the Chinese leave. In addition, there are also criticisms that Africans are losing jobs to Chinese because most Chinese-funded projects tend to employ or bring in workers from China to the detriment of many of the unemployed Africans. In situations where Africans find jobs on Chinese projects or businesses, their labour rights are abused. In most cases, they are maltreated and work in inhumane conditions. Some have also observed some Chinese migrants disrespect Africans, their hosts. This could be because of their ignorance about Africa and Africans or else it is outright racism. To deepen China–Africa relations, it is highly recommended that the Chinese authorities attend to this issue with all the seriousness that it deserves. If not, it could have a serious impact on China–Africa relations.

The Chinese investment in and foray into Africa have also brought with it Chinese migrants. Some of these migrants have made Africa their home, others are working on Chinese projects in Africa and some are transient, using Africa as a platform to enter Europe or get to the Americas. This new phenomenon can have both positive and negative consequences for Africa. It is therefore imperative that African governments and policy makers handle this phenomenon with care. Hence, it is important that they know why these Chinese are migrating to Africa and the attendant impact that it has on the countries involved. They also need to gauge the reactions from their citizens to Chinese migrating into their respective countries. The agitations and hostilities towards Chinese migrants in some African countries should not be swept under the carpet. This is because they could drive a wedge between China and Africa. Hence, both Chinese and African governments should work together to address this phenomenon.

When considering how African countries can position themselves to benefit from China's foray into Africa, it is first important to assess whether the Chinese and their capabilities mesh with Africa's needs. African countries need infrastructure, the development of their agriculture and the development of their manufacturing sectors, to name but a few. All these needs should be based on a realistic and pragmatic strategy on how to effectively direct Chinese investment to these sectors to achieve these goals. Without any strategic planning on the part of African leaders, they could easily gravitate towards prestige projects like presidential palaces and other gaudy edifices. The focus should be on the development of Africa's dilapidated infrastructure and manufacturing industries as well as the development of agriculture.

It is equally important that African countries have a clear idea and knowledge of what China "really" wants from Africa if they are to have the opportunity to effectively negotiate win–win outcomes for both partners, but it is particularly important for Africans to effectively harness the benefits that will flow out of this relationship in a sustainable manner. In positioning themselves to benefit from China's foray into Africa, leaders and policy makers should insist on technology transfer and skills development in the Chinese projects undertaken in Africa.

The book has also observed that China's investment and current engagement with Africa will definitely have an impact on the interests of other external players who are equally interested in Africa and its resources. These include the US, European countries, Asian countries and international organisations. For European countries, the impact is on their losing their influence on their former colonies as well as access to their rich natural resources and the market for their manufactured goods. For the US, its interest as a hegemon is to sway influence in Africa. Previously, during the Cold War era and using the Central Intelligence Agency (CIA), the US interfered with the internal affairs of some African countries, and in some cases got leaders removed from power. It is also about having access to Africa's natural resources, particularly some of the strategic minerals. Finally, it is about the export of their manufactured and other products to the African market. For most of the Asian countries, like India, it is about losing out to China in the demand for Africa's rich natural resources, as the Chinese have deeper pockets and can offer more aid to African countries than they can. It is also about competing with the Chinese for the export of manufactured products to Africa. Finally, international organisations see China as a "disruptor," in that it does not impose conditionalities like respect for human rights, good governance and requiring that African countries abide by the rule of law to benefit from their aid and investment. Thus, the Chinese are said to be propping up dictators in Sudan, Equatorial Guinea and Zimbabwe, to mention a few.

The final chapter of this book looks at the way forward for China and Africa, especially how they can enhance this current engagement despite the numerous challenges they face and will face moving forward. The first is that there should be a continuous engagement between African and Chinese leadership and policy makers to enhance the relationship. It is also suggested that they should forge stronger partnerships at international fora and speak with one voice on issues that affect them or their growth and development interests. They should also increase cultural exchange as a way of fostering a better understanding between their peoples. Hopefully, this will go a long way toward dispelling the warped beliefs and stereotypes the Chinese and African people have about each other. It is hoped that this will go a long way to reducing some of the worrying clashes and attacks on Chinese migrants in Africa and vice versa.

Furthermore, it is strongly observed that into the future, the China–Africa relationship should focus more on enhancing trade and investment between China and Africa, moving away from aid and hand-outs. This does not mean that aid is not important but that it should form a small percentage of the engagement. It is the belief of this author that the best way for Africa to attain sustainable growth and development is to move away from the export of raw materials and the import of manufactured goods. It needs to add value to its resources before exporting them. China will be able to help Africa attain this end, and indeed, Africa can learn from China's experience of how it emerged from being a poor country to become an economic and political power to be reckoned with in the world.

There are other bilateral measures and ways the Chinese and Africans can strengthen their relations moving forward. This can be through exchanges between law makers as well as policy makers. At the end of the day, China's current foray into and investment in Africa will benefit both China and Africa if both partners do not take each other for granted. Efforts should always be made to achieve win–win outcomes for both partners. It is also imperative that African countries harness the benefits that will accrue to them through their current engagement with China productively. This engagement should be used as leverage to help them in their growth and development efforts.

Bibliography

Abdulai, David N. (2007) *China's New Great Leap Forward: An Emerging China and its Impact on ASEAN*, Kuala Lumpur: MPH Publishing.

— (2004) *Can Malaysia Transit to the K-Economy? Dynamic Challenges, Tough Choices, and the Next Phase*, Kuala Lumpur: Pelanduk Publications.

— (2000) *African Proverbs: Wisdom of the Ages*, Denver and Accra: Dawn of a New Day Publications.

Achebe, Chinua (1987) *Anthills of the Savannah*, London: Heinemann.

Adebajo, Adekeye (2007) "Who are the good, the bad and the ugly on our shores?" *Business Day*, November 30, p. 13.

Adebajo, Adeke (2008) "An Axis of Evil?: China, the United States and France in Africa"; in Kwaku Ampiah and Sanusha Naidu (eds.), *Crouching Tiger, Hidden Dragon?: Africa and China*, Scottsville, South Africa; University of KwaZulu-Natal Press.

Alden, Chris (2009) *China and Africa's Natural Resources: The Challenges and Implications for Development and Governance*, Johannesburg: South African Institute of International Affairs.

Aning, Kwesi (2010) "China and Africa: Towards a new security relationship," in Fantu Cheru and Cyril Obi (eds.), *The Rise of China and India in Africa*, London: Zed Books.

Aning, Kwesi and Delphine Lecoutre (2007) "China's ventures in Africa," *African Security Review*, Vol. 17, No. 1.

Asia Tomorrow (2004) "China's great commodity grab," November 2004, pp. 10–14.

Balfour, Frederik, Mark L. Clifford, Moon Ihlwan and Michael Shari (2002) "How the crisis changed Asia, and how it didn't," *BusinessWeek*, July 1, pp. 19–22.

Bauer, Peter (1950) *United States Aid and Indian Economic Development*, Washington, D.C.: American Enterprise Association.

Behrman, Greg (2008) *The Most Noble Adventure: The Marshall Plan and How America Helped Rebuild Europe*, New York: Free Press.

Bertant, July (1916) *Napoleon in his own words*, Chicago: A.C. McClure and Co.

Bhattasali, Deepak, Li Shantong and Martin Will (eds.) (2004) *China and the WTO: Accession, Policy Reform, and Poverty Reduction Strategies*, Washington, D.C.: World Bank and Oxford University Press.

Botequilla, H. (2006) "Da utopia para a realidade," *Visão*, No. 286, pp. 8–12.

Bowman, Andrew (2012) "Africa's Chinese diaspora: Under pressure," *Financial Times*, August 8.

Boyle, Brenda (2007) "Beware the ties that bind China and Africa," The *Times*, September 23, p. 6.

Booysen, Joseph (2015) "Imports Killing SA textile industry," *Business News*, July 3.

Brahm, Laurence J. (2001) *China's Century: The Awakening of the Next Economic PowerHouse,* Singapore: John Wiley and Sons.

Brautigam, Deborah (2009) *The Dragon's Gift: The Real Story of China in Africa,* London: Oxford University Press.

— (2011) "Aid with Chinese Characteristics: Chinese Foreign Aid and Development Finance meet the OECD-DAC Aid Regime" *Journal of International Development (2011).* Wiley online library, DOI: 10.1002/jid.1798

— (2015) *Will Africa Feed China?* London: Oxford University Press.

Broadman, Harry (2007) *Africa's Silk Road: China and India's New Economic Frontier,* Washington, D.C.: The World Bank.

Brooks, Peter and Shin Ji Hye (2006) "China's influence in Africa: Implications for the United States," *Backgrounder,* No. 1916, February 22.

Brown, Kerry (2012) *Hu Jintao: China's Silent Ruler,* Singapore: World Scientific Publishing.

Brown, Stephen and Chandra Lekha Sriram (2008) "China's role in human rights abuses in Africa: Clarifying issues of culpability," in Robert I. Rotberg (ed.), *China into Africa: Trade and Influence,* Washington, D.C.: Brookings Institution Press.

Business Day (2013) "China's new president aspires to realise 'great renaissance'," March 18, p. 6.

Business Week (2003) "The rise of India" Dec 8, p. 42–50.

Business Week (2004) "Reform picks up speed," March 8, pp. 18–19.

— (2004) "The rise of India," December 8, pp. 42–50.

Buckley, Chris (2010) "China 'tried' to quash report on arms in Sudan," *Business Day,* October 22, p. 8.

Campbell, Horace (2008) "China in Africa: Challenging US global hegemony," *Third World Quarterly,* Vol. 29, No. 1, pp. 89–105.

Central Intelligence Agency (2003) *The World Fact Lecture.*

Chang, Gordon G. (2001) *The Coming Collapse of China,* New York: Random House.

Chang, John K. (2010) *Industrial Development in Pre-Communist China (1912–1949),* New Jersey: Transactional Publishers.

Cheng, Pei-Kai, Michael Lestz and Jonathan Spence (1999) *The Search For Modern China,* New York: W. W. Norton and Company.

Cheung, Tai Ming (2014) *Forging China's Military Might: A New Framework for Assessing Innovation,* Baltimore: John Hopkins University Press.

Ching, Frank (2004) "China embarks on strategy of gradual reform," *New Straits Times,* September 30, p. 23.

Chin-Hao, Huang (2008) "China's renewed partnership with Africa: Implications for the United States," in Robert I. Rotberg (ed.), *China into Africa: Trade, Aid and Influence,* Washington, D.C.: Brookings Institution Press.

China Daily (2004) "China's development of an opportunity for Asia," April 26, p. 7.

— (2004a) "World watching China's actions carefully," *New Straits Times,* February 26, p. 12.

— (2004b) "Emergence of China as a new diplomatic player," *New Straits Times,* March 4, p. 12.

Cliff, Roger (2015) *China's Military Power: Assessing Current and Future Capabilities,* London: Cambridge University Press.

Cochrane, Joe (2005) "A threat? No, an economic lifeline," *Newsweek,* May 9, p. 19.

Correa, Carlos M. (2000) *Intellectual Property Rights, the WTO and Developing Countries: The TRPS Agreement and Policy Options,* London: Zed Lectures; Penang, Malaysia: Third World Network.

Corkin, Lucy (2007) "The strategic entry of China's emerging multinationals into Africa," *China Report*, Vol. 43, No. 3, pp. 309–322.

— (2008) "All's fair in loans and war: The development of China–Angola relations," in Kweku Ampiah and Sanusha Naidu (2008) (eds.), *Crouching Tiger, Hidden Dragon?: Africa and China*, Scottsville, South Africa: University of KwaZulu-Natal Press.

Copson, R.W. (2007) *The United States in Africa*, London and Cape Town: Zed and David Philip, pp. 34–36.

Council of the European Union (2005) *The E.U. and Africa: Towards a strategic partnership*, (Brussels: Council of the European Union, 19 December, 2005), p. 2.

Curtis, Devon (2008) "Partner or predator in the heart of Africa? Chinese engagement with the DRC," in Kweku Ampiah and Sanusha Naidu (2008) (eds.), *Crouching Tiger, Hidden Dragon?: Africa and China*, Scottsville, South Africa: University of KwaZulu-Natal Press.

Davidson, Basil (1991) *The Black Man's Burden: Africa and the Curse of the Nation-State*, New York: Times Books.

Devlin, Larry (2008) *Chief of Station, Congo: Fighting the Cold War in a Hot Zone*, New York: Public Affairs.

De Witte, Ludo (2003) *The Assassination of Lumumba*, 2nd Edition, London: Verso.

Dhikari, R. and Yang Y. (2002) "What will WTO membership mean for China and its trading partners?" *Finance and Development*, Vol. 39, No. 3, September.

Dikötter, Frank (2010) *Mao's Great Famine: The History of China's Most Devastating Catastrophe (1958–62)*, London: Bloomsbury.

Dillion, Michael (2015) *Deng Xiaoping: The Man Who Made Modern China*, London and New York: I.B. Tauris and Co.

Doriye, Elirehema (2010) "The next stage of sovereign wealth investments: China buys Africa," *Journal of Financial Regulation and Compliance*, Vol. 18, No. 1, pp. 3–31.

Draper, Peter, Tsidiso Disenyana and Gilberto Biacuano (2010) "Chinese investment in African network industries: Case studies from Democratic Republic of Congo and Kenya," in Fantu Cheru and Cyril Obi (eds.), *The Rise of China and India in Africa*, London: Zed Books.

Diao, Ying (2009) "Trade with Africa Gallops," *China Daily*, February 12, p. 14.

Economist, "The hopeless continent," May 13, 2000 (front cover).

Economist, "Is the awakening giant a monster?" February 13, 2003.

Economist, "The dragon and the eagle," October 2, 2004.

Economist, "The new colonialist," March 15, 2008.

Economist (a), "Cornering foreign fields," May 21, 2009.

Economist (b), "Outsourcing's third wave," May 21, 2009.

Economist, "Towards the end of poverty," June 1, 2013.

Efande, Peter (2003) "China cancels African debts," *The Tribune*, December 17, 2003.

Elliot, Larry (2015) "Western countries fail to meet Gleneagles aid pledges" *The Guardian*, https://www.theguardian.com/global-development/2011/apr/06/g8-fails-to-meet-gleneagles-aid-pledges (accessed 4/4/2016).

England, Andrew (2013) "Chinese trade cuts both ways for Africa," *Financial Times*, March 25.

Farndon, John (2007) *China Rises: How China's Astonishing Growth Will Change the World*, London: Virgin Books Ltd.

Federal Trade Commission and U.S. Department of Justice (2009) "Report on charting the future course of international technical assistance at the Federal Trade Commission and U.S. Department of Justice," Washington, D.C., October.

Fehrenbacher, Don E. (1989) *Lincoln: Speeches and writings 1832-1858*, New York: Library Of America.

Financial Times (2015) "Chinese 'Warren Buffet' caught in Beijing's anti-corruption drive," December 12–13, p. 1.

Fisher-Thompson, J. (2005) "China no threat to United States in Africa, US official says," U.S. State Department Information Service, July 28. (http://iipdigital.usembassy.gov/st/english/article/2005/07/200507281821401ejrehsif0.5898096.html#axzz4HfjsNXki)

Flint, Julie and Alex de Waal (2008) *Darfur: A New History of a Long War*, second edition, London: Zed Books.

Flynn, Daniel (2008) "India and China are new colonialist: Soros," *Reuters*, February 7.

Foster, Vivien and Cecilia Briceno-Garmendia (eds.) (2010) *Africa's Infrastructure: A Time for Transformation*, Washington, D.C.: World Bank.

— (2008) "Africa infrastructure country diagnostic: Overhauling the engine of growth: Infrastructure in Africa," Washington, D.C.: World Bank.

Foster, Vivien, William Butterfield, Chuan Chen and Nataliya Pushak (2008) *Building Bridges: China's Growing Role as Infrastructure Financier for Africa, Trends and Policy Options*, No. 5, Wash. D.C.: World Bank.

Francois, Joseph F. and Dean Spinanger (2004) "WTO Accession and the Structure of China's motor vehicle sector," in Deepak Bhattasali, Li Shantong and Martin Will (eds.), *China and the WTO: Accession Policy Reform and Poverty Reduction Strategies*, Washington, D.C.: World Bank and Oxford University Press.

French, Howard (2014) "*China's Second Continent: How a Million Migrants are Building a New Empire in Africa*," New York: Alfred A. Knopf.

— (2004a) "China in Africa," *The New York Times*, August 8.

— (2004b) "A fruitful African date," *New Straits Times*, August 9.

Furst, Michael J. (2001) "China WTO accession – The big picture," in Laurence J. Brahm (ed.), *China's Century: The Awakening of the Next Economic PowerHouse*, Singapore: John Wiley and Sons.

Gera, Y.K. (ed.) (2012) *Trade Commerce and Security in the Asia Pacific Region*, New Delhi, India: Vij Books.

Gerard, Emmanuel and Bruce Kuklicks (2015) *Death in the Congo: Murdering Patrice Lumumba*, Cambridge: Havard University Press.

Gillis, Malcolm, Dwight H. Perkins, Michael Roemer and Donald R. Snodgrass (1996) *Economics of Development*, New York and London: W.W. Norton and Company.

Gorbachev, Mikhail S. (1988) *Perestrioka: New Thinking for Our Country and the World*, New York: Perennial Library.

GRAIN (2008) *The 2008 Land Grab for Food and Financial Security*, GRAIN, Barcelona.

GU, J. (2009) "China's Private Enterprises in Africa and the Implications for African Development," *The European Journal of Development Research*, Vol. 21, pp. 570–587.

Guest, Robert (2010) *The Shackled Continent: Power, Corruption and African Lives*, Washington, D.C.: Smithsonian Books.

Guijin, Liu (2004) "China-Africa relations: Equality, cooperation and mutual development," speech of Chinese ambassador to South Africa, Liu Guijin, presented at a seminar on Sino-African Relations organized by the Institute for Security Studies, November 9.

Habib, Adam (2007) "Scramble for an African response," *Business Day*, June 26, p. 13.

Halper, Stefan (2010) *The Beijing Consensus: How China's Authoritarian Model Will Dominate the Twenty-First Century*, New York: Basic Books.

Hanson, Stephanie (2008) "China, Africa and oil" Council on Foreign Relations, http://www.cfr.org/china/china-africa/p9557.

Hayes, Peter (2004) *Chinese New Nationalism: Pride, Politics and Diplomacy*, Berkley: University of California Press.

Hochschild, Adam (2006) *King Leopold's Ghost: A Story of Greed, Terror and Heroism in Colonial Africa*, Basingstoke and Oxford: Pan Lectures.

— (1998) *King Leopold's Ghost: A Story of Greed, Terror and Heroism in Colonial Africa*, New York: Mariner Books.

Hogan, Michael J. (1989) *The Marshall Plan: America, Britain and the Reconstruction of Western Europe, 1947–1952*, London: Cambridge University Press.

Holslag, Jonathan (2006) "China's new mercantilism in Central Africa," *African and Asian Studies*, Vol. 5, No. 2, pp. 133–169.

Hope, Kempe R. and Bornwell C. Chikulo (eds.) (1999) *Corruption, and Development in Africa*, Basingstoke, U.K.: Palgrave Macmillan.

Hornby, Albert Sydney, Joana Turnbull, Diana Lea, Dilys Parkinon, and Patrick Philips (2010) *The Oxford Advance Leaner's Dictionary*, London: Oxford University Press.

Hornby, Lucy and Deborah Kan (2010) "China looking beyond resources in Africa," *Business Day*, November 25, p. 2.

Hsiung, James C. (ed.) (2015) *The Xi Jinpin Era: His Comprehensive Strategy Towards the China Dream*, New York: CN Times.

Hu, Xiao (2004) "Hu: Chinese growth offers opportunity for others," *China Daily*, April 26, p. 162.

Human Rights Watch (2011) "You'll be fired if you refuse," in the report "Labour abuses in Chinese state-owned copper mines," 1–5.

Hutt, David (2014) "The not-so-dark continent," *South-East Asia Globe*, October 8.

Information Office of the State Council of the People's Republic of China (2010) *China–Africa Economic and Trade Cooperation*, December, Beijing.

Jacoby, Ulrich (2007) "Getting together: The partnership between China and Africa for aid and trade," *Finance and Development*, Vol. 44, No. 2, June.

Jinping, Xi (2014) *The Governance Of China*, Beijing: Foreign Languages Press.

John, Mark (2007) "E.U. moves to challenge China in Africa," *Business Day*, June 28, 2007, p. 9.

Kale-Dery, Severious (2014) "13 African journalists tour China," *Daily Graphic*, November 18, p. 47.

Kaufman, Alison Adcock (2010) "The 'Century of Humiliation,' then and now: Chinese perceptions of the international order," *Pacific Focus* Vol. 25, No. 1, pp. 1–33.

King Jr., Martin L. (1967) *Where Do We Go from Here: Chaos or Community*, New York: Harper & Row Publishers.

Kirkpatrick, Jean (1979) "Dictatorship and double standards," *Commentary*, Vol. 68, No. 5, November, pp. 34–35

Kissinger, Henry (1979) *The White House Years*, New York: Simon & Schuster (Reprinted edition, May 24, 2011).

— (2011) *On China*, London: Allen Lane.

Kristensen, Hans M. and Robert S. Norris (2011) "Chinese nuclear forces 2011," *Bulletin of the Atomic Scientist*, Vol. 67, No. 6, November/December, pp. 81–87.

Kroslak, Daniela (2004) "France's policy towards Africa: Continuity or change?" in Ian Taylor and Paul Williams (eds.), *Africa in International Politics*, London: Routledge, pp. 61–82.

Kurlantzick, Joshua (2006) "Beijing's safari: China's move into Africa and its implications for aid, development and governance," *Policy Outlook*, November 2006, Carnegie Endowment for International Peace.

Kwang, Ng Aik, (2001) *Why Asians are Less Creative than Westerners*, Singapore: Prentice Hall.

LaGrone, Sam and Dave Mujumdar (2014) "Chinese weapons that worry the pentagon," *USNI News* (www.news.unsi.org).

Langeni, Loyiso (2010) "U.S. wakes up to Chinese expansion in Africa," *Business Day*, November 17, p. 2.

Lake, D. (1993) "Leadership, hegemony, and the international economy: Naked emperor or tattered monarch with potential? *International Studies Quarterly*, Vol. 37, No. 4, December, p. 461.

Lampton, David M. (2014) *Following the Leader: Ruling China from Deng Xiaoping to Xi Jinping*, Berkley: University of California Press.

Lary, Diana (2012) *The Movement of People, Goods and Ideas Over Four Millennia*, Washington, D.C.: Rowman and Littlefield Publishers.

Lee, Ann (2012) *What the U.S. Can Learn from China: An Open-Minded Guide to Treating Our Greatest Competitor as Our Greatest Teacher*, San Francisco: Berrett-Koehler Publishers.

Lee, Margaret (2006) "The 21st century scramble for Africa," *The Journal of Contemporary African Studies*, Vol. 24, No. 3, pp. 303–330.

Lee, Matthew (2011) "U.S. warns Africa of 'new colonialism,'" *Business Report*, June 13, 2011, p. 9.

Leong, Apo (2009) "Working conditions and labour relations in China," in Anthony Yaw Baah and Herbert Jauch (eds.), *Chinese Investments in Africa*, Accra and Widhoek: Africa Labour Network.

Le Pere, Garth (2008) "The geo-strategic dimension of the Sino-African relationship," in Kweku Ampiah and Sanusha Naidu (2008) (eds.), *Crouching Tiger, Hidden Dragon?: Africa and China*, Scottsville, KwaZulu-Natal: University of KwaZulu-Natal Press.

Liu, Melinda (2001) "A China's century?" *Newsweek* (Special Issue), July–Sept., p. 13.

Lloyd, J.T. (1887) *Henry Ward Beecher: His Life and Work*, London: Walter Scott (Digitized on 22nd May 2009).

Lumumba, Patrick (1961) "Concluding speech at the All African Conference in Leopoldville," August 31, 1960, in *Fighter for Africa's Freedom*, Moscow: Progress Publishing, 1961, pp. 26–33.

Machiavelli, Niccolo (1515 [2007]) *The Prince on the Art of Power*, London: Duncan Baird Publishers Edition.

Mansfield, E. (1975) "East-West technological transfers issues and problems, international technology transfers: Forms, resource requirements and policies," *American Economic Review*, Vol. 65, No. 2, pp. 372–376.

Manji, Firoze and Stephen Marks (eds.) (2007) *African Perspective on China Africa*, Nairobi and Oxford: Fahamu.

Manson, Katrina (2002) "China attacks Clinton's Africa comments" *Financial Times*, August 3, 2012.

Mark, John (2007) "E.U. moves to challenge China in Africa," *Business Day*, June 28, p. 9.

Maskus, Keith E. (2000) *Intellectual Property Rights in the Global Economy*, Washington, D.C.: Institute for International Economics.

Mbaku, John M. (2010) *Corruption in Africa: Causes, Consequences and Cleanups*, Lanham, Maryland: Lexington Books.

Mbeki, Moletsi (2005) presentation at the Conference of Sustainable Development, Beijing, China, September.

Mearsheimer, J. (2006) "China's unpeaceful rise," *Current History*, Vol. 105, No. 690, p. 160.

Meyer, Riaan (2008) "China could usher in a new era of banking in Africa," *Business Day*, October 6, p. 9.

McGreal, Chris (2007) "Chinese aid to Africa may do more harm than good, warns Benn," *The Guardian*, February 8.

Michalopoulos, Constantine (1989) "Assistance for infrastructure development," in Anne O. Krueger, Constantine Michalopoulos and Vernon W. Ruttan (eds.), *Aid and Development*, Baltimore, MD: Johns Hopkins University Press.

Ministry of the Foreign Affairs of the PRC (2003) "Chinese government issues African policy paper," Beijing, January 12.

Mohan, Giles and May Tan-Mullins (2009) "Chinese migrants in Africa as new agents of development? An analytical framework," *European Journal of Development Research*, Vol. 21, No. 4, pp. 588–605.

Mohan, Giles and Lampert, Ben (2013) "Chinese migrants in Africa: Bilateral and informal governance of a poorly understood south–south flow," draft paper prepared for UNRISD conference on Regional Governance of Migration and Socio-Political Rights: Institutions, Actors and Processes, January 14–15, 2013, Geneva, Switzerland.

Mohan, Giles (2013) "Migrants as agents of south–south cooperation," in Justin Dargin (2013) (ed.), *The Rise of the Global South: Philosophical, Geopolitical and Economic Trends of the 21st Century*, Singapore: World Scientific Publishing.

Mohamad, Mahathir (1999) *A New Deal for Asia*, Kuala Lumpur: Pelanduk Publications.

Monson, Jamie (2009) *Africa's Freedom Railway: How a Chinese Development Project Changed Lives and Livelihoods in Tanzania*, Bloomington: Indiana University Press.

Moritz, F.A. (1982) "Chinese leaders tour Africa with few gifts in their sack," *Christian Science Monitor,* December 22.

Moyo, Dambisa (2010) *Dead Aid: Why Aid is Not Working and How There is Another Way for Africa*, London: Penguin Books.

Moyo, Jason (2011) "Working for Chinese is 'hell on earth'," *Mail & Guardian*, June 24–30, p. 31

Muekalia, Domingos Jardo (2004) "Africa and China's strategic partnership," *African Security Review*, Vol. 13, No. 1.

Mueller, Milton and Peter Lovelock (2004) "The WTO and China's ban on foreign direct investment in telecommunications sector: A game-theoretic analysis," *Telecommunications Policy*, No. 24, pp. 731–759.

Mwanza, Kevin (2015) "Cheap Chinese imports killing Ghana's textile industry," *AFKInsider*, May 21.

Naidu, S. and Davies M. (2006) "China fuels its failure with Africa's riches," *South African Journal of International Affairs*, Vol. 13, No. 2.

Ndulo, Muna (2008) "Chinese investments in Africa: A case study of Zambia," in Kweku Ampia and Sanusha Naidu (eds.), *Crouching Tiger, Hidden Dragon?: Africa and China*, Scottsville, KwaZulu-Natal: University of KwaZulu-Natal Press.

New Straits Times (2004a) "Terrorism tops Asean army chiefs' talks," September 28, p. 28.

New Straits Times (2004b) "Rising income gap in Asia amid high growth," August 27, p. B9.

New Straits Times (2004c) "China pays tribute to Deng Xiaoping," August 23, p. 20.

New Straits Times (2004d) "Lee: Democracy not a must for economic progress," August 18, p. 21.

New Straits Times (2004e) "China enshrines private property," March 15, p. B22.

New Straits Times (2004f) "Matsushita announces major shift to China," January 9, p. F.

New Straits Times (2003) "Foreign direct investment in China hits record US$52.7b," January 15, p. B16.

Nkrumah, Kwame (1963) "We Must Unite Now or Perish," Speech of Kwame Nkrumah at the founding of the OAU, 24 May 1963. Quoted in *New Africa Magazine*, 3 May 2013.

Norbrook, Nicholas (2015) "When the dragon sneezes, does Africa catch cold?" *The Africa Report*, No. 75, November, pp. 22–23.

Obi, Cyril (2010) "African oil in the energy security calculations of China and India," in Fantu Cheru and Cyril Obi (eds.), *The Rise of China and India in Africa*, London: Zed Books.

OECD (2006) *2005 Development Co-operation Report* Vol. 7, No. 1, Paris: OECD.

Prunier, Gerard (2008) *Darfur: A 21st Century Genocide*, Third Edition, Ithaca: Cornell University Press.

Pangestu, Mari and Debbie Morongowius (2004) "Telecommunications services in China: Facing the challenges of WTO accession," in Deepak Bhattasali, Li Shantong and Martin Will (eds.), *China and the WTO: Accession, Policy Reform and Poverty Reduction Strategies*, Washington, D.C.: World Bank and Oxford University Press.

Panitchpakdi, Supachai and Mark L. Clifford (2002) *China and the WTO: Changing China, Changing World Trade*, Singapore: John Wiley & Sons.

Park, Yoon Jung (2009) "Chinese Migration in Africa" SAIIA, Occasional Paper No. 24, January, 2009.

Pilling, David (2009) "Criticism of China in Africa rings hollow," *Business Day*, December 11, p. 9.

Piore, Adam (2003) "Views from the inside: Unsparing new images of the Cultural Revolution," *Newsweek*, November 10, pp. 54–55.

Raine, Sarah (2009) *China's African Challenges*, London: The International Institute for Strategic Studies.

Reuters (2011) "Report pans Chinese for staff abuse," *Business Report*, November 4, p. 5.

Rongji, Zhu (2013) *Zhu Rongyi on the Record: The Road to Reform, 1991–1997*, Washington, D.C.: Brookings Institution Press.

— (2001) "A brighter future," in Laurence J. Brahm (ed.), *China's Century: The Awakening of the Next Economic Powerhouse*, Singapore: John Wiley & Sons.

Rotberg, Robert I. (2008) "Preface," in Robert I. Rotberg (ed.), *China into Africa: Trade, Aid and Influence*, Washington, D.C.: Brookings Institution Press.

Rozenberg, Gabriel (2006) "Africa's future is a Chinese Story," *New Sunday Times*, July 9, p. 22.

SAPA (2008) "China pumps up Africa growth," *Sunday Times*, July 13, p. 18.

Schoeman, Maxi (2007) "China in Africa: The rise of hegemony?" *Strategic Review for Southern Africa*, Vol. 29, No. 2.

Segal, Gerald and Richard H. Yang (eds.) (1996) *Chinese Economic Reform: The Impact on Security*, New York: Routledge.

Shambaugh, David L. (1984) *The Making of a Premier: Zhao Ziyang's Provincial Career*, Boulder, CO: Westview Press.

— (2013) *China Goes Global: The Partial Power*, New York: Oxford University Press.

Snow, Philip (1988) *The Star Raft: China's Encounter with Africa*, New York: Weidenfeld and Nicholson.

Srinivasan, Sharath (2008) "A marriage less convenient: China, Sudan and Dafur," in Kweku Ampiah and Sanusha Naidu (2008) (eds.), *Crouching Tiger, Hidden Dragon?: Africa and China*, Scottsville, KwaZulu-Natal: University of KwaZulu-Natal Press.

Stockwell, John (1978) *In Search of Enemies: A CIA Story*, New York: W.W. Norton.

Suliman, Kabbashi M. and A. A. Badawi Ahmed (2010) *An Assessment of the Impact of China's Investments in Sudan*, Kenya: African Economic Research Consortium.

Taylor, Ian, Dominik Kopinski and Andrzej Polus (2012) *China's Rise in Africa: Perspectives on a Developing Connection*, London and New York: Routledge.

Taylor, Ian (2006) "China's oil diplomacy in Africa," *International Affairs*, Vol. 82, No. 5, pp. 937–959.

Tecson, Gwendolyn R. (2003) "Confronting regionalism in Asia: A view from the Philippines," in Ryokichi Hirono (ed.), *Regional Co-operation in Asia*, Singapore: Institute of South East Asian Studies.

The Star (2003) "Return student policy pays off," October 14, p. 34.

The Times of London (2011) "Chinese get up African noses," July 17, p. 8.

Trinh, T. and Voss S. (2006) "China's commodity hunger: Implications for Africa and Latin America," Deustsche Bank Report, Frankfurt, June 13.

Tse-Tung, Mao (1936) "Problem of strategy in China's revolutionary war," *Selected Works*, Vol. 1, p. 179.

Tull, Denis M. (2008) "China in Africa: European perceptions and responses to the Chinese challenge," *SAIS Working Papers in African Studies*, February, Washington, D.C.: John Hopkins University.

— (2006) "China's engagement in Africa: Scope, significance and consequences," *Journal of Modern African Studies*, Vol. 44, No. 3, pp. 459–479.

Van de Looy, Judith (2006) "Africa and China: A Strategic Partnership?" *ASC Working Paper 67/2006*, Lieden, The Netherlands: African Studies Centre.

Vines, Alex and Indira Campos (1998) "China and India in Angola," in Fantu Cheru and Cyril Obi (eds.), *The Rise of China and India in Africa*, London: Zed Books.

Wade, Abdoulaye (2008) "The responsibility of growth," *Corporate Africa*, Issue 44, Vol. 2, No. 888, p. 30.

Wang, Jian-Ye (2007) "What drives China's growing role in Africa?" IMF working paper, August.

Wang, Jian-Ye and Abdoulaye Bio-Tchané (2008) "Africa's burgeoning ties with China," *Finance and Development*, March, Vol. 45, No. 1.

Ware, Gemma (2012) "I've told the Chinese: When you are in Rome, do as Romans do," *The Africa Report*, No. 36, December 2011–January 2012, pp. 44–46.

Warren, Patrick Nell (2009) "Obama's July speech in Accra – How it looks today," *Corporate Africa*, Issue 47, Vol. 2, November 8, p. 48.

Weber, Max (1947) *The Theory of Social and Economic Organization*, London: Oxford University Press.

Wedeman, Andrew (2012) *Double Paradox: Rapid Growth and Rising Corruption in China*, New York: Cornell University Press.

Wehrfritz, George (2004) "Going global: Flush with billions in foreign reserves, China is embarking on a buying spree," *Newsweek*, March 1, p. 28.

Wen, Jiabao (2003) "Promoting peace and prosperity by deepening cooperation in all-round way," speech delivered by Premier Wen Jiabao at the Seventh China–ASEAN Summit in Bali, Indonesia, on October 8, 2003.

Wheatley, Jonathan (2016) "China volatility adds to pressure on emerging markets," *Financial Times*, January 11, p. 2

Wills, James Austin (1937) *The letters and Speeches of Theodore Roosevelt*, New York: Billington and sons.

World Bank (1997) *China 2020: China Engaged*, Washington, D.C., World Bank.

— (1991) *Managing Technical Assistance in the 1990s: Report of the Technical Assistance Review Task Force*, Washington, D.C.: World Bank.

World Economic Forum, (2007) *Africa Competitiveness Report 2007*, Washington, D.C.: World Bank.

Wrong, Michela (2010) *It's Our Turn to Eat: The Story of a Kenyan Whistle-Blower*, New York: Harper Perennial.

Xiaoping, Deng (1962) "It doesn't matter if it is a black cat or a white cat, as long as it can catch mice, it's a good cat." In *Chambers Dictionary of Quotations* (1993).

Xiaoping, Deng (1978) excerpts from the speech "Emancipate the mind seek truth from facts and unite as one in looking to the future," December 13, 1978. In Pei-Kai Cheng, Michael Lestz and Jonathan Spence (1999) *The Search for Modern China: A Documentary Collection*, New York: W.W. Norton.

Xiaoping, Deng (1989) Deng speaking to officers enforcing martial law after the Tiananmen Square protest on June 9, 1989.

Xiaoping, Deng (1982) "Combat economic corruption," speech at a meeting of the Political Bureau of the Central Committee of the CPC on April 10, 1982, in Xiaoping, Deng (1984), *Selected Works of Deng Xiaoping (1975–1982)*, Beijing: Foreign Languages Press.

— (1981) "On opposing wrong ideological tendencies," a talk with leading comrades of the General Political Department of the Chinese People's Liberation Army on March 27, 1981, in Xiaoping Deng (1984) (ed.), *Selected Works of Deng Xiaoping (1975–1982)*, Beijing: Foreign Languages Press.

— (1980) "Answers to the Italian journalist Oriana Fallaci," in Xiaoping Deng (1984) (ed.), *Selected Works of Deng Xiaoping (1975–1982)*, Beijing: Foreign Languages Press.

— (1980) "The present situation and the tasks before us," speech at a meeting of cadres called by the Central Committee of the CCP on January 16, 1980, in Xiaoping Deng (1984) (ed.), *Selected Works of Deng Xiaoping (1975–1982)*, Beijing: Foreign Languages Press.

— (1984) "Crossing the river by feeling the stones," in *Selected Works of Deng Xiaoping (1975–1982)*, Beijing: Foreign Languages Press.

Xinhua News Agency (2009) "China to continue aid, investment in Africa," February 6.

Xun, Zhou (ed.) (2012) *The Great Famine in China, 1958–1962: A Documentary History*, New Haven: Yale University Press.

Yardley, Jim (2005) "Deng got the credit, but they were Zhao's ideas," *New Straits Times*, January 18, p. 19.

Yikona, Stuart, Brigitte Slot, Michael Geller, Bjarne Hansen and Fatima el Kadiri (2011) *Ill-gotten Money and the Economy: Experiences from Malawi and Namibia*, Washington, D.C.: World Bank.

York, Geoffrey (2014) "Japan battles China for influence in Africa," *The Globe and Mail*, January 10, 2014.

Yu, George and David J. Longenecker (1994) "The Beijing–Taipei struggle for international recognition: From the Niger affair to the U.N.," *Asian Survey*, Vol. 34, No. 5, pp. 475–488.

Yuan, Wu (2007) *China in Africa*, Beijing: China International Press.

Zemin, Jiang (1996) "China and Africa usher in the new century together," speech delivered by Jiang Zemin to the Organisation of African Unity, Addis Ababa, May 13, 1996.

Zhang, Chi (2011) "China's energy diplomacy in Africa," in Christopher M. Dent (ed.), *China and Africa Development Relations*, New York: Routledge.

Zhang, Weiwei (2006) "The allure of the Chinese model," *The International Herald Tribune*, November 2.

Zhao, Ziyang (2009) *Prisoner of the State: The Secret Journal of Chinese Premier Zhao Ziyang*, New York: Simon and Schuster.

Zhu, Zhiqun (2010) *China's New Diplomacy: Rationale, Strategies and Significance*, Farnham: Ashgate Publishing.

Internet Resources

Aglionby, John, "Tokyo takes on Beijing in Africa, claiming quality over speed," *Financial Times*, January 11, 2016, http://www.ft.com/cms/s/2/564df09e-824a-11e5-a01c-8650859a4767. html#axzz4HfkSw6Y2 (accessed 18/2/16).

BBC, "Kenya breaks 'Chinese-run cybercrime network,'" December 4, 2014. http://www.bbc.com/news/world-africa-30327412 (accessed 27/1/16).

Bloomberg Business (2005) "Angola president seeks more non-oil deals in his visit to China," http://www.bloomberg.com/news/articles/2015-06-12/angola-president-seeks-more-non-oil-deals-in-his-visit-to-china (accessed 26/9/15).

Cheru, Fantu, "Decoding the evolving China–Africa relations," http://www.cebri.org/midia/documentos/eventos_03_ucla_paper9.pdf.

"China-Africa economic, trade cooperation," The 2007 Annual Meeting of the African Development Bank Group, http://adb_english.people.com.cn/81811/5687470.html.

"China's Hu urges more African ties," BBC News, http://news.bbc.co.uk/2/hi/africa/4949688.stm.

"China not to reduce assistance to Africa despite financial crisis," Ministry of Foreign Affairs of the Republic of China, http://www.focac.org/eng/zxxx/t528005.htm.

FOCAC, "Xi announces 10 major China–Africa cooperation plans for coming 3 years," www.focac.org/eng/zfgx/dfzc/t1322068.htm (accessed 26/1/16).

Gosh, Palash (2012) "Nigeria to deport Chinese migrants engaged in illegal trading," *International Business Times*, http://www.ibtimes.com/nigeria-deport-chinese-migrants-engaged-illegal-trading-699724 (accessed 20/12/15).

Handson, Stephanie (2008) "China, Africa and oil," Council on Foreign Relations, http://www.washingtonpost.com/wp-dyn/content/article/2008/06/09/AR2008060900714.html.

Hill, Matthew (2007) "Hu Jintao pledges action to reduce China–SA trade imbalance" http://www.polity.org.za/article/hu-jintao-pledges-action-to-reduce-chinasa-trade-imbalance-2007-02-07.

Kabemba, Claude, "Chinese involvement in Zambia," Open Society Initiative for South Africa, October 4, 2012. www.osisa.org/books/zambia/chinese-involvement-zambia (accessed 8/2/16).

KPMG (2014) "Manufacturing in Africa: Sector Report," www.kpmg.com/Africa/en/IssuesAndInsights/Articles-Publications/General-Industries-Publications/Documents/Manufacturing%20in%20Africa.pdf (accessed 28/1/16).

LaGrone, Sam, and Dave Majumdar (2014) "Chinese weapons that worry the Pentagon," https://news.usni.org/2014/06/09/chinese-weapons-worry-pentagon (accessed 17/12/15).

Marshall, Andrea, "China's mighty telecom footprint in Africa," http://ela-newsportal.com/china%E2%80%99s-mighty-telecom-footprint-in-africa/ (accessed 25/1/16).

Ministry of Foreign Affairs of the People's Republic of China, "The Asian–African Conference," http://www.fmprc.gov.cn/mfa_eng/ziliao_665539/3602_665543/3604_665547/t18044.shtml (accessed 2/22/16).

Okonjo-Iweala, Ngozi (2006) "Viewpoint: China becomes Africa's suitor," http://news.bbc.co.uk/go/pr/fr/-/2/hi/business/6079838.stm.

Philips, Tom, "Chinese 'gangsters' repatriated from Angola," *The Telegraph*, August 20, 2012, http://www.telegraph.co.uk/news/worldnews/asia/china/9500517/Chinese-gangsters-repatriated-from-Angola.html (accessed 2/12/16).

Powell, A. (2007) "Ethnic Somali rebels kill 74 at Chinese oilfield in Ethiopia," *The Guardian*, 25 April 2007, https://www.theguardian.com/world/2007/apr/25/ethiopia (accessed 5/11/2015).

Quartz Africa, "Robert Mugabe: China is doing everything that Africa's colonizers should have done," (Robert Mugabe's speech at 2015 FOCAC Summit in Johannesburg) *Quartz Africa*, www.qz.com/565860/robert-mugabe-china-is-doing-everything-that-Africans-colonizers-should-have-done.

Reuters, "China premier says Sino-Africa disputes just 'growing pains'," May 4, 2014. http://www.reuters.com/article/us-china-africa-idUSBREA4300L20140504 (accessed 2/21/16).

Romei, Valentina, "China and Africa: Trade relationship evolves," *Financial Times*, December 3, 2015. http://www.ft.com/cms/s/0/c53e7f68-9844-11e5-9228-87e603d-47bdc.html#axzz4HfkSw6Y2 (accessed 27/1/16).

Smith, David, "China denies building empire in Africa," *The Guardian*, January 12, 2015, www.theguardian.com/global-development/2015/jan/12/china-denies-building-empire-africa-colonialism (accessed 2/21/16).

"Social costs for China's entry into the WTO," http://www.asiafeatures.com/business/0111,2915,02.html.

Stamp, Gavin (2006) "China defends its African relations," http://news.bbc.co.uk/go/pr/fr/-/2/hi/business/5114980.stm.

Swain, Jon (2008) "Africa, China's new frontier," *Timesonline*, February 10, 2008, http://www.thesundaytimes.co.uk/sto/news/world_news/article80075.ece.

Wade, Abdoulaye (2008) "Time for the West to practise what it preaches," *Financial Times*, http://www.ft.com/cms/s/0/5d347f88-c897-11dc-94a6-0000779fd2ac.html#axzz4GqLQSGG7 (accessed 20/10/15).

Wikipedia, "Technology transfer," https://en.wikipedia.org/wiki/Technology_transfer (accessed 5/12/15).

World Intellectual Property Association (WIPO), "Overview of contractual agreements for the transfers of technology," http://www.wipo.int/export/sites/www/sme/en/documents/pdf/technology_transfer.pdf (accessed 1/1/16).

Yeebo, Yepoka, "Chinese counterfeits leave Ghanaian textiles hanging by a thread," *The Christian Science Monitor*, May 31, 2015. http://www.csmonitor.com/World/Africa/2015/0531/Chinese-counterfeits-leave-Ghanaian-textiles-hanging-by-a-thread (accessed 2/21/16).

Yusuf, Mohammed, "Chinese imports threatens Kenya's textile industry," *VOA*, July 12, 2013, http://www.voanews.com/content/chinese-imports-threaten-kenyas-textile-workers-merchants/1700819.html.

Index

For Product Safety Concerns and Information please contact our EU
representative GPSR@taylorandfrancis.com Taylor & Francis Verlag GmbH,
Kaufingerstraße 24, 80331 München, Germany

Printed and bound by CPI Group (UK) Ltd, Croydon, CR0 4YY
01/05/2025
01858432-0001